IN SEARCH OF THE GRAND TRUNK

IN SEARCH OF THE GRAND TRUNK

Ghost Rail Lines in Ontario

Ron Brown

DUNDURN
NATURAL HERITAGE
TORONTO

Editor: Jane Gibson
Copy Editor: Allison Hirst
Design: Jesse Hooper
Printer: Webcom

Library and Archives Canada Cataloguing in Publication

Brown, Ron, 1945-
   In search of the Grand Trunk : ghost rail lines in Ontario / Ron Brown.

Includes bibliographical references and index.
Issued also in an electronic format.
ISBN 978-1-55488-882-5

   1. Railroads--Ontario. 2. Railroads--Ontario--History. 3. Ontario--History, Local. I. Title.

HE2809.O5B75 2011   385.09713   C2011-900952-8

1 2 3 4 5   15 14 13 12 11

Conseil des Arts du Canada / Canada Council for the Arts

Canadä

ONTARIO ARTS COUNCIL
CONSEIL DES ARTS DE L'ONTARIO

We acknowledge the support of the **Canada Council for the Arts** and the **Ontario Arts Council** for our publishing program. We also acknowledge the financial support of the **Government of Canada** through the **Canada Book Fund** and **Livres Canada Books**, and the **Government of Ontario** through the **Ontario Book Publishers Tax Credit** program, and the **Ontario Media Development Corporation**.

Printed and bound in Canada.
www.dundurn.com

Front cover photo: Peterborough Grand Trunk station, *circa* 1890. *Courtesy of the Ron Brown collection.*
Back cover photos: (top) The restored Stirling rail station in 2009. It was originally built by the Grand Junction Railway, but later became a CN station; (bottom) the Lakefield Rail Trail in July 2010. *Both images courtesy of the Ron Brown collection.*

Unless otherwise indicated, images are credited to the author.

FSC
www.fsc.org

MIX
Paper from responsible sources
FSC® C004071

Dundurn Press
3 Church Street, Suite 500
Toronto, Ontario, Canada
M5E 1M2

Gazelle Book Services Limited
White Cross Mills
High Town, Lancaster, England
LA1 4XS

Dundurn Press
2250 Military Road
Tonawanda, NY
U.S.A. 14150

For the many rail enthusiasts who have given their time and energy to preserve the memory of Ontario's rail heritage

CONTENTS

ACKNOWLEDGEMENTS

There are, it seems, many rail lovers in Ontario. I would like to thank a few who helped me chase down the abandoned lines and garner the information needed to share my love of railways.

Chris Ryan of the Windsor Essex Tourism board helped ease the way to research the many ghost lines in southwestern Ontario. Melissa Johnson of Ottawa Valley Tourism offered the generous hospitality found in that scenic and historic section of the province. A one-time hotel in Eganville, now a gift shop and inn, Serendipity on the River, was part of that hospitality. Cheryl Norman of Middlesex Tourism provided key information on rail trails which followed the Grand Trunk in that area.

Ron Tozer of the Algonquin Park Archives shared on-site observations on the two ghost lines that pass through that historic park, as he has done in the past. And thanks, too, to Jamie Lee Everatt of Bruce County Tourism and to the friendly hosts at the Gar-ham Hall bed and breakfast in Paisley, one of Ontario's hidden heritage treasures.

To the many individuals whom I encountered along the way, and to the dedicated volunteers who operate the railway museums and who keep the rail trails safe and open, I offer my deepest appreciation.

Not everyone promotes our railways on the ground. In researching this volume, however, we have encountered a great many individual websites dedicated to the history of the railway lines that form part of Ontario's history. Those run by Rob Hughes and Charles Cooper, as referenced in the back, are two of the best in this regard.

HISTORIC RAIL LINE ABBREVIATIONS

AER:	Algoma Eastern Railway	**CAL:**	Canada Air Line
B&P:	Bytown and Prescott Railway	**CAR:**	Canada Atlantic Railway
B&LH:	Buffalo and Lake Huron Railway	**CASO:**	Canada Southern Railway
B&NH:	Belleville and North Hastings Railway	**CNER:**	Canadian National Electric Railway
B&W:	Brockville and Westport Railway	**CNoR:**	Canadian Northern Railway
BB&G:	Buffalo, Brantford, and Goderich Railway	**CNR (also CN):**	Canadian National Railway
BM&A:	Bruce Mines and Algoma Railway	**COR:**	Central Ontario Railway
BN&PB:	Brantford, Norfolk, and Port Burwell Railway	**CPR (also CP):**	Canadian Pacific Railway
BQ:	Bay of Quinte Railway	**CVR:**	Credit Valley Railway
C&P:	Cobourg and Peterborough Railway	**CW&LE:**	Chatham, Wallaceburg, and Lake Erie Railway

G&G:	Guelph and Goderich Railway	**M&K:**	Montreal and Kingston Railway
GB&S:	Georgian Bay and Seaboard Railway	**M&NS:**	Manitoulin and North Shore Railway
GB&W:	Georgian Bay and Wellington Railway	**MR:**	Midland Railway
GJR:	Grand Junction Railway	**N&NW:**	Northern and Northwestern Railway
GRR:	Grand River Railway	**N&PJ:**	Northern and Pacific Junction Railway
GT:	Grand Trunk Railway	**NFP&RR:**	Niagara Falls Park and River Railway
GW:	Great Western Railway	**NGR:**	North Grey Railway
H&LE:	Hamilton and Lake Erie Railway	**NSC&T:**	Niagara, St. Catharines, and Toronto Railway
H&NW:	Hamilton and Northwestern Railway	**NSR:**	North Simcoe Railway
IB&O:	Irondale, Bancroft, and Ottawa Railway	**NT&Q:**	Napanee, Tamworth, and Quebec Railway
K&P:	Kingston and Pembroke Railway		
L&LE:	London and Lake Erie Railway	**O&NY:**	Ottawa and New York Railway
LB&P:	Lindsay, Bobcaygeon, and Pontypool Railway	**O&Q:**	Ontario and Quebec Railway
LE&N:	Lake Erie and Northern Railway	**OA&PS:**	Ottawa, Arnprior, and Parry Sound Railway
LH&B:	London Huron and Bruce Railway	**ONR:**	Ontario Northland Railway
LH&NO:	Lake Huron and Northern Ontario	**OPR:**	Ontario Pacific Railway
LSJ:	Lake Simcoe Junction Railway	**OS&H:**	Ontario Simcoe and Huron Railway
L&PS:	London and Port Stanley Railway	**PA&D:**	Port Arthur and Duluth Railway

PAD&W:	Port Arthur, Duluth, and Western Railway	**TIR:**	Thousands Island Railway
PEC:	Prince Edward County Railway	**TSR:**	Toronto Suburban Railway
PD&H:	Port Dover and Lake Huron Railway	**VR:**	Victoria Railway
PHL&B:	Port Hope, Lindsay, and Beaverton Railway	**WG&B:**	Wellington Grey and Bruce Railway
PSC:	Parry Sound Colonization Railway	**WPP&L:**	Whitby, Port Perry, and Lindsay Railway
PW&PP:	Port Whitby and Port Perry Railway	**Y&D:**	York and Durham Heritage Railway
S&AR:	Schomburg and Aurora Railway		
S&H:	Stratford and Huron Railway		
SFP&P:	Spruce Falls Power and Paper Company Railway		
SM&W:	St. Marys and Western Railway		
SSR:	South Simcoe Steam Railway		
T&N:	Toronto and Nipissing Railway		
T&YRR:	Toronto and York Radial Railway		
TG&B:	Toronto Grey and Bruce Railway		
TH&B:	Toronto, Hamilton, and Buffalo Railway		
TLE&P:	Tillsonburg, Lake Erie, and Pacific Railway		

INTRODUCTION

To be clear, this book is not about the Grand Trunk Railway. Rather, the long defunct line is a metaphor for the growth and decline of Ontario's once extensive network of railways. Admittedly, for a heady period of nearly forty years, the Grand Trunk Railway was, along with the Canadian Pacific Railway and the Canadian Northern Railway, one of the province's largest owners of tracks and stations. And it all began very modestly.

The Laying of the Tracks

In the 1830s, barely forty years after pioneer settlers had begun clearing the first crude trails through Ontario's woodlands, railways had become the rage. In 1832, Canada's first railway began operating between La Prairie on the St. Lawrence River and St. Jean on the Richelieu. An eighteen-kilometre year-round route, it had replaced a 120-kilometre seasonal water route.

Little wonder then that the business interests in Upper Canada (Ontario), especially those in Toronto, started talking trains. Ontario's first railway charter went to the City of Toronto and Lake Huron Railway in 1836. The proposed line would link Toronto with Collingwood on Georgian Bay and reduce a 420-kilometre shipping route by water to less than two hundred kilometres over land. There were few means by which to raise the funding needed to survey the route and lay the tracks, however, and by 1850 only eighty kilometres of track existed in all the Canadian colonies.

Between 1848 and 1851, Upper Canada's finance minister, Frances Hincks, introduced three vital pieces of legislation that would kick-start the railway age in Ontario. The Railway Guarantee Act of 1849 allowed government the authority to guarantee up to 6 percent of the interest on railway loans. The Municipal Corporations Act of the same year created new municipalities with the power to raise money themselves for the financing of railways. And the Mainline Railway Act, also of 1849, guaranteed both the interest and principal on the building of trunk lines that would cross the entire province.

These acts proved to be the catalyst. Within months of their enactment, the government granted more than twenty-five railway charters. But the American Civil War slowed rail construction to a halt, largely because money from Britain was feared to be heading to support the rebels.[1] But with Confederation a reality in 1867, track-laying boomed again. Between 1870 and 1890, trackage increased five-fold. By 1910 more than 115 separate railway charters had been granted in Ontario.

Most of those charters, though, were little more than pipe dreams. Grand destinations fell miserably short of their proclaimed intent and many rail lines were never even built. Many eventually amalgamated with other lines, or were absorbed by more prosperous lines. In fact, by 1888 the Grand Trunk Railway owned and operated most of Ontario's rail network. But by 1910 two other players, the Canadian Pacific and the Canadian Northern Railways, also had created extensive networks across Ontario.

In 1884 another form of railway appeared on the scene. With the evolution of Ontario's hydroelectric power grid, the age of the electric streetcar arrived, and by 1925, interurban streetcars were linking many of Ontario's major urban areas.

But despite Ontario's extensive network of rail lines, the decline of those golden days of rail was not far off.

The CPR's Owen Sound station sits overgrown, awaiting a new use. The building was constructed in 1946–47, and saw its last train in 1994. It is now owned by the City of Owen Sound, and is a designated heritage railway station.

The Lifting of the Tracks

The year 1918 marked the first time in Ontario that more tracks were lifted than were laid. It was also the year that the Canadian National Railway (CNR) was created to own and operate the country's bankrupt rail lines.[2] By 1923, the CNR had taken over the Canadian Northern Railway, the Intercolonial Railway in eastern Canada, and the once mighty Grand Trunk.

Now the owner of many redundant routes, the CNR began to consolidate its operations, and the lifting of tracks began. The 1930s ushered in the Depression and the Canadian government began directing its money toward road-building schemes rather than providing the financing the railways needed to maintain their infrastructure. The auto age tempted people into private cars, an improvement over standing on a frigid station platform waiting for tardy trains, and buses began to replace the radial streetcar lines.

Suburbia arrived in the 1950s, and more and more housing developments were built farther and farther from any train station. In 1955, the government removed the lucrative mail contracts from the railways and handed them to truck operations. In the 1960s, with the government of Canada claiming that rail passenger service was outdated, many train stations fell silent. To increase their profits, especially in the face of competition from the trucking industry, the railway companies began chopping their less profitable branch lines. With no short-line operators yet on the scene, these routes too fell silent.

Between 1970 and 1990, Ontario lost three-quarters of its rail lines. But, with the resurgence of short-line operations in the 1990s, that decline has slowed. Commuter gridlock forced the government into introducing commuter rail service, albeit much more slowly than it was needed. One is left to wonder if a new age of rail is about to dawn. But even if that should happen, Ontario retains a vast network of ghost rail lines along which the heritage of a vanished rail era is there to explore.

The Heritage of the Tracks

Rail heritage along the ghost lines assumes many forms. Although the province has lost far too many of its heritage stations, others have been preserved. Following the mass demolition of railway stations during the 1970s, federal legislation was enacted to protect them. But that did little to prevent demolition by neglect. Thus "protected" stations were left to rot, while others tempted thoughtless arsonists.

But Ontario's railway heritage is not confined to its stations. Bridges were (and remain) among the engineering marvels of their time. Many still stand, though some have been refitted as part of a rail trail. Landscapes that evolved around the railways included hotels, feed elevators, rail-workers' homes, and trackside industries. Many outlived the demise of the rail lines that created them, and they, too, form part of Ontario's ghost-line heritage.

Ghost rail lines occur throughout Ontario. It is hoped that this book will help celebrate the heritage of a time that is too often neglected.

PART ONE:

The Ghost Rail Lines of Central Ontario

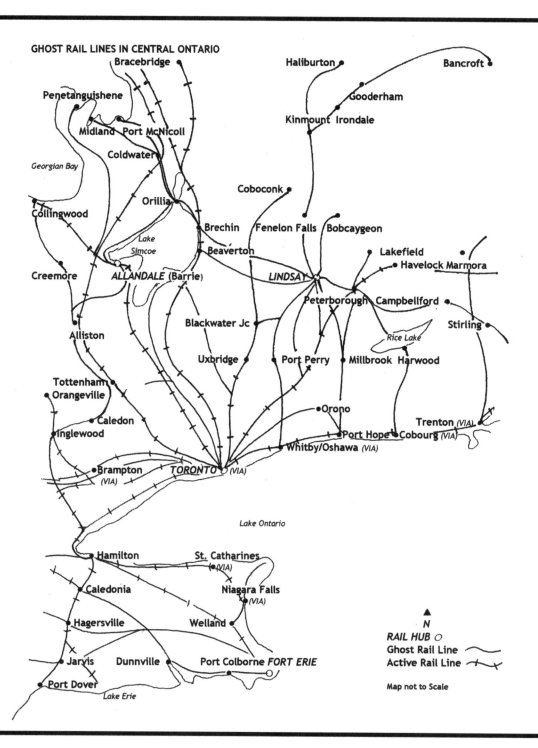

GHOST RAIL LINES IN CENTRAL ONTARIO

Bracebridge
Penetanguishene
Haliburton
Bancroft
Gooderham
Midland Port McNicoll
Kinmount Irondale
Coldwater
Georgian Bay
Orillia
Coboconk
Collingwood
Brechin
Fenelon Falls Bobcaygeon
Beaverton
Lake Simcoe
Lakefield
Creemore
ALLANDALE (Barrie)
LINDSAY
Havelock Marmora
Peterborough Campbellford
Blackwater Jc
Stirling
Alliston
Rice Lake
Uxbridge
Port Perry Millbrook Harwood
Tottenham
Orangeville
Orono
Caledon
Trenton (VIA)
Inglewood
Port Hope Cobourg (VIA)
Brampton
Whitby/Oshawa (VIA)
(VIA)
TORONTO ○ (VIA)

Lake Ontario

Hamilton
St. Catharines
● (VIA)
Caledonia
Niagara Falls
● (VIA)
Hagersville
Welland ●
Jarvis Dunnville ● Port Colborne FORT ERIE ○
Port Dover
Lake Erie

▲
N
RAIL HUB ○
Ghost Rail Line ∿
Active Rail Line ┼┼┼

Map not to Scale

CHAPTER 1

The Ghosts of the Grand Trunk

The History

The Grand Trunk Railway (GT) was originally incorporated in 1852 to construct a line between Toronto and Montreal. At first, the eastern section went by the name of Kingston and Montreal Railway and the western portion as the Toronto and Kingston Railway. By 1855, the GT had not only started construction of the Grand Trunk Railway, but had acquired the charters of five other lines, as well, including the Guelph and Toronto Railway.

Construction went quickly, and in 1855 the Toronto to Montreal portion was open. Two years later an extension from Toronto to Sarnia was also operating. By 1867, the Grand Trunk Railway extended from Portland, Maine, to Port Huron, Michigan, an empire of more than two thousand kilometres. Shortly after that, its tracks had reached Chicago.

The GT was Canada's first major trunk line (even though Canada didn't exist as a country at that time). While the Great Western Railway (GW) had begun operating in 1853, it primarily served American interests across Ontario's southwestern peninsula. The Grand Trunk, on the other hand, was determined to prove to Canadians that it was not going to be an "American style" line with cheaply built stations. Therefore, it adopted a truly British station design, copying the design of the station at Kenilworth, England. This building was a wide structure with a shallow sloping roof and a series of French windows on all sides. Thirty-eight such buildings appeared between Toronto and Montreal (a more distinctively French style was chosen for the line in Quebec).

Throughout the 1880s the Grand Trunk began to acquire the many lines that were suffering from financial troubles. These included such major lines as the Midland Railway, the Great Western, and the Wellington Grey and Bruce, as well as a few smaller ones. As profits improved, the GT began to upgrade its lines, replacing the older, cheaper stations with more stylish structures and double-tracking its main line between Toronto and Montreal. In so doing, it rerouted its older single track, which had been built too close to Lake Ontario. These tracks fell largely between Port Hope and Oshawa, and by 1900 were a ghost railway.

But the Grand Trunk would also fall on hard times. By 1923 it had, along with other bankrupt lines, become part of the government's railway rescue effort known as the Canadian National Railway (CNR).

The next section of the GT's early line to fall silent was that which ran between Cornwall and Cardinal, along the St. Lawrence River. In the 1950s, the CNR needed to relocate its track some distance from the rising floodwaters created by new dams on the St. Lawrence Seaway. Indeed entire towns had to be relocated.

The latest section of the GT/CNR to lose its tracks, in the 1980s, was the line that connected St. Marys Junction in Perth County with Point Edward on the St. Clair River. It duplicated the line already running from the town of St. Marys, through London, and along the former Great Western tracks to Sarnia. With few customers along the route, it was ripe for abandonment.

The Heritage of the Eastern Ghost Line

When the Grand Trunk first opened this section of track in 1856, it ran close to the banks of the St. Lawrence River, but far enough back to avoid building the long trestles necessary to cross the wide estuaries flowing into the big river.

When the plans for the St. Lawrence Seaway[1] became known, residents of places like Iroquois, Morrisburg, Aultsville, Farran's Point, Wales, Moulinette, and Mille Roches were distressed. They, along with people in other hamlets, realized they were about to lose their long-time homes. The CNR would lose its old Grand Trunk line.

By 1956, however, a new track and five new stations were open for service at Cornwall, Long Sault, Ingleside, Morrisburg, and Iroquois. Built in a modernistic style

with glass and steel material, and a flat roof, they bore no resemblance to the previous traditional-style stations.

Cardinal

The ghost line begins in the west at the village of Cardinal (between Morrisburg and Prescott), where the former right-of-way can be seen bending southeasterly from the new route. Being some distance from the original village on the river, the former station attracted a small satellite settlement where a few homes yet stand. But, as Cardinal did not receive a new station, little evidence remains of the old station grounds. East of Cardinal, the right-of-way has become private land, although in the village of Iroquois the 1815 Carmen House Museum marks the location of that community's station grounds. Between Iroquois and Morrisburg, County Road 2 was constructed on the right-of-way, the "welcome" sign in the latter community representing the station grounds.

Aultsville

Much of the community of Aultsville remained above the inundating waters, leaving its sidewalks and a few foundations visible. The station building now rests on Chrysler Beach Road where it, along with a Grand Trunk #88 (later CN #1008) steam engine, pays silent tribute to the heritage of the rail line. East of Aultsville, the right-of-way is still visible above the water, while at Farran's Point a walking trail follows the old railway roadbed.

Thanks to a dedicated group of heritage enthusiasts known as the Lost Villages Society, the little flag station from Moulinette has been rescued. It stands on the Lost Villages Museum grounds managed by that society.

Relocated to avoid the rising flood waters of the St. Lawrence Seaway, the Aultsville station stands near Upper Canada Village. Built in 1889, it now serves as a museum display.

Cornwall

While a modern new Cornwall station remains a busy stop on the new alignment for VIA Rail, the former right-of-way that ran through the city has become part of 10th Street East. A CNR spur still occupies the old Grand Trunk tracks at the east end of the street, while another occupies the GT tracks at the west end of 9th Street West. The economic mainstays of Cornwall included the Domtar Pulp Mill, until its closure in 2006, and the cross-border traffic using the international bridge over the St. Lawrence River.

Port Hope to Oshawa

When undertaking upgrades in the 1890s, the Grand Trunk identified two hurdles that needed to be overcome. One was the section extending west from the Port Hope station. Having been built too close to the shoreline of Lake Ontario, parts of it were being washed away. As a result, the GT relocated its tracks two to three kilometres farther inland. The former roadbed has now become a residential laneway in Port Britain — once a busy grain port, even before the GT arrived. The other involved the Port Britain to Wesleyville section, where some portions along the beach had fallen into the water. Where the original track swung inland toward the Newtonville station, a massive electric-generating station now stands, although the plant has never been fired up.

The old line passed behind the little ghost town of Wesleyville, located on Lakeshore Road, then on to the site of the first Newtonville station. Today, those foundations lie on Townline Road, hidden in underbrush, while a pair of early workers' homes is all that remains of the station village. At this point, the new CN tracks come into view and mark the location where the old and the new came together.

Between Newtonville and Bowmanville, the GT decided that, rather than widening the existing single track through the large glacial hills, it would simply find a newer and straighter route. Those original cuts through the hills remain visible both east and west of Bowmanville. To the west, the old roadbed is clearly identifiable along Highway 401 but only as a grassy mound.

While the other similar first-generation Grand Trunk stations had their French doors filled in to create windows and an operator's bay, the station at St. Marys Junction retains its French doors, although the openings have been replaced with stone.

The Heritage of the Western Ghost Line

St. Marys

Although now abandoned, the Grand Trunk's original historic route to Sarnia remained in use until 1988, and still contains some of that line's more significant heritage features.

At the top of that list is the St. Marys Junction station. Built in 1858, it is the only one of the GT's stone stations that remains unaltered. A small workers' settlement once existed at the site, as did other railway buildings, but all are now gone except for the wonderful old station. After it sat neglected for many years, local volunteers have begun to restore the structure to its former condition.

While the current tracks of the CN line to London still shine on the east side of the building, the former route of the original GT line on the west side is now a lawn. A short distance west, however, the St. Marys Grand Trunk Trail follows the ghost rail route, crossing that other feature of historical importance, the Grand Trunk's "Sarnia Bridge" over the Thames River. Resting on six stone piers, it was purchased by the town in 1995 and restored as part of the 2.8-kilometre Grand Trunk Trail.

The town of St. Marys is one of Ontario's most stunning, containing some architectural treasures such as the stone "opera house," along with an entire street of pre-railway buildings of stone architecture. A water tower, likewise constructed of stone, survives but is no longer in use. The newer Grand Trunk station on the London branch of the Grand Trunk is also an architectural treat with its buff-brick, bell-caste gable, and rounded corners. Built in 1901, it now serves VIA Rail passengers and functions as a tourist information office.

Lucan

From St. Marys, the route then led west to the village of Granton. While nothing remains of the track area, a feed mill still marks the site of the rail line. The wooden Granton station, though, stood neglected in a nearby field until it finally crumbled into a pile of rotting lumber.

Best known as the location of the infamous Donnelly massacre,[2] Lucan was the next station stop. Many landmarks survive to commemorate the Donnelly story, including the family grave at nearby Saint Patrick's Church. But of the railway, little remains, although feed mills still stand where the rail tracks once ran.

A few kilometres west of Lucan, road maps display a dot with the name "Lucan Crossing." For many years this marked the location where the tracks of the Grand Trunk crossed over those of the London, Huron, and Bruce (LH&B) railway, which ran from London to Wingham. Today that "hole in the wall" can still be seen in the GT embankment beside County Road 20, though the ghost LH&B line is now nothing more than a cornfield.

Ailsa Craig, the next station on the line, was named for founder David Craig, and is still a true farm town. A fertilizer plant marks the station grounds, but other than a one-time railway hotel, the only rail-related structure that remains here is the Grand Trunk trestle, located right in the town.

Parkhill

A historical town with a main street lined with early buildings, Parkhill still has a feed mill on the right-of-way and a walking trail that follows the rail line east through town. The local newspaper, the *Parkhill Gazette*, occupies what was once a railway hotel.

An unusual interpretative kiosk, built in the style of the Grand Trunk station in Sarnia, marks the Howard Watson Rail Trail in Sarnia.

Between Parkhill and Thedford, the right-of-way has been turned over to adjacent property owners and has largely vanished from the landscape. While Parkhill has retained much of its heritage townscape, that in Thedford has been replaced with newer development. Although a former Grand Trunk warehouse still stands near the location of the former rail yards, the rest of the railway grounds are today home to a park and a fire hall.

In Forest, the next station stop, new downtown development has obliterated the rail line, but an attractive library was built — a replica of the town's towered station.

Sarnia

As the rail line route makes its way toward Sarnia, much of the land it once occupied has been ploughed under and the line has vanished from view. Camlachie, now nearly a ghost town, retains an abandoned general store and a very old grain elevator, but much of the original right-of-way is gone. This all changes as one approaches Sarnia.

A few metres west of Camlachie marks the eastern end of the Howard Watson Rail Trail.[3] This well-groomed cycling and walking rail trail runs parallel to the shore of Lake Huron. Hikers and cyclists can freshen themselves at fast-food outlets along the way, or take a dip in Lake Huron at one of the public beaches at Telfer Sideroad. The sixteen-kilometre trail runs through rural or lakeside area for most of its length, but ends up in Sarnia on the north side of Confederation Drive near Macgregor's Junction, a switching point on the still-active tracks of CN Rail.

Indeed, the VIA Rail station in Sarnia is one of the Grand Trunk's most distinctive. Designed by former Great Western architect Joseph Hobson, it exhibits steep hip gables on the front and at both ends of the large brick building. This station and the two in St. Marys make for fitting heritage "bookends" to this ghost section of the Grand Trunk line.

CHAPTER 2

The Grand Junction Railway: Belleville to Peterborough

The History

It was 1852, a time when Ontario's railways were either American shortcuts or resource lines to Ontario's interior, a time when a group of Belleville business interests decided on a "loopy" plan. They would build a loop line that would wind toward Peterborough and then loop back down to Lake Ontario at Toronto — or at least at some lake point west of Port Hope. When the Grand Trunk indicated that it was also planning such a route, the Belleville bunch backed off.

But when the 1870s rolled around and the GT had not yet started building its own loop line, Belleville sprang back into action and chartered the Grand Junction Railway (GJR). But of all the rail lines south of the Canadian Shield, the route proved to have some of the greatest physical hurdles. First, it had many rivers to cross, including the Trent, the Indian, the Ouse, and the Moira. Then there was the lay of the land; near Peterborough lies one of the world's most spectacular fields of drumlins, those long rounded hills shaped by the retreating glaciers of the last Ice Age. Creating a rail line through them meant a very winding route. As a result, construction moved slowly, not reaching Peterborough until June of 1880.

It then became a matter of determining the best way back to the lake. One suggestion was to complete the line as far as Lindsay, where it was thought that the new line could siphon away some the grain traffic flowing along the Midland Railway (MR) from Georgian Bay to Port Hope. The Midland Railway, however, pre-empted that possibility by acquiring the GJR in 1880. By extending the route west from Peterborough to Omemee, it could connect with the MR's own line, and then via the Toronto and Nipissing Railway; the "loop" to Toronto would thus be complete.

Through the years that the line was in use, it was used primarily to transport grain, but was also used to haul coal and some manufactured goods.

A century later, however, freight traffic began to dwindle, and the section between Peterborough and Corbyville (north of Belleville) was finally abandoned in 1987. By

1990, the Peterborough to Lindsay section was no more. Gone, too, was the Grand Junction, dreams and all.

The Heritage

Belleville to Stirling

The original Belleville station of the Grand Junction Railway stood at the wharf, while another stood on Pinnacle Street in what was formerly a Methodist church. At the north end of town, the Grand Junction shared the Grand Trunk's station (which still stands) on that railway's main line, before heading straight north.

The first stop north of Belleville was in the distillery town of Corbyville — whisky was big business here from 1869 until the H. Corby Distillery was closed in 1991. Most of its structures have since been removed. From Tank Farm Road, just south of Corbyville, the GJR roadbed becomes a trail, crossing the Moira River at Foxboro. No evidence of rail structures remains at the station site, which lies on Mudcat Road, about two kilometres west of the town.

The line then winds its way to Madoc Junction, where the route of Belleville and North Hastings Railway (B&NH) split off for the golden boomtown of Eldorado, the site of Ontario's first gold mine, established in 1867. The line was abandoned in 1984, and this route is now a trail known as the Two Lakes Trail, which extends to the southern limits of Madoc. The most visible remnant of the route is the trestle over Moira Lake. The portion that ran from Madoc north to Eldorado was abandoned in 1913, and is overgrown and largely unusable as a trail.

As the GJR swings westward, it enters the scenic and historic village of Stirling. From 1879 to 1962, goods moved in and out of the Stirling station. Outbound products were largely farm and lumber products, while arriving goods were those manufactured elsewhere and shipped in to suit the community's needs. But truck traffic put an end to that, and the station stood empty until 2004, when the Stirling Rotary Club, along with the historical society and the municipality, moved the building onto its new foundation.

It was at Anson, a small station in Hastings County just west of Stirling, that the tracks of the GJR met those of the Central Ontario Railway (COR). The junction of the two rail trails (one being the Hastings Heritage Trail) is located just south of County Road 8. Because Stirling was so close, no settlement of any size ever grew around this station site.

The village of Hoards developed around its station, which, for some strange reason, stood across the tracks from the community and the feed mill, the most substantial structure. Although the place hasn't seen a train in years, the name "Hoards Station" remains in use. Indeed, a feed mill still stands by the silent right-of-way, while the station name board rests on the side of a nearby building.

Campbellford

The trail portion of the right-of-way halts at Dant Road on the eastern end of the town of Campbellford, reappearing at Alma Street on the other side of the wide Trent River. A substantial bridge was needed here, and when the Trent Canal finally opened to through traffic in 1907, the old bridge was replaced with a high-level one that would allow boats to pass beneath. A smaller bascule-type lift bridge (in which a heavy weight at one end lifts the span into the air) was built a bit south of the bridge, permitting access to the Gair Pulp Mill (closed in 1964) and the Breithaupt Leather Company (closed in the 1920s), both located on an island in the river.

It is in Stirling that one finds Ontario's only surviving example of a true Van Horne station.[1] The two-storey building has gable ends and a freight-shed extension. It has been moved a few metres east of its original site and now houses a railway museum and meeting room. In 2004, the Stirling-Rawdon Historical Society and the Stirling Rotary Club bought the station and restored it to its former glory.

The original station here was a two-storey structure, later replaced with a single-storey building that lasted into the early 1980s. Enduring a bit longer were a freight building and a large, square grain elevator. Sadly, everything has now gone from this community that seems to care little for the preservation of its railway heritage. The bridge was removed in 1987, the station site is now a parking lot for Canadian Tire and Tim Hortons, and the freight building and the grain elevator were removed, the land they sat on just vacant fields. A plaque erected beside the remaining piers of the bridge is the only lasting memorial to what has been lost.

Campbellford to Peterborough

The trail resumes at the corner of Alma and Simpson Streets in Campbellford, and makes its way amid the imposing summits of the Peterborough drumlin field to Godolphin, where it then strikes north toward the town of Hastings. At Concession Road 13, east of the town, Cedar Drive picks up the right-of-way and follows it along the banks of the Trent River.

A bustling tourist village on the Trent Canal, Hastings still possesses a historic mill on the north side of the canal, but not the station nor any other vestige of its railway heritage. The station served as an antique shop until the 1990s, when it burned, while new businesses and roads occupy the right-of-way. The Grand Junction Railway crossing of the Trent can be seen at the western end of Hastings on Homewood Avenue, west of Highway 45. North of the Trent Canal, the trail resumes, passing through the station stop of Birdsalls, where the former station hotel survives as a private residence.

The station at Keene, which stood well to the north of the village, has disappeared, the site now occupied by a small industrial operation. The village, however, retains a variety of heritage features, including a popular tea room, a café, and the remains of its dockside streets that date from the early days when Keene was a busy steamer port on the north shore of Rice Lake.

Peterborough

The trail portion of the Grand Junction Railway ends at the south end of Peterborough, roughly where the GJR took over the trackage of the defunct Cobourg and Peterborough Railway (C&P). For a time, the Grand Junction used the C&P's Ashburnham yards and station on the east side of the Otonabee River before moving into the larger GT station located on Bethune Street, on the western fringes of downtown Peterborough. The latter station was originally part of the Midland Railway, which had built a branch line from Millbrook Junction into Peterborough. When the Midland Railway assumed the Grand Junction, it amalgamated the lines as well as the stations. The Midland Railway was subsequently absorbed by the Grand Trunk.

In the 1960s, the attractive Italianate station building was demolished to make way for an apartment building, while the tracks of the Grand Junction and the Midland Railways were abandoned by CN Rail in 1987. Although the Canadian Pacific Railway still operates a line through the city, nothing remains of the Grand Junction, the Midland, or the later CNR, except for the long, low steel trestle over the Otonabee River near Lansdowne Road, which carries a short spur line to an industrial area of Peterborough.

CHAPTER 3

The Cobourg and Peterborough Railway

The History

In 1831, few people in Upper Canada had even heard of a railway, much less seen one. In that year, however, a group of Cobourg citizens familiar with the benefits that a railway could bring began to lobby for a rail link to Rice Lake. They could envision trains hauling lumber and farm produce from ports on Rice Lake to the harbour at Cobourg. Three years later they received their charter as the Cobourg Rail Road Company, and began to raise funds. Their efforts failed; however, they tried again the next year, and this time completed surveys to the Rice Lake port villages of Bewdley, Gores Landing, and Harwood. Once again they hit a snag, this time the construction of the Trent Canal, which was viewed by prospective railway promoters as a more economical way to transport goods.

Not to be outdone, another Cobourg group, led by D'Arcy Boulton, a local businessman and grandson of the one-time chief justice of Upper Canada, D'Arcy Boulton, decided the route should go all the way to Peterborough. He was more successful in raising funds from the municipalities en route, and, in 1852, construction on the Cobourg and Peterborough Railway (C&P) began. From Cobourg the route followed the banks of Cobourg Brook, through the hills of the Oak Ridges Moraine, and on to the Rice Lake shore at Harwood. From here they needed to cross the lake.

To do this, the railway builders undertook what was at the time one of the continent's most ambitious bridge-building schemes. From the south shore of the lake, they constructed a pile-trestle bridge more than 1,500 metres in length to the middle of the lake at Tic Island. Another 3,000 metres to the north shore still remained to be crossed. From Tic Island, they sank stone cribbings at intervals of thirty metres, each connected by a truss-bridge span. In the middle, they placed a swing bridge to allow the passage of lake vessels.

On December 29, 1854, a train full of delighted but freezing revellers piled into the open cars for the journey to Peterborough. Just two days after the excursion trouble began when ice movement damaged the trestles, a hint of what was to come — damage from shifting ice necessitated costly annual repairs. In 1860, after an excursion carrying the Prince of Wales was halted at the causeway because of safety concerns, the rail line ceased operations.

However, there was potential in a different direction. To the northeast of Rice Lake, a rich bed of iron ore was discovered at Blairton, near Marmora. In 1867, the railway quickly built a new line from the east end of the lake at Trent Narrows to the bustling new town of Blairton. They renamed their line the Cobourg Peterborough and Marmora Railway and Mining Company. By 1893, however, the ore was depleted and

the line shut down for good. Rails were lifted during the First World War to supply steel for the war effort.

The Heritage

Cobourg

Being primarily a resource line, the Cobourg and Peterborough Railway built few stations and had little impact on the development of communities. A two-storey

On the south shore of Rice Lake, the remains of the ill-fated Cobourg and Peterborough Railway causeway form an eroded ridge that extends a few hundred metres into the lake and provides a perch for local fishers.

wooden station stood at Cobourg's harbour, as did several tracks and warehouses. Today the harbour has been refurbished, and walkways, condos, and marinas cover the site of the station grounds. The old station, however, still stands, now a house on Stuart Street, a short distance west of the harbour.

Except for a small industrial spur that runs north from the CN tracks near the VIA station, no other trackage remains anywhere from this line.

Harwood

North of Cobourg the roadbed, only occasionally visible as an overgrown berm (a ridge of soil), winds through the Cobourg Brook Valley, then descends to the shore of Rice Lake at Harwood. For the last few kilometres, the raised berm is clearly visible a few metres west of County Road 15, which ultimately follows the roadbed. Here a plaque was erected in 1987 to commemorate the final resting place of fourteen German rail-construction workers who died after contracting cholera during the rush to complete the line.

A gangly wooden station once stood at the Rice Lake shoreline. A storey and a half high, it once stood on the west side of the tracks, with three doors facing a wooden platform. A water tank could be found on the opposite side of the tracks. Sometime prior to 1910, the Harwood station was disassembled and rebuilt in nearby Roseneath, where for nearly a century it served as a community hall. A small plaque by the door commemorated its origins. Today the building lies in pieces once more while a local community group tries to raise the funds to reassemble it on or near its original location. The original station site has been cleared to make way for a small community beach.

Extending out into the waters of Rice Lake is one of the most unusual of Ontario's ghost rail-line relics — the remains of the four-thousand-metre causeway that once crossed the lake. North of Tic Island lay the now submerged cribbings of the trestles — a hazard for unwary boaters. On the north shore, the roadbed resumes at Hiawatha, on First Nations land, where a business calling itself The Old Railroad Stop Store and Restaurant commemorates this long-lost rail line.

Peterborough

From Hiawatha to Peterborough the roadbed is scarcely traceable, other than as an overgrown berm or bush line. It re-emerges on Rice Lake Road about three kilometres west of Mather's Corners, where a large brick building with a porch beside the right-of-way once served as a stopover/station for Cobourg and Peterborough travellers.

As the line approached Peterborough, its track merged with those of the Grand Junction Line for a short distance. The C&P built their Peterborough station in what was then called Ashburnham, near Rogers Road, north of Hunter Street. The tracks and the building later served the CNR for a number of years, until finally all vestiges were removed to create a park and a rail trail during the 1990s.

Although the C&P's bridge over Peterborough's Otonabee River no longer stands, a pair of rail-workers' homes identify the right-of-way on the west side of the river. To this day they stand on Elcombe Crescent, just south of Parkhill Road.

Chemong Lake

In 1859, the Cobourg and Peterborough Railway extended its tracks northwest from Peterborough to the shores of Chemong Lake (two kilometres east of Bridgenorth) to ship timber and farm products to

Peterborough. The route, however, is no longer traceable and is little more than an elevated bush line or tree line. From Selwyn Road, Fire Road 6 follows the roadbed to the shore of the lake.

Blairton

No evidence remains of the old mining portion of the line, known as the Cobourg Peterborough and Marmora Railway. However, the once busy iron town of Blairton, on Blairton Road north of Highway 7, is now a ghost town — one of Ontario's earliest. While its population peaked at five hundred during the time when the Blairton Mine was in operation, by 1900 it had plunged to a mere twenty-five. The grid of streets lined with homes and boarding houses fell eerily silent. Today, a few scattered wooden structures, once workers' homes, still lie along the old, overgrown streets, although newer structures and a trailer park have infiltrated the "ghostly" ambience of the location.

CHAPTER 4

The Midland Railway: Port Hope to Midland

The History

During the 1830s, Ontario had yet to see its first railway. But ports such as Port Hope and Cobourg were already planning to create rail links to the rich natural resources of Ontario's interior regions. Cobourg was first off the ground (or rather, into the ground) with its Cobourg and Peterborough Railway. This early line, completed in 1854, rebuffed Port Hope's dreams to access the same region. In fact, the first proposed name for Port Hope's dream line was the Peterborough and Port Hope Railway. With the opening of the Cobourg and Peterborough Railway, however, the proposal was abandoned.

Instead, Port Hope sought bigger dreams — Georgian Bay and the western grain trade. But that would be a few years off, and the new line began more modestly in 1857 with a route that extended only as far as Lindsay. Its new name became the more realistic Port Hope, Lindsay, and Beaverton Railway (PHL&B), and reached Beaverton, on the shores of Lake Simcoe, in 1871. By that time,

however, the name had been changed again, this time to the Midland Railway (MR).

In 1879, the link to Midland was complete. While the Cobourg and Peterborough sank, literally, into the waters of Rice Lake, the Midland prospered and expanded. Links to Lakefield through Peterborough were added, and several lines were absorbed, such as the Whitby and Port Perry, the Victoria (Lindsay to Haliburton), the Toronto and Nipissing (Toronto to Coboconk), the Grand Junction (Belleville to Peterborough), and the Belleville and North Hastings (Belleville to Eldorado). In 1884, however, the Midland Railway was leased by the burgeoning Grand Trunk, which took over the running of the Midland in 1893.

At its peak, the Midland line ventured northwest from Port Hope, across the Oak Ridges Moraine, and into Lindsay, which was at that time a major rail hub with lines extending to Haliburton, Bobcaygeon, Whitby, and Peterborough. The line then headed off across country to Beaverton. From there it followed the shore of Lake Simcoe into Orillia, which also was evolving into a major rail hub with the Georgian Bay and Seaboard (GB&S, soon to be a subsidiary of the CPR), the Northern, and the Midland railways converging here. Even the Canadian Northern had extended a branch line into Orillia from its main line at Udney, just east of the town.

From Orillia, the Midland line continued northwest, crossing the CPR at Medonte and finally tracing the Georgian Bay shores from Waubaushene into Midland. Because its main role was that of a portage line for grain coming from the upper lakes and bypassing the locks of the Welland Canal,[1] its fate was sealed with the improvements to the Welland Canal that were made in the 1930s and by the opening of the St. Lawrence Seaway in 1959. By then the grain ships had stopped, and the Lindsay station came down four years later.

In 1966, the link between Beaverton and Lindsay was abandoned. The last section to go was the line from Orillia to Midland. By the year 2000, not a metre of track remained in either Lindsay or Orillia. The Midland Railway had vanished from the landscape.

The Heritage

Port Hope

Headquartered in Port Hope, the Midland line built its main office here, a handsome three-storey stone structure a few blocks southwest of today's town hall. The original site is now a parking lot. The roadbed between that point and the town's stunning main street, Walton Street, is now a walkway that passes the railway's little-noticed downtown "station." To service passengers from the downtown hotels, such as the Midland and the St. Lawrence Hotels, both still standing, the line opened a waiting room in the rear portion of a store. The building remains (currently occupied by Furby Books and Lents Travel), and the doorways that opened into the waiting room are still visible on one side of the building.

From the downtown area the line ran north along Cavan Street, where a number of older industrial buildings still linger. The railway then wound its way into hill country northwest of Port Hope, but very few settlements of any size sprang up in its wake. At Millbrook, once a pivotal junction for the branch line to Peterborough, little evidence remains — only one building, once a railway hotel located at the west end of the town, reflects the rail era and the track alignment. Otherwise, the station grounds are obliterated, replaced with new developments. Despite the absence of its railway heritage, Millbrook's main street retains many historic stores, an early fire hall, and a mill. Because of this undisturbed townscape, Millbrook has begun attracting the attention of Hollywood; the 2003 made-for-TV movie *Music Man* was one of the films shot there.

Lakefield

In 1869, the Midland Railway extended its line from Peterborough through Auburn Mills, on the northern fringe of Peterborough, and on to the town of Lakefield. Early trains with nicknames that included the "Cannonball Express" and "Boosterville Buzzer" would carry vacationers to the Lakefield docks on the shore of the Trent River. Freight shipments would haul cement out from the Lakefield Cement Plant.

Since its demise as a railway, the route has become the Rotary Greenway Trail, which runs from Peterborough north to the Trent University campus. From there to Lakefield it is known as the Lakefield Rail Trail.

In Lakefield, rail heritage lives on, not just in the rail trail but in the form of an early station, built by the GTR

Much of the Lakefield Rail Trail follows a scenic route along the banks of the Trent River, offering shelter for trail-users, as well as providing information plaques at various intervals.

after taking over the Midland line. It remains on its original site, in its original form, and is now a popular used-book store. An information plaque on the rail trail in front of the station describes the rail-era story of Lakefield.

Peterborough

Today, the only tracks in Peterborough belong to the CPR. The line continues to haul freight, such as nepheline syenite, used in the manufacturing of glass and ceramics, and mined north of Havelock, and products from local industry such as the Quaker Oats plant. Locals, however, yearn for the return of passenger service to Toronto, which, until abolished by the Mulroney government in 1990, was provided by VIA Rail.

In Peterborough, the Midland alignment has become a walking trail commencing near the historic 1837 Hutchinson House,[2] located at the corner of Brock and Bethune Streets, and winding its way through Jackson Park en route to Lindsay.

Halfway between Peterborough and Omemee, the trail crosses the Doube trestle, a dizzying thirty metres above Buttermilk Creek. The trestle, originally five hundred metres long, was later partly filled in. Today, it consists of a nine-span, two-hundred-metre iron bridge. In Omemee, the rail trail crosses a much lower trestle over the Pigeon River, then passes the site of the former station, now located in a nearby schoolyard, where it is used for storage.

The section of the Midland Railway between Omemee and Peterborough was originally a branch line, whereas the main line ran directly from Millbrook through Omemee to Lindsay. From the scenic community of Bethany north to the west end of Omemee, County Road 38 has been built over much of the roadbed. Halfway between these two locations sits the ghost town of Franklyn with its vacant, overgrown lots and a sign that marks the site of a lone cemetery.

From Omemee, the Midland's main line leads west toward Lindsay, as does the continuation of the rail trail from Peterborough.

Lindsay

The town of Lindsay, the county seat and gateway to the Kawarthas, could once boast a proud railway heritage. Rails converged on it from five directions, giving rise to no fewer than five stations at various times.

The first was the Midland Railway station on Paul Street. The original route of the Midland took it along the east side of the Scugog River to a bridge that crossed the river near Colborne Street. The alignment then led north before swinging west. Later, when the Victoria Railway (VR) entered town, it crossed the tracks of the Midland at Victoria Junction and shared the Midland station. Later still, it extended its tracks down Victoria Street, and,

in conjunction with yet another newly arrived line, the Whitby, Port Perry, and Lindsay (WPP&L), constructed a "union" station at Victoria and Melbourne Streets.

Eventually, when all three lines fell under the ownership of the Grand Trunk, the new owners decided to bring the Midland tracks into town farther south so that all three lines could use the same station on Durham Street. After it burned down, a new two-storey wooden station, with offices and sleeping quarters on the second floor, replaced it. This station remained in use until 1966, when the CNR demolished it. The fifth station, located on Lindsay Street North, belonged to the CPR. It was never a component of the Grand Trunk or the CNR. The Grand Trunk built a new bridge over the Scugog River in 1901 to replace the original three-span truss bridge, a structure that still stands near the east end of Durham Street.

From Lindsay, the Midland line lead across country, the only station stops on this stretch being at Grasshill and Cambray — small hamlets located amid farm fields west of Lindsay. Farther along, at Lorneville Junction (in Victoria County, now the City of Kawartha Lakes), it crossed the route of the Toronto and Nipissing Railway. Once a busy rail hub, Lorneville Junction has almost become a ghost town, with only a handful of early rail-workers' homes scattered along a typical grid of streets. The rail station still survives and sits behind a farmhouse a short distance to the north, barely visible from the road.

At Beaverton, the route originally terminated at the shores of Lake Simcoe, where a marina and boathouses have now taken over the site. When the MR extended its tracks to Midland, it built a new station farther inland. The station grounds from the later building are now the site of a health centre, located near the corner of Centre and Franklin Streets. The original connection to the wharf is still discernable between Mara Road and King Street.

Between Beaverton and Orillia, evidence of the route has faded from the landscape, although the grassy ridge that was once the roadbed can be seen adjacent to today's CN lakeside line at Mara Beach. Vanished station stops at Brechin and Uptergrove, however, are unmarked, leaving no evidence of the rail heritage of the area.

Orillia

Atherly, situated on the east shore of The Narrows that connect Lake Simcoe with Lake Couchiching, was a rail-junction village. Here, the Midland's tracks converged with those of the Georgian Bay and Seaboard (GBS) and the Northern and Pacific Junction Railway (N&PJ) to cross the narrow channel of water. The Midland's CNR swing bridge over The Narrows is still in place, while that of the GBS is an overgrown causeway. Both are visible from the new Highway 12 bridge.

Through much of Orillia, the roadbed has been converted to a walkway. Happily, Orillia's wonderful stone-and-brick Grand Trunk junction station, which replaced that of the Midland, still survives at Lake and King Streets.

The former Grand Trunk station in Orillia is well-preserved, both outside and in. It is now used as a bus terminal and tourist office. Outside, the platforms remain in place along with various railway artifacts, such as signals and baggage carts.

The yards of the Northern and Pacific Junction Railway once lay west of Matchedash Street and south of King Street, but this is now the site of new development. The location of the original Midland Station at the foot of Mississauga Street has, for a number of years, been home to a collection of heritage rail coaches, which served as the popular Ossawippi Restaurant, just recently closed.

Coldwater

From Orillia to Coldwater, a rough rail trail known as the Lightfoot Trail follows the roadbed. North of Orillia the line passes through the scant vestiges of the ghost towns of Uhtoff, which formerly had three sawmills, an Orange Hall, a church, and a half-dozen workers' homes, and Foxmead, also once a sawmill village with a school, church, and lime kiln. When the post office moved to nearby Bradley Corners in 1940, the latter rail-side hamlet became a ghost town. A sign marks its location. In both places, vague cellar holes and foundations lining the right-of-way are the only evidence that busy rail-side villages once existed here.

In Coldwater, while the roadbed is barely visible, the bridge, which once carried trains across the Coldwater River and now carries cars, is part of a private laneway

Midland's last station was that built by the CNR in a more modern international style. Constructed in 1952, it was demolished by the CN in the late 1980s.

leading to a collection of private homes, one of which is the two-storey former Coldwater station. Fortunately, the owners have preserved much of the building's external appearance.

Midland

From Coldwater to Waubaushene the line once again vanishes from view; however, the Tay Shore Rail Trail more than compensates.

This scenic trail follows the Midland Railway's roadbed along the shore of Georgian Bay from the historic village of Waubaushene through the one-time lumber-mill town of Victoria Harbour, where John Waldie reigned as the second largest lumber baron at the time, surpassed only by J.R. Booth. It then continues on to the outskirts of Midland. Along the route, historic plaques depict such features as the now-dismantled Hogg's Bay Trestle, while offering conveniences such as benches and washrooms for trail-users.

The trail ends near the popular Saint-Marie among the Hurons mission village, where the trail crosses the Wye River on a surviving railway trestle. While new developments, especially condos, have obliterated the Midland's alignment to its terminus at the foot of King Street, some of the town's famous murals depict this era in history. The site of the terminus has now become a waterfront park and cruise-ship terminal.

CHAPTER 5

The Whitby, Port Perry, and Lindsay Railway

The History

From a location on the shores of Lake Scugog, the business interests of Port Perry were worried, as were those of the two neighbouring villages of Manchester and Prince Albert. They were afraid that the 1850s rail era was going to leave them behind. As in Port Hope to the east, the businessmen felt that a link with Lake Ontario was vital to their livelihood. In particular, they wanted a rail line to link Port Whitby with Georgian Bay, which they saw as a valuable route that could carry lumber and wheat through their region and provide an outlet for their own goods. In 1853, they received a charter from the government to form the Port Whitby and Port Huron Railway. With few municipalities along the proposed route prepared to provide the needed funding, this charter, like so many others, lapsed.

Meanwhile, they watched as Port Hope began the Midland Railway to Lindsay, Beaverton, and Georgian Bay (although many years would pass before it was completed). Also, George Laidlaw[1] and the owners of the Gooderham and Worts Distillery in Toronto started

the Toronto and Nipissing Railway (T&N), established to bring raw materials to the distillery. These two lines would likely nullify any attempt by Port Perry to obtain the longed-for rail connection.

In 1868, however, these businessmen received a charter to build the Port Whitby and Port Perry Railway (PW&PP). Although it fell well short of their preferred terminus on Georgian Bay, it was a start. But with both Manchester and Prince Albert wanting to be on the route, the line was forced to adopt a winding route through both communities, each located a few kilometres south of Port Perry.

But those dreams of an extension continued to burn, and the charter was soon revised to become the Whitby, Port Perry, and Extension Railway, which would allow it to build from Port Whitby to the shores of Lake Muskoka, where it would connect with the steamers *Ogemah* and *Victoria*, also owned by the railway. Again, the reality fell short. The extension went to Lindsay instead, with a connection from there to the Trent Canal and then to the Victoria Railway, with its links to Haliburton.

Construction began in 1869 with the Prince of Wales turning the sod in Whitby. By 1871, trains were running between Port Whitby and Port Perry. The link to Lindsay was finished in 1876. But other railways were in an expansion mode and in 1881 the Whitby, Port Perry, and Lindsay Railway (WPP&L) became part of the Midland system, which, in turn, was absorbed by the Grand Trunk.

Having also acquired the Toronto and Nipissing line to the west, the new owners built a connecting link between the WPP&L and T&N between Cresswell (renamed Manilla Junction), located about twenty kilometres north of Port Perry, and Wick, about eight kilometres to the west. Wick became Blackwater Junction.

The combination of an excessive number of rail lines, the decline in lumbering, and the arrival of the automobile meant that the WPP&L was doomed. The section between Port Perry and Manilla Junction disappeared as early as 1937, and that between Port Perry and Port Whitby four years later.

The remaining route continued in use until 1991, with trucks finally replacing the boxcars, when this line, too, fell silent.

Whitby's decorative Grand Trunk station, which marked that line's junction with the Whitby, Port Perry, and Lindsay Railway, now serves as the Station Gallery, which offers free admission to exhibits by local artists as well as permanent displays.

The Heritage

Whitby

The terminus of the Whitby, Port Perry, and Lindsay Railway lay at the harbour in Port Whitby. Originally known as Windsor, the Lake Ontario port developed into a busy shipping centre with wharfs and grain elevators. The village of Port Whitby developed on a network of streets nearby. A number of the heritage homes here date from the days when Port Whitby was a busy harbour. The line linked with the Grand Trunk at Whitby Junction, where an attractive wooden Grand Trunk station with three towers stood until 1970, at which time it was relocated to start a new life as an art gallery. The aptly named Station Gallery is located near the corner of Henry and Victoria Streets in Whitby.

From that point, the WPP&L led straight north into downtown Whitby, where a simple two-storey station served passengers. The station survived until the 1970s and the engine house was home to an auto-repair shop until the 1990s. Today, both are gone, as is the right-of-way.

From Whitby the line continued northward, passing through Brooklin — the right-of-way is now incorporated into the local street system — and then on to Myrtle. The stations built were simple wooden affairs. The one at Myrtle, on Myrtle Road west of Highway 12, lacked even an operator's bay window. Later, a separate community known as Myrtle Station would grow up around the CPR station on the Ontario and Quebec (O&Q) line, which was under a 999-year lease to the CPR. The WPP&L then wound its way through the hills of the daunting Oak Ridge Moraine, prompting local travellers to nickname it the "Nip and Tuck," since it was nip and tuck whether the little engine could make the grade. Atop the moraine was a flag station with the appropriate name of High Point.

Two more little stations stood at Manchester and Prince Albert, the former three kilometres to the south of the village, on Highway 12. Only a line of trees and a single building mark the site. The roadbed through Prince Albert is no longer discernable, nor is the one in Port Perry.

Port Perry

Despite the significant role that the railway played in the growth of this town, there is very little left to commemorate that role. The station grounds, the siding, and the lumberyards are now part of Palmer Park, and the docks have been replaced by new waterfront redevelopment. Today a popular sightseeing boat, the double-decker *Woodman* (one of the lake's original steamers carried the same name), departs from a new dock located at the foot of Queen Street.

The station was dragged across Water Street and is now a flower shop, retaining much of the building's original shape. Looming above the north side of Queen Street, however, is a rare and significant relic of the days of rail — Currie's Grain Elevator. Built in 1874 with the arrival of the railway, it stands twenty metres high and rests on a nearly one-metre-thick stone foundation. The building, having survived the fires that ravaged the downtown in the 1880s, is likely the Whitby, Port Perry, and Lindsay's most significant surviving heritage feature.

Port Perry to Lindsay

From Palmer Park, the right-of-way follows Old Rail Lane, and then continues on as a walkway through Port Perry Wildlife Park. It then promptly vanishes again. Station stops in Sonya and Seagrave have vanished, as well, although a few early rail-era buildings, such as a store and a former hotel in Seagrave, still linger.

Not until the town of Cresswell does some evidence of the right-of-way re-emerge. Station Street, which was built along it, leads to the site of Manilla Junction, just a few metres north of the town. The main street of Cresswell retains several early structures, including a fine one-time hotel, now a private home.

East of Cresswell the old roadbed becomes the Kawartha Trans Canada Trail. Under the jurisdiction of the City of Kawartha Lakes, this section of the WPP&L trail follows the right-of-way east into Lindsay at Angeline Street, then west to Blackwater Junction, where it meets the Beaver Meadow Wetland Trail on the Toronto & Nipissing. At Eldon Road, where the family of Marg Fevang erected an Inukshuk to honour her memory, a shelter offers respite to trail-users.

A small country station at Mariposa, east of Manilla Junction, served the farm villages of Oakwood and Little Britain. While a village didn't develop at Mariposa, the location did contain the substantial feed-mill operations of Hogg and Lyttle. Although both station and feed mill have gone, the trail is well-maintained and passes a former WPP&L freight shed, the only significant heritage structure other than the feed mill left in Port Perry to mark the history of this long-lost rail line.

CHAPTER 6

The Toronto and Nipissing Railway: The Coby Connection

The History

Despite the rather short length of the abandoned portion of this line, the Toronto and Nipissing Railway (T&N) boasts a surprising number of surviving stations.

In 1869, railway promoter George Laidlaw, along with William Gooderham, owner of Toronto's Gooderham and Worts Distillery, decided to extend a line northeast of Toronto to provide a reliable shipment of grain to the distillery and to link with the planned CPR transcontinental line at Nipissing Junction, close to North Bay. The name Nipissing Junction still exists but now refers to the junction between today's CN and CP lines.

As happened with many others, this route fell short of its intended destination and terminated at a tiny lumber town called Coboconk, located in the heart of the Kawartha Lakes area. While most of Ontario's other existing lines were built at what was called "provincial" or broad gauge (five-foot six-inch rails, as required by the province in order to obtain grants), the T&N went the opposite way and built a less costly narrow gauge (three-foot six-inch rails).

From Toronto, the T&N negotiated running rights on the existing Grand Trunk line as far as Scarborough Junction. This entailed adding a third rail so that the narrow gauge would fit within the Grand Trunk's standard-gauge tracks.

The T&N's Toronto terminal was not in the Grand Trunk's newly built Union Station, but in a smaller building located on the south side of the Gooderham and Worts Distillery.

In September 1871, a trainload of dignitaries travelled to the new station in Uxbridge for the line's opening ceremony. The following year, the route reached Coboconk. During the 1870s, with a depression dragging down the economy, the T&N's expected revenues failed to materialize. As a result, in 1881, the Midland Railway absorbed the line and altered the tracks to match its own standard gauge. About the same time, Midland also acquired the faltering Whitby, Port Perry, and Lindsay line, and connected the two routes at Blackwater Junction, just east of Uxbridge. From here, the Midland Railway built a new link eastward into Lindsay to join up with its original main line.

With the Midland Railway now owning the Grand Junction Railway (Belleville to Peterborough) as well, that portion of the Toronto and Nipissing south of Blackwater Junction became part of a busy Belleville–Peterborough–Lindsay–Toronto line. Between Blackwater Junction and Coboconk there was little business except for the Coboconk sawmill and stones from a massive quarry at Kirkfield, located between those two points. However, when the quarry closed in 1961, that portion of the line was abandoned. The remainder — from Uxbridge to Lindsay — fell out of use in 1991.

GO trains now carry passengers along the route from Stouffville to Toronto, past a pair of original Toronto and Nipissing stations at Unionville and Markham, both of which have been rehabilitated.

From Stouffville to Uxbridge, the York and Durham Heritage Railway (Y&D) offers scenic trips through the Oak Ridge Moraine using vintage coaches and diesel engines. Beyond that, the ghost line begins.

The engines and coaches of the York and Durham Heritage Railway bring the ghosts of the Toronto and Nipissing Railway back to life beside the restored Uxbridge station.

The Heritage

Stouffville

The Toronto and Nipissing built eleven stations along its line between Blackwater Junction and Toronto, and a further ten between the Junction and Coboconk. From Stouffville, a branch line, the Simcoe Junction Railway, angled north to Sutton, near the shore of Lake Simcoe. At nearby Jackson's Point, tourists could disembark at the lakeside landing. The main station stood farther south, right in the village of Sutton. In the 1980s, following the closing of the line, the Sutton station was moved to its new home on the grounds of the Georgina Pioneer Village on Civic Centre Road. No other stations have survived on this branch line, and the right-of-way remains barely visible.

A new station in Stouffville, built in 1995, serves GO Transit commuters travelling to Toronto, as well as tourists travelling on the popular York and Durham Heritage Railway between Stouffville and Uxbridge. Using vintage diesels and coaches, the heritage train snakes through the woods and fields of the Oak Ridges Moraine, pausing at the village of Goodwood before reaching its yards in Uxbridge.

Uxbridge

The historic station in Uxbridge (on Durham Regional Road 47) was built in the 1890s. Now restored, it displays the distinctive "witch's hat" style, with its conical roof above the waiting room. In the yards are the three heritage locomotives and the half-dozen coaches that tourists ride.

Blackwater Junction

From Uxbridge, the now-empty right-of-way leads to Blackwater Junction on Highway 12, where it is now a snowmobile trail. At the junction, the station, with its bay windows on either side of the building, once stood between the two sets of tracks. But today there is no sign of this building nor of the elevators, sawmill, or stockyard that were once at the site.

Within the village, the Bric-A-Brac Shoppe occupies what was once the railway hotel, although few other rail-era buildings remain.

Lorneville Junction

On its way to Lorneville Junction, the T&N route travels north, passing the villages of Sunderland and Cannington. Although no rail buildings remain in Sunderland, the historic main street offers a townscape of vintage stores. Along the south side of the village of Cannington, the station grounds, near the corner of Shedden (named for railway-builder John Shedden) and St. John Streets, are overgrown. A number of rail-era structures, however, still survive on Shedden Street, including a one-time hotel that is now a private residence.

But Cannington does have a "station." The one from Mt. Albert, built by the Canadian Northern Railway around 1908, was relocated here in the 1980s. Today, it stands on Peace Street as part of the Cannington Centennial Museum's heritage village. The collection also includes a caboose (poorly maintained), two log cabins, and the town hall from the nearby hamlet of Derryville.

Lorneville Junction (on County Road 47) owes its origins to its position at the junction of the Toronto and Nipissing and the Midland rail lines. Its grid of streets lies between the two rights-of-way, although neither remains visible. Cracked sidewalks, the small homes of the railway employees, and the historic general store all evoke the ghosts of the days when puffing engines would pause at the crossing, waiting for another train to cross.

The diminutive Lorneville station lurks behind a farmhouse a short distance north, just barely visible from the road.

Kirkfield

North of Lorneville Junction, the Toronto and Nipissing came to the hamlet of Eldon Station, which contained a store, a gristmill, and stockyards. Today, this quiet and somewhat remote place resembles a ghost town on Eldon Station Road, a few kilometres east of Kawartha Road 46.

Kirkfield is significant, not because of the T&N but because it was the birthplace of the Canadian Northern Railway's co-builder, William Mackenzie, whose grand summer home is a village landmark.

The Kirkfield quarries kept the trains of the T&N running until the 1960s; one of the quarry engines is on display at the Simcoe County Museum near Barrie. Located north of the village, the quarries were close to one of the Trent Canal lift locks, well worth a visit on its own. The right-of-way that crossed County Road 6 just north of 46 is also scarcely visible, although the station survived the demise of the line for many years. It was lost to fire in 2001.

Victoria Road

This historic village, which appeared in conjunction with the construction of the Victoria Colonization Road in the 1860s, was built to encourage settlement on land to the north. But the soil in the area proved infertile, and today the road comes to an end in a marsh just north of the town. The village did grow considerably, however, once rails were laid. Today, the station remains on the same site, although its exterior has been altered and it is barely visible behind a cedar hedge.

East of Victoria Road, en route to the terminus at Coboconk, the line passed by the Raven Lake cement plant (now just a ruin on private property), and the little logging town of Corsons' Siding. During the winter logging season the latter was nicknamed "Hell's Half Acre," because the Georgian Bay sailors who made their home there were often drunk, their behaviour outraging the year-round inhabitants.

The last obstacle for the building of the railway was the 160-metre-long trestle needed to cross Cameron Lake's north bay. The crossing, a pile-trestle bridge once located some six kilometres west of Coboconk, is now gone.

Coboconk

Coboconk, located on Highway 35, about forty kilometres north of Lindsay, is now a busy centre for Kawartha Lakes cottagers. Downtown, the popular Pattie House Restaurant occupies an early hotel built when the Toronto and Nipissing Railway arrived in 1873.

The station, the village's second (the first was lost to fire around 1900), has been relocated from its original site (where a Rona store now stands) and was placed in the Rotary Park, half a kilometre to the north. It is gradually undergoing restoration as an event venue. Coboconk is also home to one of the province's more unusual structures, the Coby "gaol," a tiny two-cell stone lockup located a few paces from Highway 35. Rescued from demolition by a community group after it had sat vacant for fifty years, it now houses a small gift shop.

CHAPTER 7

The Lindsay, Bobcaygeon, and Pontypool Railway: Burketon to Bobcaygeon

The History

Situated at the vital link between Pigeon and Sturgeon Lakes, Bobcaygeon was, from its inception, the industrial heart of the Kawartha Lakes country. It was here in 1833 that, to facilitate the lumber industry, the first lock was built on what would become the Trent Canal system.

Among the first and most influential of the lumber companies was the Boyd Lumber Company. Starting with a single sawmill in 1846, Mossom Boyd and his sons expanded their lumber empire to include tugs and barges. The family-run company, the Trent Valley Navigation Company, became a vital outlet for lumber and farm commodities, while bringing in various other products and providing passenger service for the many small communities along the Kawartha Lakes. But moving lumber and passengers was slow and seasonal, and the Boyds began to press for a rail link to Lindsay, where the Midland Railway had its main line.

When that initiative failed, the Boyds persevered, this time proposing a link to the more recently built Ontario and Quebec Railway (O&Q), which, unlike the Midland Railway, had the advantage of providing a more direct link to Peterborough, and, more importantly, to the port of Toronto. In 1890, they succeeded in acquiring a charter to build the line from Bobcaygeon, through Lindsay, and then to Pontypool on the O&Q. A financial depression, however, delayed the start, and it was not until 1904 that the Lindsay, Bobcaygeon, and Pontypool Railway (LB&P) began construction. It quickly became apparent that the terrain around Pontypool was too rugged, and the link was switched to another point on the O&Q, Burketon, a small settlement west of Pontypool. North of Burketon the landscape was flatter and the line was completed in a matter of weeks.

At about the same time, the CPR was building the Georgian Bay and Seaboard line, its point of origin also at a junction on the O&Q. The two lines converged in Lindsay, where they shared a short section of track and a station. Timetables show a dozen stations along this LB&P line, but as the CPR was now running two duplicate lines between the O&Q line and Lindsay, it opted to abandon the southern portion of the LB&P, between Burketon and Lindsay, in 1932.

When the opening of a newer and bigger Welland Canal reduced traffic on the Georgian Bay and Seaboard, a section of that line between Lindsay and Atherly was closed in 1937. At that time, the remaining track of the LB&P, between Lindsay and Bobcaygeon, and that of the GB&S, between Dranoel and Lindsay, were amalgamated as the "Bobcaygeon subdivision" of the CPR.

Finally, with little traffic originating on the Lindsay to Bobcaygeon section, those tracks were finally lifted in 1961, and the entire route of the Lindsay, Bobcaygeon, and Pontypool Railway fell silent.

The Heritage

Burketon

This little village lies nestled in the steep sandy hills of the mighty Oak Ridge Moraine, a little west of County Road 57, between Lake Scugog and Lake Ontario. The road that runs directly through the village, the Scugog Road, dates back to the 1840s, when it provided the pioneer settlers in the Lake Scugog area with their only link to Lake Ontario, at Port Darlington.

The first station here was a two-storey "Van Horne–style" building, the same style as nearly all of those built along the Ontario & Quebec line. It was later replaced with a small shed, which was built solely for passengers travelling on the once-busy Havelock to Toronto commuter train.

From this point the LB&P led northward. The *Y* that formed the junction between the two lines has now mostly vanished, and only the western arm remains visible as a lane.

Burketon to Lindsay

Where the route makes its way across farmers' fields to Nestleton, a small village to the north, it has mostly been ploughed under or remains visible only as a line of vegetation. The station at Nestleton was built in the style of the CPR's standard plan, known as the "Swiss Cottage," a simple but elegant single-storey structure with a bell-caste roof extending over the full front of the building and with a wrap-around at each end. In fact, all the smaller LB&P stations copied this pattern. The Nestleton station served as a private home until the late 1980s, when it was replaced with a new house.

The next rural station to the north, Janetville, was constructed in the same style as the one in Nestleton. It also survived the demise of the line as a seasonal dwelling, but succumbed to fire in the 1990s. Few other buildings remain to mark this settlement, which was also known as Viewlake.

Farther north, the River Road follows the shores of Lake Scugog. The causeway, which carried the rails across East Cross Creek, remains visible from the road.

Lindsay

The two sets of rails, those of the LB&P and the GB&S, met at a point called Lindsay Junction, where a converted boxcar filled the role of station for many years. The in-town station, which the two lines shared, was one of the CPR's rare "witch's hat" styles, with a conical roof atop the waiting room. Located near the corner of Wellington Street and Lindsay Street North, the station, which had a brief period as a museum in the 1960s, was torn down later that same decade.

Lindsay to Bobcaygeon

As the line to Bobcaygeon was more recently abandoned, its remains are more visible today. From Lindsay, it can be discerned as a line of vegetation up to Heights Road where, for seven kilometres, it becomes the Dunsford Nature Trail.

The Dunsford station was also built in the popular Swiss Cottage style and survives today as a private home on the shores of Emily Creek.

From Dunsford to Bobcaygeon, County Road 24 was built along the rail bed and provides the same scenic views for drivers that the trains once offered their passengers. Originally, summer stations were built en route at the popular Ancona and Kenstone beaches.

Upon entering Bobcaygeon, the former roadbed crosses the bridge over Little Bob Channel, once a busy shipping point for the town. Today, the roadbed ends at the corner of Mansfield and Park Streets, where the station was once situated. Another of the CPR's standard-plan stations, it was a large one-and-a-half-storey building with a steep bell-caste roof punctured by a small dormer. Unfortunately, the attractive structure was demolished shortly after the line was abandoned in 1961. With new

The diminutive Dunsford station was typical of the station plan which the CPR used on this short rail line. It survives today as a cottage on Emily Creek.

homes having been built all around the site, not a scrap of evidence remains to show that a railway once brought in tourists and shipped out lumber.

Although the Boyd family, who ran the Trent Valley Navigation Company, is celebrated on historic plaques in the area, the once-grand Boyd mansion fell into disrepair and eventually burned down sometime in the 1980s. Only portions of the stone fence remain today. The Boyd Building, which now houses the Boyd Heritage Museum, was built in 1889 by Mossom Boyd's son, Mossom Martin Boyd, and originally served as the office for the Navigation Company.

Sitting close to the centre of the town, the Boyd Building looks across to the most visual link to the town's heritage — the lock and bridge on the historic Trent Canal. In fact, the original lock at Bobcaygeon was the first to be built on the Trent-Severn Waterway. Known as Lock 32, it was rebuilt in 1919 and is the third replacement lock at this site. The swing bridge here is the only one of its type along the Trent system.

CHAPTER 8

The Victoria Railway:
Into the Haliburton Highlands

The History

Unlike the scene today, the town of Lindsay of the 1850s was evolving from a remote mill town into one of Ontario's main railway hubs. In 1857, the first trains of the Midland Railway arrived here from Port Hope. In the late 1860s, the Canada Land and Immigration Company, responsible for luring settlers into the Haliburton area, was anxious to build a rail line that linked Peterborough, which had been the destination for Peter Robinson's Irish settlers in the 1820s, to Lindsay. It was suggested that the line would be constructed of wood, with iron rails covering the surface. But this initial proposal failed.

However, railway promoter George Laidlaw was determined that the railway he had in mind would succeed. His proposed line would extend from a junction with the Midland Line in Lindsay and run as far as Fenelon Falls. In 1871, it was chartered as the Fenelon Falls Railway. But the route was too short to gain much interest. Not to be deterred, Laidlaw next proposed a line called the Fenelon Falls and Ottawa Valley Railway.

Included was a mandate to construct its line well beyond Fenelon Falls, or even Haliburton, with the intent of building all the way to Mattawa on the upper Ottawa River and making a connection with proposed tracks of the transcontinental CPR. The justification was not just to bring settlers into the Haliburton area but to tap the timber and mineral riches thought to abound in those distant hills.

This, however, left the Peterborough proponents of the earlier line quite unhappy, and they refused to help fund the Lindsay-based line. As a result, the more northerly group of townships through which the line would pass separated themselves municipally from Peterborough County and formed the provisional county of Haliburton.

Sod was turned in 1874, and construction began at Victoria Junction on the Midland line in the north end of Lindsay. Since this location was well north of the town, the new railway was allowed to use the existing Midland station, where the Victoria line crossed the MR tracks. Soon afterward the line's name was changed to the Victoria Railway with the hope that the "royal" nomenclature would encourage funding. Fortunately, it was relatively easy to build through the terrain, with bridges being required in only a few locations. Nor were the rocks of the Canadian Shield an obstacle; in fact, much of the route passed through large tracts of level land.

The expected mineral and the timber riches to the north, however, proved meagre, and the line proceeded no farther than the lumber town of Haliburton. Tourism here was not as vibrant as in places such as Algonquin Park, and both passenger and freight traffic remained light. The last of the Haliburton Highlander tourist trains ran the line in 1955, although a farewell excursion train did make a final run in 1974. The CN abandoned the line entirely in 1983, after proposals to develop a tour train came to nought, and the rails were lifted. Ironically, the route has once more become a popular tourist attraction for snowmobilers, hikers, and cyclists using the Victoria Rail Trail and Haliburton Rail Trail year-round.

Even before the tracks of the Victoria Railway were lifted in 1983, this station in Haliburton had become an art gallery. Established in 1980, the Rails End Gallery and Arts Centre features exhibits by local artists. The building, still in its original location, now rests upon a new foundation.

The Heritage

Lindsay

In 1877, the Victoria Railway built its first station in downtown Lindsay. Later, along with the Whitby Port Perry and Lindsay Railway (WPP&L), they constructed a union station at Victoria and Melbourne Streets. When the Midland Railway acquired the WPP&L, it re-routed its line more directly into Lindsay, building a bridge over the Scugog River and running its track along Durham Street to meet up with those already built by the WPP&L. However, after the station burned, the Grand Trunk, by now having absorbed both the Midland and the Victoria Railways, built a large two-storey station that served both that line and the subsequent CNR until 1966, when it was demolished.

Although an asphalt pathway follows the path of the Victoria line from downtown Lindsay at Victoria Street, no railway heritage has survived there. Both stations and tracks have all been removed, and the land they once occupied largely remains vacant at the time of writing.

Along the more southerly section of the trail, the landscape is one of lakeside marshes and rolling farmlands. Cameron, a rural community on the route, has a few historic homes and an old general store. Its former station site, a few metres east of Highway 35, offers some early rail-era homes, but no surviving railway buildings.

Fenelon Falls

Although the right-of-way has been altered through the town, rail heritage in Fenelon Falls abounds. On Highway 121, the attractive little Italianate wooden station still stands on its original site, and is now home to a Chamber of Commerce office. The rail bridge that crosses the Trent Canal has been decked in for trail-users, except during the summer months, when it remains open to allow boat traffic from the Trent Canal to enter Cameron Lake.

From Fenelon Falls, the trail follows the shore of Cameron Lake and exposes trail-users to some very scenic views across the lake. After leaving the lakeshore, it follows the east bank of the Burnt River, passing Fell Station, where the only feature was the two-storey wooden station/section man's house, now gone.

The trail next comes to one of the route's more interesting bridges, the "Iron Bridge," which carries the trail across the Burnt River. This 1952 replacement had originally been constructed for use in China before the Second World War. But the war and the post-war politics of that country foiled the plan, and, instead of being shipped to China, the fifty-metre-long bridge with its web of iron beams looming above the tracks now spans the river.

The trail then continues into the community of Burnt River (originally named Retties Station). When the first station burned down, it was replaced by a long wooden building on the north side of the tracks. While that station, too, is now gone, the name board for the Burnt River station has been placed at the northern approach to this quiet village.

Kinmount

The village of Kinmount offers perhaps the best example of rail preservation on the line. Originally the juxtaposition of two main colonization roads, the Monck and the Bobcaygeon,[1] Kinmount's riverside location attracted several mill operations, as well as the route of the Victoria Railway.

Among those who boarded the train for Kinmount in 1874 was a hardy group of 350 Icelanders fleeing economic hardship in their native country. Housed in poorly ventilated shanties around Kinmount, more than two dozen people, mostly children, perished in the bitter winter while others tried in vain to conquer the area's difficult soils. Ultimately, they decided to go back to Toronto and then head to Manitoba, where an Icelandic community still thrives at Gimli. A provincial plaque in Kinmount commemorates their early efforts.

The Grand Trunk station, built after the GT assumed the Victoria Railway, today forms the focus of a heritage park. Repainted in its Tuscan-red and yellow paint scheme, the building now houses a model railway layout of the Irondale, Bancroft, and Ottawa Railway line (IB&O), which ran eastward from the Victoria Railway at Howland Junction, just to the north. The Kinmount Model Railway and Museum is located in what was once the agent's office and baggage room of the well-preserved station. The former waiting room now houses a tourist information office. Also located in the park is the old Austin mill, the community's historic water-powered sawmill, which has been painstakingly restored.

Kinmount to Haliburton

From Kinmount, the trail resumes its route along the banks of the Burnt River to the key railway intersection of Howland Junction. It was here that the tracks of the IB&O Railway branched eastward to the iron mines of Irondale, then on to its junction with the Central Ontario Railway north of Bancroft.

Today, a pair of rail-era homes still stand at the junction, as does the neglected little Howland station. Basically little more than a waiting room, it replaced an earlier and larger station building.

Lurking in the undergrowth are the remains of the hand-operated turntable. A few paces north leads to one of the Victoria Railway's loftiest bridges, built over Kendrick's Creek, a small tributary of the Burnt River. Constructed in 1896, and known as the "High Trestle," this iron structure looms sixteen metres above the water and stretches for 150 metres from one side to the other.

Cemetery Road leads from County Road 1 to not just the cemetery, but to the site of the Gelert station and the ghost town of Gelert. One of the railway's larger standard stations, the building measured twenty-five metres long by seven metres wide. Inside, along with the waiting room, freight room, and ticket office, were the agents' quarters, which included two bedrooms, a kitchen, and a small living room. Sawlogs, tanbark, and cattle were often shipped from this location. But not only has the rail era ended here, but so, too, has the life of the town. A handful of early buildings still line Cemetery Road, the main street, but with several of them now vacant, the quiet place now has a "ghost town" air.

Just a few paces to the north leads one to another trestle, this one crossing the Drag River. Here a small iron bridge, known as a "pony truss" bridge, was constructed in 1939. North of Gelert, the railway and the county road both swing to the east, where the trail parallels the road. Amidst a region of flat farmer's fields, the community of Lochlin faces the track. With the boomtown-style general store and a trio of early houses facing the track from the opposite side of the road, the scene evokes the image of a prairie station village.

But perhaps the most striking scene along the trail is that of the gaunt concrete shells of the Standard Chemical Plant in Donald. Of the string of company houses that once lined the track, only one pair survives, as does the Donald store, now a bakery. Newer homes have also appeared around the village, while the station grounds now contain the community mail boxes.

Built in 1900, the Standard Chemical plant in Donald used the ample supply of local wood to manufacture charcoal, acetate of lime, and wood alcohol. The operation ceased in 1946. Here the three massive shells of the ghost plant loom in the brush.

Haliburton

Haliburton was a bustling lumber town even before the tracks arrived. Unfortunately for the community, the tracks were to end here, and the line would not continue on to Mattawa as originally proposed by George Laidlaw. The station was the usual attractive Grand Trunk station plan consisting of gable ends and a gable above the operator's bay. The wooden sides were of board-and-batten construction.

Today, the lumber yards are gone, as are the tracks and all the sidings. The lakeshore where they stood has become a busy community park, and the station now sits on a higher foundation and houses an art gallery. Behind the building, the presence of a boxcar and a nearby caboose keep alive the history of the railway. Walking paths follow the right-of-way to the intersection of Highland Street and County Road 1, where the rail trail begins. At this intersection, in front of the Haliburton District High School, CN steam engine #2616 now rests on a pedestal, a reminder to visitors of the town's place in Ontario's railway history.

CHAPTER 9

The Georgian Bay and Seaboard Line: Dranoel to Port McNicoll

The History

As grain traffic from the booming Canadian West grew, the CPR's facilities were becoming taxed to the limit. Since 1884, grain traffic had been shipped into Owen Sound, and then transported south along the Toronto Grey and Bruce Railway (TG&B) to the CPR's terminus at the foot of Toronto's Bathurst Street. But the facility soon became overburdened, and attention was given to finding a new route to Montreal.

The first vision was a CPR route, to be called the Atlantic and Northwest Railway, that would run from Montreal through Ottawa and across the central portion of Ontario via Renfrew and Eganville and on to Parry Sound. But this proposal lost out to J. R. Booth's Ottawa, Arnprior, and Parry Sound Railway (OA&PS), which won the rights to the route. The CPR's line would go no farther than Eganville.

Forced to change its plans, the CPR decided to construct a line from what was then its main Toronto to Montreal line, built as the Ottawa and Quebec Railway

(Q&O). Thus the corporation received a charter to construct a line from Peterborough, through Lindsay and Orillia, and on to Georgian Bay at Midland. But the Grand Trunk Railway, which had taken over the Midland Railway's facilities at Midland, refused to share that location.

Once again, the CPR was forced to alter the route. This time it would run from Bethany Junction on the O&Q to a location then known as Victoria Harbour (later renamed Port McNicoll in recognition of David McNicoll, a CPR executive), where the railway dredged out a vast new harbour. The new Georgian Bay and Seaboard (GB&S), a subsidiary of the CPR virtually from the start, opened in sections, the first from Port McNicoll to Orillia in 1911, and the following year to Bethany Junction (renamed Dranoel to recognize James W. Leonard, his last name reversed, who lived in nearby Bethany and served as a senior staff of the CPR). The total length of the route was 110 kilometres.

That route ran across the countryside from Dranoel to the east side of the Scugog River at Lindsay, where it shared a short section of track with the Lindsay, Bobcaygeon, and Pontypool Railway (LB&P), then crossed the Scugog River north of Lindsay. From there it left the LB&P tracks and travelled cross-country again to Atherley, where it crossed the Narrows between Lake Simcoe and Lake Couchiching, continuing along the west shore of Lake Couchiching to its Orillia station.

From Orillia, it was once more across country to Port McNicoll. Here the Georgian Bay and Seaboard dredged out a deep harbour, building massive grain elevators on the east side, and a station on the west. The grain elevators were capable of holding six and a half million bushels of wheat. The line accessed the site by constructing one of Ontario's most ambitious trestles, the Hogg's Bay Trestle. The CPR also needed to plan a new town site, to be laid out using the standard railway-style street grid.

In 1937, the Depression and decreasing traffic forced the CPR to abandon the section between Lindsay and Orillia, and reroute grain shipments on the CPR's Toronto to Sudbury line at Medonte Junction, near Coldwater. Meanwhile, the remaining eastern section

The famous Hogg's Bay Trestle stretched for 750 metres across the marshes of Hogg's Bay. The structure stood fifteen metres above the water and also crossed the tracks of the Midland line. The now demolished wooden trestle, however, was difficult to maintain, and trains were required to slow to eight kilometres per hour while crossing it.

between Dranoel and Lindsay was incorporated into the Bobcaygeon "sub," along with the surviving section of the LB&P route (the section from Lindsay to Burketon had been abandoned about the same time). Then, to simplify matters even more, in 1971 the CPR obtained running rights over the CNR's Midland line and abandoned its Port McNicoll to Medonte link.

Soon afterward, no longer needed, the Hogg's Bay Trestle, Ontario's most historic, was removed. Canada's longest wooden trestle, it stood from 1908 to 1978. Then, in 1989, the federal government ended its grain subsidy, forcing most of Ontario's grain elevators to close, including those in Midland, Goderich, and Port McNicoll. It was the end of an era.

When the Lindsay to Orillia section was discontinued during the 1930s, rail trails were unheard of, and much of the right-of-way was sold to adjacent farmers, who, for the most part, simply ploughed the sections under. However, the Dranoel to Lindsay and the Orillia to Coldwater sections, abandoned in more recent times, have been converted to rail trails.

The Heritage

Dranoel

Now part of the Victoria Heritage Trail, the Georgian Bay & Seaboard right-of-way starts at the site of the Dranoel station, on the Toronto to Havelock line of the CPR. Still visible in the clearing are the foundations of the station and water tower, and the *Y* that provided the connecting link. The station, a storey-and-a-half standard-plan structure, was replaced in later years by a small waiting room that served travellers on the Havelock to Toronto commuter train. The site lies

about a ten-minute walk south along the trail from Syer Road.

From Syer Road the trail then proceeds northwest, passing through the picturesque community of Bethany, where it closely follows the alignment of the Midland Railway, now County Road 38. The trail continues northward to the site of Fleetwood Station — although the little ghost town of Fleetwood is situated a couple of kilometres west of the old station grounds, on Fleetwood Road. The route then passes through the hamlet of Hillhead before entering the town of Lindsay.

Lindsay

Along the Logie Road the trail meets the now-vanished right-of-way of the long abandoned Lindsay, Bobcaygeon, and Pontypool Railway at a location once known as Lindsay Junction. Here it passes beneath the Grand Trunk's steel-girder bridge, becoming a paved riverside walkway to its end point at King and St. Paul Streets.

The former station grounds at Wellington and Lindsay Street North are vacant now, although the station survived a few years as a museum after the closure of the Bobcaygeon sub. Unfortunately, a demolition mentality remained supreme at the time, and the delightful wooden station with its "witch's hat" roof above the waiting room survives only in photographs.

Lindsay to Orillia

The Lindsay to Orillia portion of the line, abandoned since 1937, is scarcely visible amid the fertile farm fields of Victoria County. At a location called Camray, the Georgian Bay and Seaboard had a small station and water tower. At Birches Road and County Road 9, a one-time section house remains standing, while buried in the grass near the roadside lie the foundations of the water tower and a concrete culvert dated 1912.

Because the GB&S was built long after the communities of Argyle and Brechin came into being, the stations were situated well away from the town sites, where the cost of acquiring land for the route and the station was lower. As a result, the established villages did not experience growth with of the arrival of the railway. Interestingly, however, the CPR stations at both locations still stand in their original spots.

The station at Argyle is well-preserved and is now a private home on County Road 46. The one at Brechin enjoys new life as the Wild Wings Restaurant. The former track-side portion of the latter has been modified and

The Argyle station served as such for only three decades. Its style reflects the Canadian Pacific Railway's typical station pattern for this line, a style that was used for most of CP's country stations in Ontario. The large second floor was to accommodate the agent and his family, making it ideal for conversion to a residential dwelling.

now sports an old boxcar. The highway side retains much of its original appearance.

Orillia

Between Brechin and Orillia, the GB&S ran side by side with the tracks of the Midland line, and relics of both lines have largely vanished from the countryside. One exception is found on the GB&S right-of-way, where Ellesmere Junction endures as a private railway museum. The site contains a caboose, freight cars, and the Sir Adam Beck steam locomotive used to help build the hydroelectric facilities at Niagara Falls. The latter has since been offered to the Niagara Railway Museum.

The Georgian Bay and Seaboard continued to parallel that of the Midland Railway until it reached the railway junction known as Atherley Junction, where the GB&S built a bridge to cross the Narrows between lakes Simcoe and Couchiching. A causeway in the centre of the Narrows was linked to the eastern shore by a trestle and to the western shore by a swing bridge. While the Midland Railway's bridge, still in use by the CNR into the 1990s, remains in place, the GB&S swing bridge and trestle have been removed, leaving only traces of the causeway.

Despite the obliteration of the GB&S right-of-way along Orillia's shoreline, the station here still stands. Located by the water at the foot of Mississauga Street, the building retains most of its original shape and is now home to the Orillia Legion. From the north end of Orillia's waterfront park, both the Midland and GB&S rights-of-way now serve as rail trails. The trail that follows the line of the GB&S is known as the Uhthoff Trail, after the village of the same name, likely christened by Baron Adolphe von Hugel, one-time German president of the Midland Railway.

Orillia to Port McNicoll

The Uhthoff Trail, with crushed stone as its base, generally has a straight route. Starting at Jarvis Street at Couchiching Beach Park, it crosses through one-time farmer's fields and brings hikers and cyclists to the site of the New Uhthoff quarry, where the GB&S formerly had built a large railway station.

At Medonte, on Southhorn Road near Coldwater, the complex of rail crossing and connections, which included the tracks of the Midland Railway, the GB&S, and the CPR's later Sudbury branch, is still very much in evidence. The only line still in use is the CP's busy main line between Toronto and Sudbury. The trail terminates in Coldwater, near Gray Street and Fire Hall Lane. Although all traces of rail operations within Coldwater are gone, the former bridge across the Coldwater River remains, although it is no longer usable.

West of Coldwater, the right-of-way is only occasionally recognizable. Beside Highway 12, west of Waubaushene, an arch bridge known as the "Hole in the Wall" still stands. Opposite, in a picnic ground along the Tay Shore Trail (the route of the Midland Railway), is a provincial plaque commemorating the engineering feat of constructing the Hogg's Bay Trestle.

The station grounds and docks at Port McNicoll are currently the site of a new waterfront housing development (which will include a replica railway station and a new home for the former CPR steamer, the *Keewatin*) but the extent of the harbour facility is very much apparent. The town still displays the usual network of streets consistently laid out by the railways, with many early railway homes and buildings still in evidence.

CHAPTER 10

The Hamilton and Northwestern Railway: Port Dover to Meaford

The History

By the 1860s, Ontario was in the grip of rail fever. Ontario's first steam operation had puffed north from Toronto to Machell's Corners (now Aurora) in 1853, and by the following year the Great Western Railway was running trains from Niagara Falls to Hamilton, and would soon push on to Windsor and Sarnia.

With the arrival of the Grand Trunk into Toronto in 1856, however, it appeared that that city would become the rail hub of Ontario, not Hamilton. By 1860, Toronto had the Ontario, Simcoe, and Huron (OS&H) — later renamed the Northern Railway — as well as the Great Western and the Grand Trunk railways all converging on its waterfront. Hamilton was left with only the Great Western and grand dreams.

Rail lines for Hamilton were on the drawing boards as early as 1834, with plans afoot for both the London and Gore and the Hamilton and Port Dover railways. Like Toronto, Hamilton saw the economic benefit of resource lines drawing lumber and farm produce to its main line and lake port. But a decade and a half would pass before the Port Dover line would finally incorporate as the Hamilton and Lake Erie Railway (H&LE), and another four years before its trains began running.

Because of these delays, the H&LE lost the opportunity to occupy the better lands on the west side of Port Dover Harbour to the Port Dover and Lake Huron Railway (PD&LH), and had to settle for more cramped space on the east side. Then, in 1875, the Hamilton and Northwestern Railway (H&NW) published its intent to build a line northward, with a line to Collingwood that would compete with the Northern Railway, as well. It also extended a branch line into Barrie, building stations there and in the village of Allandale (now also part of Barrie).

In 1877, the H&NW and the H&LE amalgamated to become the Hamilton and Northwestern Railway. Four years later, it and the Northern Railway recognized that they had duplicated each other, and amalgamated as the Northern and Northwestern Railway (N&NW).

In Collingwood, the N&NW began using the elaborate new station of the Northern Railway on St. Paul

Street, as well, instead of the original H&NW terminus at Walnut and Second Streets. Meanwhile, its original Allandale station became a church hall. Both lines then used the Northern Railway station until it was replaced in 1904 with the Grand Trunk station that survives today.

Just four years after that amalgamation, however, the Grand Trunk took control of the N&NW and began improving trackage and replacing stations. One such replacement was of the station in Allandale, where, in 1904, the GT constructed an elaborate wooden structure that still stands today, and counts, in my opinion, as Ontario's most elegant wooden station.

During the same period, the trackage into Barrie's downtown Sophia Street station was relocated, and in Port Dover a bridge was built over the Lynn River, connecting the N&NW to a new Grand Trunk station on the west side of the harbour.

But by 1920, even the Grand Trunk was in financial trouble, and was absorbed into the government-owned Canadian National Railway system. In the years that followed, the CNR began to abandon its excess lines.

In 1935, the rails to Port Dover were lifted and the Lynn River bridge removed. By 1957, the section between Alliston and Collingwood was gone. Finally, by 1990, the entire route had been abandoned except for a few small sections. A short spur line still led into Barrie to serve the Barrie and Collingwood short line, while the section between Hamilton and Caledonia was made part of a new line, meant to serve the industrial growth at Nanticoke. A short section of track between Tottenham and Beeton became part of the popular South Simcoe Steam train attraction, Ontario's only tourist steam train.

Only the section between Burlington and Georgetown continues to operate as part of the CN system. Much

of the Northern Railway's trackage, on the other hand, remains in place, serving GO Transit passengers from Toronto to Barrie and as a short-line operation from Barrie to Collingwood.

The Heritage

Port Dover

After the Grand Trunk closed the original H&NW Port Dover station in 1896, it built a new one, designed in one of its more common architectural plans. Constructed of board-and-batten, it sported a hexagonal operator's bay window with a gable above. After passenger service ended in 1957, the station was relocated a short distance away and the waiting room was removed. Here it served as a carwash until subsequently moved again to become a gift shop on St. George Street, south of Walker.

The next main stop en route to Hamilton was at Jarvis. Although two earlier stations, those of the Canada Air Line (CAL) and the H&NW, are long gone, the one built by the Grand Trunk in 1906, at the junction of the two lines, remains in place. Its elegant features, including the hip-roofed waiting room and the operator's bays on each side of the building, have been restored and repainted in original Grand Trunk colour scheme. The right-of-way for CAL remains visible while that of the H&NW is scarcely identifiable. The station is now the home of Michaud Fine Woodworking, situated on the east side of Highway 6 at the north end of the town. A historic grain elevator still standing near the station marks the CAL right-of-way.

Another of the line's stations has also managed to survive at Garnet. It is here that the still active Nanticoke section diverts from the H&NW's original alignment. As a station it was a waiting shelter. Today, it is a backyard storage shed in a residential yard, a short distance west of its original grounds.

At Hagersville, the altered Canada Southern Railway (CASO) station, now operated by Rail America, a company that runs short lines on a contract basis, still guards the intersection of that line with the H&NW, which here forms part of the active Nanticoke route. Opposite the station is a former railway hotel. Both are found in downtown Hagersville.

Caledonia

The restored Caledonia station is another of those labours of love. Built by the Grand Trunk in 1908 after that line assumed the H&NW, it has a bell-caste roofline beyond which extend two wings. The wooden structure formerly had an octagonal gable above the operator's bay window, but that was removed. The nicely preserved building now houses the local chamber of commerce and a tourist office.

Hamilton

From Caledonia to Hamilton, little remains from the days of the H&NW. The alignment into Hamilton is now the Escarpment Rail Trail, but all traces of its route through the city along Ferguson Avenue are gone, as are the station and crossing tower that once stood at King and Cannon Streets respectively. The rail line shared a station with the Great Western on Stuart Street, but that building was removed in 1931 when the CNR built its new and still extant James Street station.

From Hamilton, the H&NW made its way to Burlington along the beach strip, where many workers travelled by rail to enjoy a break from the smoky mills of the industrial city. Hotels, such as Dynes, the Elsinore, and the Ocean House, as well as the amusement park and the beach station have all gone, and the right-of-way was converted to a beach-side walking trail. The most prominent relic of the beach tracks is the lift bridge over the Burlington Canal, built as a combination road and rail bridge in 1962.

Terra Cotta

That section of the H&NW that runs between Burlington and Georgetown remains an active component of the CN rail system. But beyond that, it is a different story. From Terra Cotta to Tottenham, the route of the H&NW is now the Caledon Trailway, a multi-use cycling, hiking, and, in parts, equestrian trail.

On the abandoned portion of the line, no stations remain. Stations from the active section at Milton, Stewartown, and Burlington Junction have all been relocated — the Milton Grand Trunk station is now a tourist office on Martin Street, the Stewartown station has found new use as a shed on private property, and the Burlington Junction Grand Trunk station was moved back from the tracks in 2006 and awaits a new location and use. However, the one at Georgetown is a Grand Trunk original, altered around 1904 with the addition of a decorative corner tower but kept in the same location. It remains an active VIA Rail and GO Transit station.

The western trailhead for the Caledon Trailway lies on Isabella Street in Terra Cotta, although no signage or information plaque marks the site. The village, once a bustling brick-making town, sits serenely on the banks of the Credit River with a variety of heritage buildings, such as the Terra Cotta Inn, gracing its main street.

Cheltenham

One of the more unusual sights on any of Ontario's abandoned rail lines is the gaunt remains of the Cheltenham Brickworks. Built by the Interprovincial Brick Company in 1914, the brickworks could, at their peak, produce 90,000 bricks at a time. Workers living in the small village, around 1914, paid $13 a week in rent. The village has now vanished, the brickworks having closed in 1958. For thirty-five years the furnaces, chimneys, and warehouses sat vacant by the rail line. In 1993, when Brampton Brick began excavating, the company stabilized the aging structures. Located on Mississauga Road near Cheltenham's Mill Street, these remains now form a visual oddity in Ontario's rail heritage.

Although the route passed just north of the village of Cheltenham, its picturesque stores and homes in the valley of the Credit River date from the prosperity brought by the H&NW. The station now sits on private land near King Street and Mississauga Road.

The Credit Valley Flyer tour train, when travelling its route between Orangeville and Snelgrove at the north end of Brampton, pauses by the abandoned foundations of the Inglewood station. In earlier days the station served both the Credit Valley Railway and the Hamilton and Northwestern Railway.

Inglewood

The route of the H&NW next grinds its way up the Niagara Escarpment toward Inglewood where it formed a junction with the CPR's Credit Valley Railway. That line still sees both freight and tourist traffic as the Brampton and Orangeville Railway. A scenic community on the Credit River, Inglewood has long since lost its "junction" station, although the platform still lingers among the grasses where the two lines once crossed. Here, too, the Inglewood Hotel still stands as a general store, busy whenever the Credit Valley tour train stops for a break. At this point, the trail provides an interpretative historic plaque, a shelter, and a washroom facility. Inglewood lies just north of Old Baseline Road and west of Highway 10.

From Inglewood, the rail trail winds across the scenic foothills of the Niagara Escarpment, revealing vistas of cliffs, forests, and fields. Its route through Caledon East has been pleasantly landscaped just as it has in Palgrave, on Highway 50, where another shelter awaits trail-users.

The trail passes more forests and hills as it nears the hamlet of Black Horse, where the active CP main line runs just metres from the trail. Finally, the route peters out by the rails of the South Simcoe Steam Railway (SSR) in Tottenham, and ends altogether at the gates of that historic attraction.

Tottenham

The shortness of this heritage track, just eight kilometres long between Tottenham and Beeton, seems odd. Regrettably, its brevity is due to nothing more than self-serving NIMBYism.

Earlier efforts to create a steam-train operation between Georgetown and Cheltenham and later from Craiglieth to Meaford — the latter an exceptionally scenic portion — were rebuffed by adjacent property owners, who, in some cases, feared for the laundry on their clotheslines. Then, when the tour train's proponents suggested a route from Tottenham into Barrie, politicians in Innisfil Township, an unattractive community of unbridled urban sprawl through which it had to pass, lobbied the provincial government of the day to prevent the operation from extending beyond Beeton. Still, the SSR has survived for more than twenty years, drawing steam-train enthusiasts as well as moviemakers to a unique bit of Ontario's rail heritage.

The grounds of the South Simcoe Railway Heritage Corporation, which runs the railway, offer vintage coaches and rolling stock as well as, of course, the steam engines. One of these was built in 1883, and was featured in the TV special, "The National Dream."

Rails of the SSR end suddenly at Beeton, where the only rail-era structure of note is the old feed mill run by Parson Seed. One of Beeton's popular family restaurants celebrates the community's rail roots in its name, The Whistle Stop.

Originally, the line split at Alimill (Patterson Street north of the 10th Line) with one section heading northeast toward Barrie, the other northwest to Collingwood. But no trace of the split remains. The roadbed, where not ploughed under or built upon, is nothing but ruts running through the fields. The whistle stop at Randall (13th Line and Sideroad 15) offered little more than a mail hook and agent's house, of which the latter remains.

Cookstown

From Cookstown to Thornton, the Cookstown to Thornton Rail Trail follows the H&NW roadbed. It is a maintained walking and cycling trail that crosses a number of small historic trestle bridges, some dating from as early as 1895. The scenic route offers views across the farmland and makes its way through shady forests. At each trailhead, "tree spirits" — imaginative faces carved into the trunks of dead trees, meant to represent the spirit of the tree — have been carved into the old trunks to greet trail-users.

Barrie

From the community of Vine (the station is nicely preserved as a house) into Barrie, industrial spurs remain in place on the Hamilton and Northwestern line, while new sidings have been added to house the rolling stock of the Barrie and Collingwood short line. In Allandale, the grand old station, located at Essa Road and Tiffin Street, is what many regard as the finest wooden station in Ontario. Now dilapidated and vacant, it is owned by the City of Barrie, which, to date, has had little luck in finding a tenant. The H&NW Sophia Street station was in operation for only a few years, but gained subsequent life as a private residence a short distance away.

Alliston

Meanwhile, the westerly branch makes its way from the Alimill junction to the nearby "ghost town" of Thompsonville. Once a busy mill town, the site retains only a few reminders of those busy times. Here, a historic plaque recounts the story of "Trainsville," a mill operation that was named, not for its rail link, but for its owner, William Train. Although it did have a siding later installed for loading lumber, this too has vanished from the landscape.

In Alliston, the site of the track is marked by a caboose, displayed by Gibson Transport, at the east end of town, beside Tottenham Road. Within the town, the Gibson Centre for Art and Culture occupies a former trackside feed mill at the corner of Tupper and Paris Streets. At the west end a feed mill marks the right-of-way, which has otherwise vanished in this bustling town.

Abandoned since the 1950s, the H&NW right-of-way winds its way through small villages such as Everett, Lisle, Glencairn, and Avening, all of which once boasted stations; many also had feed mills. No trace remains, however, the rail bed having mostly been put to the plough.

Creemore

The town of Creemore has managed to celebrate its link to the rails. Although the station erected by the Grand Trunk in 1906 burned down in 1955, a replica station was constructed nearby in 2002. Called the "Station in the Green," it hosts community events and private functions.

A block to the east of the station is the famous Creemore Jail, a three-cell stone lockup that claims to be North America's smallest. The village's main street, dominated by its famous Creemore Springs Brewery, is lined with a variety of interesting shops and restaurants, all of which make the village a popular daytrip destination. The village is on Simcoe County Road 9, just west of Airport Road.

Once out of Creemore, the roadbed vanishes from sight again, except for a short stretch that forms Riverside Drive, west of Creemore. Communities such as Smithdale and Duntroon show no evidence of ever having a railway history.

Collingwood

In Collingwood, the route of the original Hamilton and Northwestern Railway is nowhere to be seen. However, the station that it shared with the Northern Railway has been replicated and now houses the Collingwood Museum. The spur line to the grain elevator is now a roadway, and the elevator is preserved as part of a waterfront park system.

The route of the railway, originally called the North Grey Railway (NGR) at this point, continues west, following the shoreline of Georgian Bay, parallel to Highway 26. It has become a popular and scenic rail trail known as the Georgian Trail. Here, cyclists and hikers enjoy views over the waters of Georgian Bay and can visit the historic turreted Craigleith "depot," now the Craigleith Heritage Museum. A short distance west, inside the Craigleith Provincial Park, a historic plaque recalls the short-lived shale-oil works constructed in 1859 to extract oil from the underlying bituminous shale; the earlier discovery of oil deposits at Oil Springs and Petrolia in 1858 soon put an early end to this operation.

The trail continues through Thornbury, where the old wooden trestle over the Beaver River offers views downstream toward the bay and upstream to the village. A waterfront park offers respite for hikers and cyclists.

Built in 1881, the Craigleith station closed in 1960. Eight years later, Kenn and Suryea Knapman opened it as a restaurant. In 2001, the Town of Blue Mountain bought the building and converted to a railway museum.

Although some distance inland from the shore, the trail then ventures from Thornbury on to its terminus at Meaford. Here the trailhead is marked by a gazebo and by a plaque placed on a granite boulder. Although the station has long gone, a railway freight shed still survives in the village's attractive waterfront park.

The North Simcoe Railway

The History

The North Simcoe Railway (NSR) was a short rail line chartered in 1878 to link the Northern and Northwestern Railway with the port of Penetanguishene on Georgian Bay. Promoted by the lumber interests in the then still forested hills of Tiny Township, the line opened in the same year.

A short tramway, known as the Flos Tramway, built to Hillsdale in 1882, accessed the timber stands to the east. A similar branch led from a point north of Elmvale into Midland, but the Midland Railway had occupied the waterfront there, leaving little room for the NSR.

The Heritage

As the North Simcoe Railway was never heavily used, the CN abandoned the route in 1991. Since then it has been converted into a rail trail which offers a surprising amount to see over a relatively short distance.

The southerly portion, known as the North Simcoe Rail Trail, begins just north of the Sunnidale Road, west of Barrie. After a short distance, a few paces north of Old Orchard Road, a clearing offers a wide vista across the Minesing Swamp, a forbidding wilderness that remains untamed today. A few paces from the lookout, a series of steps lead to the bluff-top site of Fort Willow. During the War of 1812, this small post was a jumping-off point for military supplies from Fort York bound for Georgian Bay. A re-creation of the small fort sits atop the bluff above the trail. This historic but little-known location lies in a conservation area on Grenfell Road.

A short distance along the trail to the east of Fort Willow sits the ghost town of Josephine. Once a sawmill village, Josephine was short-lived. Today, only a few piles of rubble indicate the location of the workers' homes. A plaque beside the trail, erected by the trail authorities, describes their story.

Minesing Station Park lies on Highway 26 and offers visitors a parking area and an information plaque. An overgrown Hendrie Station Park marks the location of the last station to remain on this line: it disappeared in the late 1970s. The trail enters Elmvale at Heritage Park, west of the town's busy main street, where a variety of heritage buildings house an array of retail businesses.

North of Elmvale the trail becomes the Tiny Rail Trail (named after Tiny Township). Between Elmvale and Penetanguishene, the trail encounters a series of fourteen small bridges that cross local roads and creeks. Most of them offer information plaques describing their history. Wyevale developed around the North Simcoe Railway station, and a facsimile name board stands on the right-of-way in the village.

Between Concession Roads 6 and 7, a sign announces the location of the Huron Ossuary, where, in 1636, more than one thousand Huron bodies were interred in a mass grave. It was part of the Huron culture to hold an occasional "Feast of the Dead" when they would re-bury their dead in a common grave. This ossuary is considered to be among the largest in Ontario, and believed to be the one recorded by Father Jean de Brébeuf in 1636.

The trail continues on to Perkinsfield, where a replica station marks the trail access on County Road 25. As the trail enters Penetanguishene, it becomes the Penetang Rotary Trail and passes through a small tunnel before ending at Robert Street. Another trail leads to Georgian Bay and eventually ends at the site of the once-elegant wooden Penetang station. The station, sadly, is now gone, the site now home to a park and marina.

CHAPTER 11

The Radials and the Belt Line: Ontario's Early Commuter Railways

The History

It is said that everything old is new again. That saying could well apply to the era of the radial electric railways and today's renewed interest in Light Rapid Transit. Linking Ontario's urban areas with its smaller communities, the radial railways were, in the early years of the twentieth century, everywhere, at least throughout central and southwestern Ontario.

Electric trains burst onto the scene in 1884 when the first of these strange devices premiered at the Toronto Agricultural Fair (now the Canadian National Exhibition, or CNE). They quickly replaced the earlier horse-drawn trams, and by 1900, Ontario could claim more than two hundred kilometres of electric railways. Unlike street railways, which served neighbourhoods within a given town or city, radials cut across the country, carrying both freight and passengers. Many travelled the lines for recreation, not just as a method of getting from point A to point B, since the railway companies would build parks along their systems to encourage more Sunday travel.

The electric railways had a booster in Adam Beck, who, as chairman of the Ontario Hydro Electric Power Commission,[1] was able to readily target them as a major user for the commission's hydro-generating facilities at Niagara. His vision encompassed a province-wide system of radial railway lines that would link Ontario with destinations as far away as the American Midwest.

But not all governments shared that enthusiasm. The Ontario government of E.C. Drury denied the municipalities provincial funding for such lines, and the system declined from its peak length of 1,280 kilometres in 1920, to less than half that just two decades later. But, by then, the auto age had arrived, and cars and buses proved more flexible in the routes and times they could travel. By 1959, the last of the electrics went out of service.

In recent decades, the rapid rise of the LRTs (Light Rapid Transit) has seen a dramatic resurgence of electric rail service in many American cities and in a few of the more progressive jurisdictions in Canada. But today, little survives of those once-popular radial networks.

The Heritage

The Toronto Belt Line

While this railway was never an electric line, its role as an early commuter line shares that story. Incorporated in 1889 as the Toronto Belt Line Land Corporation, it was, as the name implies, an effort to encourage land development around Toronto's expanding urban fringe.

The line consisted of two main loops. The first, known as the Humber Loop, used the tracks of the Grand Trunk Railway from Union Station as far as Swansea, where the line then followed the east bank of the Humber River. It then looped back east through Lambton, where the corporation built a large one-and-a-half-storey station. After heading east, north of St. Clair Avenue, it linked again with the Grand Trunk near that line's Davenport station.

The second, the eastern loop of the Belt Line, followed the GT's tracks east from Union Station and up the Don Valley, where the company established its Rosedale Station. From that point, tracks were laid up

The Toronto Belt Line bridge across Yonge Street bears the name of former city councillor Kay Gardner, who helped convert the right-of-way into a popular trail.

the Moore Park Ravine to Moore Park (a proposed land-development scheme), where the company established another large station. This building could boast four towers on its corners to reflect what the promoters hoped would be an upscale new suburb. Trains ran six times a day and cost a nickel a station. But Sunday excursions to the country proved more popular than daily commutes, and, by 1890, a depression killed any dream of a land boom and the company went bankrupt.

Although the Grand Trunk finished the line in 1892, even this corporation could not rescue this mission, and, in 1894, it put an end to passenger service. In 1910, the GT rebuilt the line to accommodate its freight shipments, portions of which were still used by the Canadian National as recently as 1988. That year, the CNR sold off the right-of-way to the cities of Toronto and York, a move that created two of Toronto's more popular walking and cycling routes, the Kay Gardner Beltline Park[2] and the York Beltline Trail.

Today, its role as a commuter route has at last been fulfilled, at least by cyclists and strollers. Despite its popularity, the route has retained few heritage relics. All stations have long since been removed, although those at both Moore Park and Lambton outlived the demise of the railway as residences. The former Dominion Coal Company silos remained a landmark where the line passed beneath Mt. Pleasant Avenue until they, too, were torn down to make way for condominiums in the 1990s. Today, only the Yonge Street Bridge and the Dufferin Street Bridge date to the days of rail, and their origins belong more to the CNR than to the Belt Line.

The eastern trail begins at the former Toronto Brickworks, which has been preserved and transformed into a community environmental centre known as the Evergreen Brick Works. After following the Moore Park Ravine to Mount Pleasant Cemetery, the trail resumes east of Yonge Street, then angles northwest to its western trailhead at Allen Road. The trail resumes west of Marlee Avenue in northwest Toronto, where, between Times Road and Bowie Street, it has been developed as the York Beltline Trail.

By contrast, neither the GT nor the later CNR showed any interest in the western loop, and the right-of-way was incorporated into the area's developing residential street pattern. Today, streets such as the South Kingsway, Old Mill Road, Humbercrest, and Florence Crescent represent the ghosts of the western loop. Its only station of any size, the Lambton station, which outlasted the demise of the line, was located at Florence Crescent, but was eventually removed to make way for new housing.

The Toronto Suburban Railway

One of the longest routes to emanate from Toronto was the one leading northwest to Guelph. Its route took the Toronto Suburban Railway (TSR) through Churchville, Huttonville, Eldorado Park (one of the line's recreation parks), thence through Georgetown, Acton, Limehouse, and into Guelph.

Construction began on the route in 1911, when the Canadian Northern Railway (CNoR) acquired the line's charter. While there were more than one hundred stops along the route, major stations were built only at Georgetown, Acton, and Guelph.

Following the demise of the CNoR, the City of Toronto took over the portion that lay within the city limits, turning it over to the Toronto Transit Commission (TTC), while the CNR assumed operations outside the city, creating its own electric division to do so, the Canadian National Electric Railway (CNER). As did many radial companies, the CNER created a park to encourage Sunday ridership, a one-hundred-hectare riverside facility named Eldorado Park, situated on the Credit River north of Churchville. At its peak, the TSR was running trains to Guelph every two hours. But, with the arrival of buses and cars, traffic plummeted to only three hundred passengers a day, and in 1935 the CNER dismantled the line and sold off the right-of-way.

For the most part, the portions of the line nearest Toronto have long since disappeared. Bridge abutments remain barely visible in Old Meadowvale, while a one-time pavilion still stands in El Dorado Park. The Georgetown

station, a large building that also doubled as a powerhouse, survived as bakery following the demise of the line, but it, too, is now gone.

The western segment has become the twenty-eight-kilometre Guelph Radial Trail, which runs between Limehouse and the outskirts of Guelph. En route, the right-of-way passes through Ontario's only streetcar museum, the Halton County Radial Railway and Streetcar Museum (located on the Guelph Line a short distance south of the village of Rockwood), where old-time radial

Abandoned for many years, the radial line from Limehouse to Guelph is now enjoyed by trail-users. Although rugged in places, and off limits in others, the trail resembles the Bruce Trail more than it does a typical rail trail.

cars still trundle along a kilometre of original right-of-way. The former Meadowvale shelter, one of the "stops" on the museum route, provides an authentic reminder of the radial's heyday. Used primarily by hikers, the trail crosses mostly private land and is available to the public only with the agreement of the property owners. As such, access is not consistently available, nor is the roadbed always discernable.

The Toronto and York Radial Railway

Chartered in 1893 as the Metropolitan Street Railway Company, this line was built from the north end of Toronto to Aurora and Newmarket in 1899. Five years later, it was renamed the Toronto and York Radial Railway (T&YRR). When acquired by the Canadian Northern Railway of William Mackenzie and Donald Mann, the tracks were extended to Sutton and ultimately to Jackson's Point in 1909.

In 1922, with the CNoR bankrupt, the T&YRR, also nicknamed the "Metro," fell to the Hydro Electric Railway Company, which cut the route back to Richmond Hill in 1930, and then finally abandoned it totally in 1948.

South of Richmond Hill, the line followed the major roads, hence no visible evidence of its existence remains. However, from the north end of Richmond Hill, it went across country, where lines of telephone poles now identify its route. The remains of a culvert survive in Newmarket, although the station, which later served as a pool hall, was torn down circa the 1960s. The Bond Lake engine house stood until the 1990s, when it was removed despite pleas from the community to save it.

Farther north, the former Queensville station still survives and is now a private home. From Keswick to Sutton, Metro Road was built along the right-of-way.

At Willow Beach, another T&YRR recreation spot, the weathered, former powerhouse and station still stand at the southeast corner of Metro Road and Kennedy Road.

In Sutton, the former station is now an office at Dalton and High Streets. Two small T&YRR shelters have found refuge in the Georgina Historic Museum, as does the CN station that once stood in the town. Another, known as Stop 17, was rediscovered in 2000 by the Society for the Preservation of Historic Thornhill, after spending fifty years as a shelter on the Thornhill Golf Course. Following restoration by the Society and the Thornhill Lions Club, it was placed near its original location on Yonge Street in Thornhill.

The Schomberg and Aurora Railway

Chartered in 1896, the Schomberg and Aurora Railway (S&AR) began running in 1902 in an effort to attract Torontonians to the surrounding farm country to purchase agricultural produce. Until taken over and electrified by the T&YRR in 1916, the line operated as a steam railway. Stations were placed at Aurora, Eversley, Kettleby, and Schomberg.

While the rail station at Aurora survived as a restaurant until the 1960s (the area is better known as Oak Ridges), the only building to remain is the house in Schomberg that served as the S&AR's terminus. Visible portions of the right-of-way include Dr. Kay Road in Schomberg, as well as Lloyds Lane and Brule Trail. Otherwise the line has, like so many others, vanished from the landscape.

The Cataract Lines

If any place could be called a radial hub, it would be Hamilton. This city at the head of Lake Ontario at one time could count no fewer than four radial lines, which radiated out like spokes from a wheel. Being operated by the Hamilton Cataract Power Light and Traction Company, they were known simply as the Cataract Lines. The terminal was in a six-storey building, built in 1907 at Catharine and King Streets in downtown Hamilton. Passengers would wait in a twenty by thirty-five-metre waiting room that contained a lofty six-metre-high ceiling.

The Hamilton and Dundas Street Railway began operation in 1876 using dummy engines, or steam engines hidden in the bodies of streetcars. It became electrified in 1897 and used the Grand Trunk station on Ferguson Avenue until 1907, when it moved with the other radial lines into a new terminal building. By 1923, service had ended and the tracks had been removed.

The Hamilton, Grimsby, and Beamsville Electric Railway operated between Hamilton and Beamsville from 1896 until 1927, when buses replaced the streetcars. The railway operated specials to Grimsby Beach Park, and carried fruit from the many farms that operated in the area prior to the urban sprawl. Many of the Victorian cottages still stand in historic Grimsby Beach, as does the power plant in Stoney Creek, now known as the Powerhouse Restaurant.

The Hamilton Radial Electric Railway provided electric-rail service from Hamilton to Oakville. Chartered in 1895, it reached Burlington in 1898 and Oakville in 1905. Efforts to extend the line to Port Credit, however, failed, and the line never linked with the streetcar system emanating from Toronto.

In 1925, service was cut back to Port Nelson, a few blocks east of downtown Burlington. In 1927, service stopped altogether. Many of the structures that originally outlasted the line came down over the ensuing years: the Burlington Beach Power House was removed in 1947, the car barn in 1962, and the nearby station in the 1980s.

Only the station in Oakville remains, and is currently a law office on Randall Street.

The Brantford and Hamilton Electric Railway, the longest of the four, began operating in 1906 on its own private right-of-way rather than sharing the roads. Its route took it from the Terminal Station in Hamilton along Main to Aberdeen Avenue, at which point the line climbed a steep grade up the face of Hamilton Mountain, offering its passengers spectacular views across the Dundas Valley below. Once on top of the Niagara Escarpment, it crossed the countryside, through rolling farm fields and woodlots. Stations were located at James Street, Summit, Alberton, Langford, Cainsville, and, in Brantford, at Mohawk Park, near the abandoned Grand River Canal. In downtown Brantford, it shared the Lake Erie and Northern station, a bi-level building where passengers entered from the upper street level and then descended to the tracks below.

In 1930, with competition from the more flexible bus operations, the line closed. Only traces of the right-of-way are discernable across farm fields in the area. In Hamilton, the right-of-way has become the Chedoke Radial Trail, a 2.7-kilometre crushed-stone path, popular with joggers, that leads from Hillcrest Avenue in Hamilton, up the escarpment to Scenic Drive. Along the way, vistas extend across the now urbanized Dundas Valley. At one location, stone walls are an odd remnant of a protective wall once used to shield passengers from a rifle range that was located in the valley below. The trail continues into the community of Ancaster, where it merges with the street network at Helson Avenue.

The Niagara Falls Parks and River Railway

Although many of the radial lines offered scenic vistas across farmers' fields, lakes, and rivers, nothing compared with the jaw-dropping spectacles that awaited travellers on the Niagara Falls Parks and River Railway (NFP&RR).

The rail line started operating in 1893 from a ferry dock in Chippewa, where tourists from Buffalo, anxious to see the falls, disembarked. The route carried them along the brink of the gorge to stations such as Table Rock, the Maid of the Mist at Clifton Hill, Niagara Glen, and Queenston. In 1899, on the American side, the Niagara Gorge Railway began a scenic line of its own, following the base of the gorge from Lewiston to Niagara Falls, New York. When a new bridge opened at Queenston, the two lines joined forces, becoming the Great Gorge Route.

Despite the spectacle of the trip, travel on this line was not without its dangers. In 1915, a radial car lost its grip on the tracks when descending the hill into Queenston and plunged into the river, killing fifteen onboard. But the arrival of the auto, as usual, meant the end of the streetcar line. In 1932, the service on the Canadian side ended, and that on the United States side three years later.

Happily, the route has not been entirely forgotten. The Niagara Parks Commission has placed plaques along the route to inform a new generation of what would be otherwise a forgotten heritage. Indeed, a handful of one-time station stops still remain. The Table Rock Restaurant and Gift Shop is located in what was a popular stop for the NFP&RR, the platform being located on the west side of the structure. Near Whirlpool Road, the line built a trestle over a gully known as Bowman's Creek. A plaque here commemorates that trestle. The Niagara Glen Gift Shop occupies the only NFP&RR station to survive on-site, although it has been much altered. A short distance away, the Niagara Parks Botanical Gardens and Horticulture School grounds contain the station from the Brock Monument stop.

Portions of the route on the American side have been incorporated into a walking trail along the foaming river.

The Niagara, St. Catharines, and Toronto Railway

Known at first as the St. Catharines and Niagara Central Railway, this line began as a steam rail operation in 1881. Seventeen years later it became the Niagara, St. Catharines, and Toronto Railway (NSC&T) and joined Ontario's growing network of radial streetcar lines.

Although it never did reach Toronto, it did extend to several locations in the eastern Niagara Peninsula. In 1901, the line entered Port Dalhousie, where, to entice Sunday travellers, it established the popular Lakeside Park. Shortly thereafter the trains were travelling along the streets of Niagara-on-the-Lake.

Then, in 1908, it became part of the ever-growing Canadian Northern Railway network, which, three years later, laid tracks into Port Colborne. When the CNoR went bankrupt, the NSC&T became part of the Canadian National Electric Railway, which added a new terminal in St. Catharines at Geneva and Welland Streets, and, in 1928, another in Niagara Falls, which it called the Terminal Inn. This elegant structure lasted only a few years, and was removed in 1940 to make way for the new Rainbow Bridge to the United States. By 1959, all of its trains had been replaced by a fleet of buses.

In the 1990s, the St. Catharines terminal was removed, as well, and today little remains to proclaim its rail heritage. Although Lakeside Park, with its five-cent carousel, still attracts visitors by the thousands, there is no evidence that there was ever a radial railway there. The same holds true throughout the breadth of its once-extensive network. Yet, its memory does live on in the railway lore of Niagara.

Ontario's Southwestern Radials

Next to the central Ontario region, no portion of Ontario was as thoroughly covered with radials as was southwestern Ontario.

The Windsor, Essex, and Lakeshore Rapid Railway carried passengers and vegetables alike between Windsor and Leamington. Although its charter dates to 1879, the line never came into operation until 1907. Despite falling ridership, the Hydro Electric Power Commission (HEPC) assumed control of the line and began an upgrade. It acquired new cars and called the line the "Sunshine Country Route." With smoking compartments and leather seats, the luxurious new coaches offered a five-metre solarium at each end. All the upgrades, however, failed to stem the rush to buses and private cars, and in 1932 the service ended.

From a waiting room at Pitt and Osborne Streets in downtown Windsor, the route followed Essex County's road system to Maidstone, Cottam, and then into Kingsville, located on the scenic shores of Lake Erie. Here, many of the trains' passengers disembarked to spend their holidays in one of the assortment of Kingsville hotels. The route ended at Seacliffe Park in Leamington. Little evidence remains of the right-of-way, although the vacant powerhouse still stands in Kingsville, overlooking the harbour.

Another Essex County line that has almost completely vanished is that of the Sandwich, Windsor, and Amherstburg Railway. Its route mostly followed the road networks along the Detroit River into Amherstburg. The service began in 1891 and was upgraded by the HEPC in 1924 when it instituted freight haulage. But, by 1937, the line folded and its vestiges have vanished.

The Woodstock Thames Valley and Ingersoll Railway had a name for its twenty-four-seat "Tooterville Trolley" —

Estelle. Estelle, it turns out, was the daughter of the line's main promoter, S. Ritter Ickes. The eighteen-kilometre route began at the McLeod Building at Dundas and Broadway in downtown Woodstock, then followed what is today County Road 9 to the Ingersoll Inn, its western terminus. En route, the railway created Fairmount Park on the banks of the Thames River, hoping to attract riders on Sundays and holidays. In 1925, the line ceased operations and all evidence of its existence has been erased.

The Chatham, Wallaceburg, and Lake Erie Railway (CW&LE) began service in 1905, primarily to link Chatham and Wallaceburg. The line was as much about hauling sugar beets from the flat, fertile farm fields of Kent County as it was about carrying passengers. But in 1908 it added an extension to Erie Beach to attract more paying customers. Although the line continued to show a profit from its freight operations, the City of Chatham, which hadn't cared much for the operation from the beginning, ordered the line to remove its poles and wires from the city streets in 1930. That was the end of the CW&LE.

The tracks left Wallaceburg from Wallace Street and River Road, then followed the shoulder of the Baldoon Road to a shipping point, which the railway appropriately named Electric. Although no rail-era buildings survive, the setback for the tracks remains evident. The hamlet of Dover Centre, a short distance south of Electric, is still home to an elevator for the storage of the sugar beets that dates back to the days of rail. In Paincourt, the heart of the county's Franco-Ontarian community, the old hotel that served customers on the trains still stands, although most of the community is now made up of more modern buildings.

South of Chatham, nothing remains of the area's railway heritage. The route carried it south through Charing Cross, where it was forced to tunnel beneath the tracks of the Michigan Central. But no evidence of that structure remains, and the Michigan Central, the route of the Canada Southern Railway, is now a ghost rail line, as well. The CW&LE continued south through Cedar Springs, where portions of the embankment are still visible, then on to Erie Beach, where the railway had erected a pavilion for summer tourists. That building survived into the 1980s, at which time it was removed. An early hotel building still stands at the western end of 4th Street.

For an all too brief period of time, Londoners could choose which railway they wanted to take to get to the popular resort town of Port Stanley. As well as the still-operating London and Port Stanley Railway (L&PS) — now the Port Stanley Terminal Railway — they could ride the streetcars of the London and Lake Erie Railway (L&LE). In addition to its passenger service, the L&LE would load fish right from the dock and carry them fresh to the markets and restaurants of London. But with the decision of the L&PS to electrify its own lines, the L&LE became the less desirable of the two choices. Its travelling time was longer (nearly two hours as opposed to fifty-five minutes on the L&PS), and, being a provincially chartered line, it could not operate on the "Lord's Day." The federally chartered London and Port Stanley faced no such restriction.

It is not surprising, then, that by 1918 the L&LE had shut down. Today its route lies largely buried beneath the asphalt of Highway 4. Its station in Port Stanley, however, has managed to remain, and the little concrete building on Main Street is now a store.

The Grand River Railway (GRR) began operating as the Galt and Preston Street Railway in 1894. Four years later, when it expanded into Hespeler, the line became the Galt, Preston, and Hespeler Railway. About the same time, the Preston and Berlin Railway was building a link from Preston to the Erb Street terminus of the Waterloo and Berlin Railway. The two lines merged in 1908, and in 1918 adopted its new name: the Grand River Railway.

In 1921, the railway altered its route through Kitchener and added a new station at Queen Street. Another new station, styled in the flat-roofed international style then coming into vogue, was added in Preston in 1943. Passenger service continued until 1955, when buses finally took over. While portions of the GRR have been incorporated into a CNR line built in 1962, and then extended more recently to the new Toyota plant between Preston and Hespeler, other sections fell silent.

Although no stations or other rail buildings have survived, the Iron Horse Rail Trail follows the GRR from Ottawa Street in south Kitchener to Caroline Street in Waterloo, near the current Waterloo and St. Jacobs Railway station. Along the trail are information plaques as well as artifacts from Kitchener's Industrial Artifacts Project.[3]

PART TWO:

The Ghost Rail Lines
of Eastern Ontario

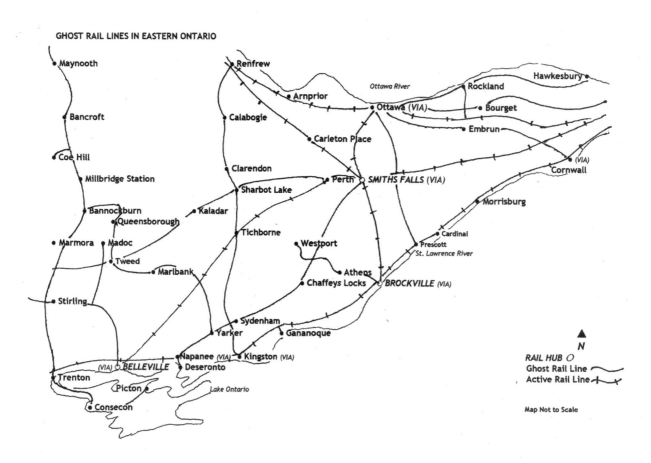

GHOST RAIL LINES IN EASTERN ONTARIO

Maynooth
Renfrew
Hawkesbury
Arnprior
Ottawa River
Rockland
Ottawa *(VIA)*
Bourget
Bancroft
Calabogie
Embrun
Coe Hill
Carleton Place
Millbridge Station
Clarendon
(VIA)
Perth
SMITHS FALLS *(VIA)*
Cornwall
Sharbot Lake
Bannockburn
Kaladar
Morrisburg
Queensborough
Tichborne
Marmora
Madoc
Westport
Cardinal
Tweed
Prescott
St. Lawrence River
Marlbank
Athens
Chaffeys Locks
BROCKVILLE *(VIA)*
Stirling
Sydenham
Yarker
Gananoque
(VIA) BELLEVILLE
Napanee *(VIA)*
Kingston *(VIA)*
Trenton
Deseronto
Picton
Lake Ontario
Consecon

N

RAIL HUB ○
Ghost Rail Line
Active Rail Line

Map Not to Scale

CHAPTER 12

The Ottawa and New York Railway: Cornwall to Ottawa

The History

It may come as a surprise to many Ottawa residents, but there was a time when they could have boarded a train in that town and travelled to New York City, direct. The Ottawa and New York Railway was conceived in 1882 by a pair of politicians, MPs Darby Bergin and Joseph Kerr. That year they were awarded a charter to build a line called the Ontario Pacific Railway (OPR), which would run from Cornwall to Ottawa. The line would continue northwest through Arnprior and Eganville to Georgian Bay, then on to Sault Ste. Marie. But the project gained neither funds nor popular support and simply died.

Then, in 1896, Bergin met an American railwayman named Charles Hibbard who wanted a route into Ottawa. And so, in 1897, the OPR was given a new name and a new charter: it would be called the Ottawa and New York Railway (O&NY) and it would run from Cornwall to Ottawa. South of the border, the American section was called the New York and Ottawa Railway and was linked with New York City.

Construction proceeded quickly because the land was flat and river crossings few, and by June of 1898 the line was in business. Originally the O&NY used the old Bytown and Prescott Railway station at Sussex Drive and McTaggart Street in lower town Ottawa, but the bridges over the Rideau River leading to that location proved unsafe, and the line was moved into Ottawa's Union Station. In 1941, it relocated again, providing passenger service from its freight yards at Mann Avenue.

The major obstacle facing this railway was the challenge of crossing the St. Lawrence River. Three segments were required: a drawbridge across the Cornwall Canal, a cantilever bridge over the river's north channel, and three steel trusses to span the south channel. In 1898, while under construction, the portion over the south channel collapsed, killing fifteen workers. Just nine years later, the span over the north channel collapsed. The bridge was later planked in to allow vehicular traffic and became the Roosevelt International Bridge.

More than a dozen stations lined the route, including a diminutive waiting shelter, possessing little more than a single door and a few benches, on Cornwall Island. Sitting on the international border, it was called, appropriately, Uscan. In fact, most of the O&NY's stations were little more than waiting shelters. The only stations of any size were those built at Cornwall and at Russell.

The O&NY later became part of the New York Central system and remained so until its abandonment. Eventually, the new age of car and truck travel caught up to the rail line. By 1951, passenger revenue had plunged from a high of $2,000 a month to only $500 a month, and in 1954 passenger service ended altogether. In 1957 the final train chugged out of Ottawa heading for New York.

The Heritage

Cornwall

Although the bridge across the St. Lawrence was dismantled following the opening of the St. Lawrence Seaway in 1959, and today's high-level bridge constructed, a few piers from the original structure remain visible in the river behind the Domtar plant in west-end Cornwall. The station stood near the corner of Hoople Street and Leonard Avenue and measured twelve by eighteen metres, with two waiting rooms, a ticket office, and a baggage room. It closed in February 1957 and was dismantled soon after.

A short distance north of the station the tracks of the O&NY crossed those of the original Grand Trunk line. The junction was called Cornwall Junction and consisted of a station and interlocking tower. These remained until 1949.

Cornwall to Embrun

Continuing along the line, small stations once stood at Black River and Harrison, the name board from the former now displayed in the Raisin River Heritage Centre at St. Andrews West.[1] The centre, a former convent (built in 1908 and closed as a convent in 1976), contains a museum and the headquarters for the Cornwall Township Historical Society. Glengarry County Road 15 generally parallels the route of the O&NY. The roadbed here is now a snowmobile trail.

The hamlet of Northfield grew around the little O&NY station, three kilometres to the west. A second station replaced the first, which had burned down. It survived the dismantling of the line and was given a new use — as a storage shed — a short distance from the right-of-way.

The next station stood in the larger village of Newington, located on County Road 12. Initially, it was large enough to warrant a full-time agent but, by 1955, he was replaced by a caretaker agent. The village retains a strong collection of early buildings, many dating from before the arrival of the railway. North of Newington, the snowmobile trail disappears from sight and much of the right-of-way is now ploughed under.

A short distance north of Newington, the O&NY crossed the tracks of the Canadian Pacific's main line (in the village of Finch) and shared the use of that railway's station. Although the CPR station was demolished, the cement foundations of the crossing tower remain visible to the east of the crossing. Finch sits at the intersection of County Roads 42 and 12.

Berwick station, the next stop north of Finch, consisted of little more than a flag stop. That building, saved from demolition, now stands on the right-of-way in the village of Embrun, marking the trailhead for the "New York Central" rail trail.

Chrysler became the site of the next station, or to be more precise, the next three stations. The first was destroyed by fire in 1908 and replaced with a two-storey structure. In 1937, it, in turn, was replaced with a smaller station about a kilometre to the north. That building, and what was presumably its freight shed, stand at the back of a property south of the village. Chrysler began life as a mill village on the South Nation River, and here the abutments of the railway bridge remain visible. Built in 1899, the steel truss bridge extended fifty metres across the river.

The village of St. Albert had another of the flag-stop stations. This small structure, also saved, now stands as a private house on Rue Notre Dame in Embrun. Embrun today is a bustling modern-looking town with a sizable Franco-Ontarian population. It was a mill town on the Castor River long before the arrival of the Ottawa and New York Railway. The extent of its rail heritage, however, is surprising. Not only do the former Berwick and St. Albert stations survive in this community but that of the Russell station as well. The Embrun station outlived the demise of the railway but unfortunately burned down

Although marked with the Embrun name board, the Berwick station, built by the New York Central Railway, has been restored to its original paint scheme and marks the Embrun end of the seven-kilometre maintained New York Central Rail Trail.

in 1970. The remains of the sixty-metre bridge that once spanned the river here are still visible.

Embrun to Ottawa

West of the village of Russell (the next station stop), the next string of villages — Pana, Edwards, Piperville, Ramsayville, and Hawthorne — had small flag stations, none of which have survived. From Edwards to the 8th Line Road, the rail trail re-appears. At Ramsayville, however, the extension of Ottawa's urban fringes and its highways has truncated the trail.

Upon its arrival in Ottawa, the O&NY moved into the station built in 1860 by the Bytown and Prescott Railway, which was situated at Sussex and McTaggart Streets. Later taken over by the CPR, it continued in use until 1964, when the National Capital Commission's urban-renewal program oversaw the removal of all of Ottawa's rail lines from its downtown core. The site of that first station is now occupied by the Lester B. Pearson Building. The only evidence of any rail lines is the piers that remain standing in the Rideau River, south of Sussex Drive.

Following its stint in the Union Station, in 1941 the O&NY moved its station facility to its freight yards at Mann Avenue. Today, no evidence survives to indicate that a railway named the Ottawa and New York Railway ever existed here.

CHAPTER 13

The Thousand Islands Railway: Gananoque to the Grand Trunk

The History

The Thousand Islands Railway has endured as a romantic icon in the annals of eastern Ontario despite its diminutive size — the line ran a mere sixteen kilometres, from the wharfs at Gananoque to the main line of the Grand Trunk Railway.

"Gan," as this picturesque St. Lawrence River community continues to be called, has been around a lot longer than the railways. Its first mills appeared in 1787, and in 1808 it was a main stop on the Montreal to Kingston stage road. Steamers began to call at a new wharf in 1819, and with the growth of the American rail network along the south shore of the St. Lawrence River, businessmen in Gananoque began to lobby for a rail link.

The first line to be built along the north shore of the river was the Montreal and Kingston Railway (M&K), which was proposing an alignment paralleling the river, but some sixteen kilometres away from the shore. Predictably, this drew considerable criticism. Shippers at ports such as Brockville and Kingston would not have

any link to the railways, a connection needed in order to be competitive. When the Grand Trunk assumed the M&K charter, the tracks were built closer to the water. Still, a harsh topography meant that the line remained well inland from Gananoque.

The GT built one of their standard stone stations with the low wide roof and French windows to serve Gananoque, but the road leading to it was tortuous at best and the station site did little for the community's economy. A rail line from the wharfs to the GT line seemed to be the only real solution. The first attempt in 1871 was to be the Gananoque and Rideau Railway, but having failed to attract funds, it was never built.

Responding to the dilemma, the Rathbun Company, whose milling, railway, and shipping empire was based in Deseronto, came to the rescue. After acquiring much of the town's waterfront property, the company received a charter to build the missing link.

Initially, this line was called the Gananoque, Perth, and James Bay Railway — a rather optimistic title. By 1883, however, when Gananoque finally has its rail link to the GT main line, it was more realistically called the Thousands Islands Railway (TIR).

The small settlement of Cheeseborough, which grew up around the junction, contained a section house, hotel, cheese factory, and a few homes, as well as the station. Meanwhile, a large wooden station appeared at Gananoque's wharf, as did a small "umbrella" station shelter on the main street.

The new railway link encouraged more tourists to come to enjoy the beauty of the Thousands Islands and vacation at the resort hotels by the river. In response, in 1899, the GT and TIR built a newer and larger station two and a half kilometres east of the first, at Gananoque Junction. In 1929, a new station was also built by the docks; a more elaborate brick building, it boasted pillars, a bell-caste roof, and a gable over the front entrance.

As with most rail lines, the demise of the Thousand Islands Railway arrived with the auto age. In 1931, a new highway was constructed along the shore of the

The tracks of the Thousand Islands Railway lie overgrown beside the station built by the Grand Trunk at Gananoque Junction. It remains a VIA Rail station stop.

river, and passenger traffic on the TIR fell to just seven thousand per year. Two decades later it carried an average of just two passengers per trip. Since the TIR's charter required that its trains meet each arrival of the Grand Trunk (by then the CN), the route quickly became uneconomical, and in the 1960s the passenger service was discontinued. In 1995, all rail service ended and the tracks were removed.

The Heritage

Gananoque

With the end of passenger service, the handsome wharf station at Gananoque became a restaurant and gift shop, a role that might have continued had it not burned down in 1990. On the site, near the cruise-ship dock, sits the newly built Arthur Child Heritage Museum.[1] Particularly notable for its striking gable and

Preserved beside the umbrella station in downtown Gananoque, the diminutive gas electric engine #500 continued to rumble along the Thousand Islands Railway from 1931 until 1966, by which time the rail line was no longer profitable.

tower, the museum offers displays of Thousand Islands history and culture.

The waterfront in Gananoque still attracts tourists, indeed more than ever. Cruises of the Thousand Islands lure visitors by the busload, while the Thousand Islands Playhouse, with its boat-in entrance, hosts thousands more. The Playhouse is housed in the historic Gananoque Canoe Club building, where, since 1982, it has staged some ninety-three Canadian productions. The redevelopment along Gananoque's waterfront, with its new shops and restaurants and a riverside walkway, has also made it an inviting destination point.

The old rail line is now a walking trail that leads from Mill Street to Highway 32, although the portion that runs through town is more professionally groomed, with a base of fine crushed stone. The trail crosses three trestles, including the iron trestle on the east side of King Street — Gan's main drag — and another on River Street. Near the King Street bridge stands the delicate little umbrella station shelter, and along King Street a number of historic structures recall not just the rail era, but the stagecoach era before that. The Gananoque Inn and Spa, recently renovated, has occupied a site on the river's edge since 1896.

Gananoque Station

The visible portion of the rail bed today ends at County Road 32, close to where the tracks first met those of the Grand Trunk at Cheeseborough, now little more than a ghost town. Even with the building of a new junction station, the original one at Cheeseborough continued to function until 1938. The newer Gananoque Junction station lies three kilometres east of County Road 32, along Station Road. Still a VIA Rail stop, the attractive wooden building with its diminutive tower has been restored. The tracks that served the Thousand Islands Railway remain visible on the south side of the building, while the busy CN and VIA line lies on the north side.

CHAPTER 14

The Brockville, Westport, and Sault Ste. Marie Railway: Brockville to Westport

The History

The ports on the St. Lawrence River were among Ontario's earliest shipping points. Places such as Brockville and Prescott had been around since the arrival of the United Empire Loyalists in the 1780s. With the first inklings of the coming railway age, these communities realized the value of rail lines to the hinterlands in getting lumber, minerals, and farm products to their wharfs.

One of the first lines to appear was the Bytown and Prescott Railway (B&P), which was open by 1855, a year before the Grand Trunk. Although interest was growing in neighbouring Brockville, B&P's difficulties securing sufficient revenue discouraged many local municipalities from financing rail ventures. The driving force behind a line from Brockville was Robert Hervey, the former mayor of Bytown (Ottawa). An American, he had successfully ushered the Illinois Midland Railway into

An early view shows the Brockville and Westport station at Athens, the community that urged the building of the line. Like many rural Ontario communities before them, Athens recognized the benefits of year-round, fast transportation links to other markets. The building burned down in 1948. Courtesy of the Ron Brown collection.

existence, and sought to repeat his success with a line he optimistically dubbed the Brockville, Westport, and Sault Ste. Marie Railway.

As early as 1871, the spirited little village of Farmersville (today's Athens) sponsored the building of a rail line from Brockville to Westport. But the defeat of John A. Macdonald's railway-mad government in 1873 and the onset of a depression brought new rail construction to a halt. With Macdonald's re-election five years later, the fever resumed, and in 1884 the Brockville and Westport Railway (B&W) was duly incorporated.

But none of the municipalities along the proposed route was as enthusiastic as Farmersville. Many refused to grant the funding needed. After considerable effort on the part of the line's promoters, however, sufficient money was raised. On January 11, 1886, sod was turned in Newboro, a village built around a lock station on the Rideau Canal a short distance east of Westport, for the building of the Newboro to Westport section. Two other sod-turnings in the months that followed brought the little line into being.

By then, however, the Grand Trunk had built its own tracks through Brockville and refused to negotiate any running rights over them with an upstart such as the B&W. In fact, the GT even refused permission to cross its line at grade level, thus forcing the little line to construct a pair of long trestles over the GT's tracks.

Interestingly, the Canadian Pacific, the Grand Trunks's main rival, allowed the Brockville and Westport line to use its tracks to the CP's Brockville wharfs on the west side of Butlers Creek. The Brockville terminus for the Brockville and Westport line was a plain three-storey wooden station located on Church Street in the west end of town.

But by 1903 the B&W was broke, and it was sold to a New York syndicate, which re-incorporated it as the Brockville, Westport, and Northwestern Railway, although there was no indication that it would even get beyond Westport.

Between Brockville and Westport, the B&W built more than a dozen stations, as well as flag stops. Its station designs were simple but elegant, with gable-end roofs, sometimes with a decorative finial and sloping overhangs over both the platform and the operator's bay window. Any difference in them was usually in the length of the structure and whether or not it had a permanent agent.

As with so many other lines, the B&W fell into the hands of a larger railway in 1910, in this case the Canadian Northern, which filled in the wooden trestles with ballast to make them more stable and reduce the risk of fire. When the Canadian National Railway was incorporated and took over the GT as well as the CNoR, the old Church Street station was closed, the trestles dismantled, and operations moved to the former Brockville Grand Trunk station. In 1925, the section of track from downtown Brockville to Lyn Junction on the CN line was abandoned and the rails lifted.

The remainder of the line from the GT tracks to Westport did remain in use, but scant shipments along the line eventually doomed its existence, and in 1953 the train whistles were silenced.

The Heritage

Brockville

From Brockville to Delta, twenty kilometres to the northwest, there is scant evidence that a rail line ever passed this way. Here and there, telltale tree lines mark the right-of-way, but a deep cut in the granite rocks, running a half-kilometre long and nearly twenty metres deep, is now so heavily forested that it resembles a natural valley.

After standing vacant for some time, the Brockville and Westport's tiny Forthton station is being restored. Its style was one that was repeated along the line. Forthton is a small hamlet situated northwest of Brockville.

All remaining evidence of the trestles that crossed the Grand Trunk was finally obliterated when the Brockville Golf and Country Club expanded.

No trace remains of the Church Street station or the CPR wharves, the land they once stood on now the site of a marina. The station from Lyn was moved and converted to a private residence that still stands today. The little station at Forthton, near the intersection of Highways 29 and 42, also remains, and is at the time of writing being restored by its new owners.

Athens

It would seem appropriate that the next station stop, Athens, where the initial push for the line began, would provide one of the more interesting, modern heritage features of the railway. In 1985, Reeve John Dancy was inspired by the increase in tourism that outdoor murals in Chemainus (British Columbia) had created. The murals there recounted that town's history and First Nations culture. He encouraged the Athens council to launch a similar initiative, and in 1986 one of the first murals to appear in Athens depicted train time at its station. Painted by Lorrie Maruscak, it graces the side of the Athens Pro Hardware on the town's main street. The station depicted in the mural, however, had burned down in 1942, and had been replaced by a simpler CN shed that later was moved to Eloida Road, where it was converted into a private home.

Although the station at Lyndhurst, several kilometres west of Athens, was located well to the east of the village, it may have been the largest station building on the line. One of the Canadian Northern's standard plan two-storey stations, it was erected following the destruction of the original B&W station by fire.

From a point west of Athens, Railway Street follows the shores of Lower Beverley Lake and traces the right-of-way as far as Delta. While all evidence of the line has vanished from the village, it does contain one of eastern Ontario's most photogenic structures, an old stone mill that dates from 1812. It is now the Old Stone Mill Museum.

The route of the rail line then passed well to the west of places such as Phillipsville and Forfar, both on Highway 42. Here, the roadbed has become a snowmobile trail, although it is unmaintained and overgrown during the summer. Forfar Station marks the trail's junction with another rail trail, today known as the Cataraqui Trail. This maintained hiking and biking trail follows the route of the Canadian Northern from near Napanee to Smiths Falls. The junction point, which contains no buildings, lies on Stone Road, west of the village of Forfar.

Newboro

The trail portion of the B&W ends at the east end of Newboro where the station once stood at the end of John Street. The village's historic Main Street with its early hotels and one-time stores lines the Rideau Canal and predates the rail line. A historic blockhouse was built in 1832 to guard the Newboro Lock on the Rideau Canal, a site that now forms part of the UNESCO Rideau Canal and Kingston Fortifications World Heritage Site. The abutments that carried the tracks across the canal are still visible from the highway bridge.

Westport

From Newboro, the barely discernable route of the B&W next crosses fertile farmlands before entering its terminus at Westport. This scenic village at the western end of Big Rideau Lake has developed into a popular day-trip destination for residents of both Kingston and Ottawa. Despite its name, the Westport Station Motel can no longer claim the station that outlived the end of the line. It was removed in recent years.

The Westport waterfront has been renovated to allow not just mooring for pleasure craft navigating the Rideau Canal, but also to allow strollers to amble along the water's edge and gaze across to the high granite ridge, known as Foley Mountain, that forms the north wall of the lake.

CHAPTER 15

The Kingston and Pembroke Railway:
Kingston to Renfrew

The History

Locals nicknamed the Kingston and Pembroke Railway (K&P) line the "Kick and Push" for a reason. The hard, rocky hills of northern Frontenac and southern Renfrew Counties are tortuous and unforgiving; in fact, they were so unforgiving that the K&P builders didn't even bother to blast. Rather, they simply opted to go around the granite outcrops. So twisting was the line that the engines could rarely garner much of a head of steam. The journey from Kingston to Renfrew could take several hours, and usually did.

The area north of Kingston was considered to be rich in resources, particularly iron and timber. Promoters C.F. Guildersleeve (a Kingston shipbuilder), C.V Price (a major Kingston shareholder and leading proponent of the line), and the influential Flower family of New York embarked on a route to tap these resources and link the port of Kingston with the booming lumber town of Pembroke. But with the CPR having entered Pembroke first, it was not economical for the K&P to build beyond Renfrew.

Instead, the line merged at that juncture with the CPR and the Ottawa, Arnprior, and Parry Sound Railway.

The first section opened to Godfrey, north of Kingston, in 1875, where a branch line led to the Glendower Iron Mine, a short distance east. The line to Renfrew, however, would not begin operating until 1885, a full decade later. The line never fulfilled the early expectations; the timber was soon gone and the iron-ore deposits proved disappointingly small.

Finally, after many years, the CPR (which had taken over the line in 1901, primarily to keep it out of the hands of the Grand Trunk) began abandoning the failing line. In 1962, the section from Snow Road to Calabogie was lifted, while the last section of the K&P, from Kingston to Tichborne, fell to the track-lifting crews in 1986.

The Heritage

Despite the numerous little stations on the Kingston and Pembroke line, few locations developed into communities of any size. While some grew with the arrival of the highways and the cottagers, others remain remote and little altered.

Much of the K&P line has been converted to a series of rail trails. The northernmost section has been opened and maintained within the last few years by the County of Renfrew. The middle section lies within the K&P Conservation Area, while the southern section is little more than a rough snowmobile track. Within the city limits of Kingston, however, the trail is better maintained.

Renfrew

Along the northern portion of the abandoned rail line between Renfrew Junction and Calabogie, the crushed-stone trail is suitable for hiking and cycling. From its northern trailhead at Riverview Street in Renfrew, the right-of-way crosses hayfields and pasture lands before reaching the historic community of Ferguslea, south of Highway 132 on the Ferguslea Road. The town was originally a stage stop on the legendary Opeongo Colonization Road, one of the government's failed colonization roads that were constructed during the mid nineteenth century to lure settlers to the north.

From Ferguslea, the rail trail follows forests and small farm fields before emerging at Ashdad, where a small station once stood. Today, a pair of early buildings is all that remains, one of which may have served as a hotel.

Calabogie

From Ashdad the trail plunges back into the woods, finally emerging at Highway 508 at the scenic village of Calabogie. Here, the trail crosses the tumultuous waters of the Madawaska River on a pair of trestles. The southern trailhead lies opposite a tourist office located on County Road 511, with breathtaking views across Calabogie Lake to Mount St. Patrick and the Black Donald Mountains.

Calabogie began as a rough-and-tumble lumber town where logs were floated down the Madawaska River from the forested mountain peaks. A dam built to help move the logs raised the waters of the lake to the level held today. Picturesque churches overlook the lake, while a rare eight-sided house can be found on one of the back streets.

Between Calabogie and Barryvale, the right-of-way crosses the lake over a lengthy causeway. Although not part of the rail trail, the causeway can be traversed partway from Barryvale. The next portion of the K&P Trail begins on the south shore of Calabogie Lake in the community of Barryvale, where a few early workers' homes mingle with newer and grander villas.

Between this point and County Road 509, the forty-kilometre trail forms the K&P Conservation Area, maintained by Mississippi Valley Conservation Authority. It is wide enough to be travelled by car. Passing can be awkward, however, especially when meeting the logging trucks that frequent this portion.

Flower Station

Past Barryvale, the route leads through hardwood forests (some, unfortunately, with clear-cuts) and along the scenic shores of Mile Lake and Clyde Lake to the remote hamlet of Flower Station. Here, by the crossing, a handful of early village buildings survive, with what is likely an abandoned railway hotel among them. The nearby community of Clyde Forks is a one-time mill town whose station sat surrounded by marshland. Here, too, an early church and several rail-era homes line the winding lanes. Campbell's Road and Black Creek Road both access this distant site.

The next station was located at Folger, a former rural logging community that is now quite difficult to access by car. A little easier to reach, Lavant Station was larger and saw the shipping of iron and lumber. Early churches and houses date to the arrival of the K&P tracks.

Wilbur Ghost Town

A short distance south of Lavant stands the ghost town of Wilbur, one of the K&P's early iron-mining villages. Unlike the other iron deposits in the area, those at Wilbur proved substantial, and between 1886 and 1900 the mines yielded 125,000 tonnes of iron ore. The population of the village grew to 250 and the community included a church and school. In 1911, the mine closed and the town was vacated. Today the mine site lies on private land, and a handful of early homes still huddle by the trail. The Wilbur Road leads from County Road 16 to this site.

The usable portion of the trail ends south of Wilbur at Highway 509 and is barely traceable at Snow Road Station, a few kilometres to the south. This village, however, is one of the route's most scenic, with pioneer churches and homes perched on a series of rolling hills.

Where the K&P crossed the Mississippi River, just south of Snow Road, the trestle has now been removed, leaving only the abutments as evidence of its existence. Highway 509 closely parallels the K&P roadbed for the next twenty kilometres until it reaches Highway 7.

Robertsville Ghost Town

South of the river, Mississippi Station, which for a half dozen years was the K&P's northern terminus, contains just a few early homes, now mixed in with newer country dwellings.

Robertsville, a short distance east of Highway 509, marks the location of another of the line's early iron-mining towns. Two mines were in operation here, the Mississippi Mine and the Mary Mine, and the railway ran a short spur line to serve them and laid out a town site nearby.

The village grew to a population of two hundred and had a store and school, as well as cabins and a boarding house for the workers. In 1885, after having yielded only 30,000 tonnes of ore, the mines were closed. Today, only a single house and the village cemetery mark the site of this ghost town, while vague cellar holes from the cabins mark the location of the little spur line.

Clarendon Station

Once a quaint rail-side community, Clarendon Station retains little of that heritage. One noteworthy exception is its original station. Little altered, the storey-and-half wooden CPR building still stands by the right-of-way, its platform now overgrown.

Sharbot Lake

A vacation destination for many early travellers as well as modern ones, the bustling lakeside village of Sharbot Lake (on Highway 38 just south of Highway 7) marks the junction of the K&P with another of Ontario's ghost rail lines, the Ontario and Quebec Railway.

At the site of the still-visible station platform where the two lines intersected, the village has created a tribute to its railway heritage. Beside the platform, which lies between the two rights-of-way, the village brought in a caboose and constructed an information kiosk. These elements form part of a station display outlining the community's railway history, and early photos depict the station area during those heady days of rail travel.

Other than the one in Kingston, the Clarendon station is the only other remaining on-site Kingston and Pembroke Railway station.

Kingston

Between Sharbot Lake and Kingston the trail is once more scarcely traceable, and is used by only the most ardent of snowmobilers. The County of Frontenac, however, has expressed interest in acquiring the route and developing it into a multi-use recreation corridor. The villages of Tichborne, Godfrey, and Verona all mark the sites of early stations, but scant evidence of their K&P era remains. Trains do still rumble through Tichborne on the CP's active Toronto to Montreal main line.

Orser Road marks Kingston's northern boundary. From this point to the shore of Cataraqui Creek, a short distance east of Sydenham Road, the city has created a crushed-stone cycling, hiking, skiing, and equestrian trail, one that is popular and well-used. But between the creek and the K&P's terminus on the waterfront, the city's urban growth has all but obliterated the right-of-way. However, down at the waterfront, opposite the domed city hall, the attractive stone K&P station with its mansard roof is now an information centre.

The historic steam engine that hauled the funeral train of Sir John A. Macdonald along the Kingston and Pembroke Railway line, appropriately named the "Spirit of Sir John A.," stands grandly before the station as it did when the prime minister came home to rest.

CHAPTER 16

Rathbun's Road, the Bay of Quinte Railway: Deseronto to Bannockburn

Although the Bay of Quinte Railway (BQ) is one of Ontario's shorter ghost rail lines, and one of the earliest to be abandoned, it contains a greater concentration of surviving on-site stations than any other.

The History

The Rathbun empire began as a milling and shipping business on the northeast arm of the Bay of Quinte, in the town of Deseronto. Because of the length of time required to transport logs from their timber limits north of Lake Ontario, Edward Rathbun chose to extend a rail line into that area. In 1879, along with other business interests, the Rathbuns launched the Napanee, Tamworth, and Quebec Railway (NT&Q), ostensibly to create a line from the Bay of Quinte to Ottawa. As often happened in those early days of railway building, the funds failed to materialize, and the route went no farther than from the port of Napanee on the Grand Trunk Railway to Tamworth, and, a few years later, to Tweed.

To directly connect their Deseronto shipping operations with the Grand Trunk west of Napanee, the Rathbuns created a rail line of their own. It was called the Bay of Quinte Railway and Navigation Company. Meanwhile, the NT&Q, now renamed the Kingston, Napanee, and Western Railway (the Quebec idea had, not surprisingly, been dropped), was also leased to the Bay of Quinte Railway, giving the Rathbuns their long-sought-after link, not just to the Grand Trunk but to their valuable interior resources. Later, in 1889, to give them access into Kingston, they extended their trackage to Harrowsmith, located on the Kingston and Pembroke Railway.

But the Rathbuns were still not content and set their minds on further expansion. To that end, the Rathbuns merged the BQ and the NT&Q lines under the single name the Bay of Quinte Railway (BQ). In 1893 they extended the line again, this time to the mica mines around Sydenham Lake. Then, in 1902, they extended a branch line from Yarker (a short distance to the northeast of Camden) to the villages of Queensborough and

Bannockburn to link with the Central Ontario Railway (COR) and thus tap the mineral fields there.

In 1910, with the BQ floundering, the builders of the Canadian Northern Railway, William Mackenzie and Donald Mann, incorporated the BQ into their network, not to access the minerals of the interior but simply to fill in a missing link in their ambitious scheme to create a main line from Toronto to Ottawa.

With the closing of the Rathbun docks in Deseronto, the end of the cement plant at Marlbank, and the depletion of the mines, the abandonments began. The CNR, which had absorbed the bankrupt CNoR in 1918, began by closing the Tweed to Bannockburn section in 1935, and six years later the Yarker to Tweed section. This left the Canadian National with what Mackenzie and Mann really wanted in the first place: a line from Napanee to Ottawa. Another forty-three years would pass before the CNR finally shut down that section as well, leaving only VIA Rail's line from Smiths Falls to Ottawa and a short spur line in Napanee as a legacy of the Rathbun days.

While the roadbed from Napanee to Bannockburn was, in nearly all areas, sold off to adjacent property owners and all evidence of its existence essentially eliminated, no fewer than five of the substantial stations built by the Rathbuns have survived, four of them as private homes. By contrast, the stations that were operated by the CNR in later years were all demolished by that railway.

The station style used by the BQ copied the popular style of the CPR, and was known as the "Van Horne." This consisted of a two-storey structure with end gables and no embellishments. The main difference between the BQ style and that of the CPR is that the operator's bay on the BQ buildings extended to the second floor, while those on the CPR did not.

The Heritage

Deseronto

As with nearly all the Rathbun structures in Deseronto, the station building no longer stands. Yet despite being away from today's busy rail and road corridors (or more likely because of it) Deseronto has retained a valuable heritage main street. Not only have the town hall and limestone post office survived, but so too has the historic Naylor's Theatre.

From Deseronto to Napanee, the right-of-way remains visible, although not developed as a trail.

Napanee

While the original Bay of Quinte Railway Station was moved to the corner of Roberts and Isabella Street to become a residence, the historic Grand Trunk station in Napanee, built of stone in 1856, still stands and plays host to VIA Rail service twice a day. Napanee, too, can claim the Gibbard Furniture Company, which, until it closed in 2009, was the oldest continuously operating industrial establishment in Canada. The county jail, built in 1864, located behind the court house, has been preserved and today houses the Lennox and Addington County Museum and Archives.

Newburgh

This section of line from Strathcona to Yarker remained part of the CN's Ottawa line until it was abandoned in 1984. Today, it forms part of the Cataraqui Rail Trail system, an extensive pathway leading from Strathcona to the western limits of Smiths Falls. The trail begins behind the Strathcona Paper Mill on Finlay Street, where it is largely hidden behind the factory buildings.

A few kilometres north of Strathcona, the right-of-way runs through Newburgh. Oddly, there are two rights-of-way here. The Bay of Quinte Railway's first route lay beside the Napanee River, but frequent flooding forced its relocation away from the river. While this original roadbed is no longer visible, the BQ station still stands on site, while across the road is a former railway hotel, now a private dwelling. Both structures are visible from Grove Street and lie just east of the main street along with rows of early stone buildings. The later right-of-way, where the rail trail now runs, had a later CNoR station, but it was demolished.

The trail continues on from here through Camden East, with its historic limestone former hotel, currently the Bookstore Café, on the main corner. The right-of-way here lies some distance to the north of County Road 2, but no station or rail structures survive.

Yarker

At Yarker, an attractive mill village situated beside a tumbling waterfall contains a variety of intriguing structures. It marks the location where the BQ once branched north to Bannockburn, then east to Sydenham via a bridge across the Napanee River. When the alignment was later straightened, a second bridge was added. The stone abutments of the original bridge still stand beside the Napanee River, while the steel girders of the newer one now carry the trail across the river.

Tamworth

Between Yarker and Bannockburn, four of the Bay of Quinte stations still survive. While the route made its way past villages such as Moscow and Enterprise, where neither stations nor roadbed remain, the one in Tamworth still stands. Now a private home, it lies on Concession Street South, a few blocks south of Bridge Street or County Road 4.

A short distance west of Tamworth and north on Highway 41, the Erinsville station stands beside a small municipal lakeside park. The Lakeview Hotel, still in operation, was built as the station hotel. The main part of village lies a kilometre to the north.

Marlbank

The right-of-way, meanwhile, angles southwest from Erinsville Station to the community of Marlbank, where another of the identical BQ stations stands by the road, now also a private home. Marlbank was the site of the Rathbuns' extensive cement works. The operation closed in 1908 following the takeover and consolidation of many of Ontario's cement plants by the Canada Portland Cement Company.

Tweed

For much of the distance between Marlbank and Stoco, Hastings County Road 13 follows the Bay of Quinte roadbed.

In Stoco, a short distance south of Tweed, the BQ station stands right by the road. Located on the west side of the Skootamatta River, where the bridge abutments are still visible in the water, the Stoco station has changed little and exhibits the same two-storey station pattern as the others on the line. Today, it is a private home.

In Tweed, on the shore of Stoco Lake, any evidence of both the Bay of Quinte and the abandoned Ontario and Quebec line has gone. The CPR station served out its last years as a lumberyard office.

Two kilometres west of Marlbank, just to the southeast of Tweed, lies the gaunt shell of the Rathbun's cement plant. Although fenced off today, the ruins can be easily seen from the road.

Beyond Tweed, the BQ has also all but vanished. Although lacking railway features, Actinolite, the next station stop, boasts a unique church and town hall, both constructed of local marble. The community of Actinolite was first founded in 1853, when it went by the name of Troy. In 1859 it became Bridgewater, and in 1895 it was renamed Actinolite after the mineral that was being extracted from open-pit mines near the town.

Queensborough

Queensborough, situated northeast of Madoc, is a village with several early heritage buildings, including the Bay of Quinte railway station, built in the same style as the others on the line, which is now a private home. It lies on Bosley Road, south of Queensborough Road.

Between Queensborough and Bannockburn, the stations that once stood at Allan and Rimington are now gone, and the right-of-way is scarcely traceable. The BQ line proceeded no farther than Bannockburn, on Highway 62, where at one time it formed a junction with the Central Ontario Railway. While the COR has become part of the Hastings Heritage Trail, the route of the BQ rail line can no longer be distinguished. Station Street, which lies west of Highway 62, in the centre of the village of Bannockburn, leads to the right-of-way, now a private fenced lane. It was here that the Bay of Quinte Railway placed its two-stall engine house and turntable. Their vestiges still lie in the woods beyond the gate.

The Queensborough station shows a modified Van Horne style copied in most of the Bay of Quinte Railway's original stations.

CHAPTER 17

The Prince Edward County Railway:
Picton to Trenton

The History

The earliest portion of what became the Central Ontario Railway was the Prince Edward County Railway (PEC). Although "the County," as it is more simply known, had a jump-start on many of the early Lake Ontario ports, the rail era had left it behind.

In 1784, Picton's harbour saw the arrival of thousands of United Empire Loyalists fleeing the barbarous persecutions that followed the American Revolution. The expression "if you're not with us, you're against us" is not a new one, as those who had opposed the revolution against British rule were at best disenfranchised, at worst killed. These fugitives sought a new home in the townships that the British government laid out for them along the British north shore of Lake Ontario and in Prince Edward County.

Throughout the 1800s, the county prospered on fishing and barley shipments. But it lacked a railway. Finally, in 1873, the Prince Edward County Railway received a charter to link the port of Picton with the Grand Trunk Railway north of Trenton. In 1879, the fifty-kilometre line opened to traffic.

In 1881, the line was purchased by American financiers and renamed the Central Ontario Railway (COR). Their vision was to look beyond the Grand Trunk and aim for the gold mines of Eldorado and the iron-ore riches of Coe Hill. In 1884, with ore flowing from the Coe Hill mines, COR built a large ore dock on Wellers Bay; however, the bay was too shallow, and the dock was useless. The shipping of canned goods, however, was far more lucrative, and Prince Edward County became the canned fruit and vegetable capital of Canada. Such shipments made up half the tonnage of goods shipped from the stations in the county. In 1909, both the COR and the PEC were acquired by the ever-expanding and ambitious Canadian Northern Railway.

But more ore was to come. In 1953, when Bethlehem Steel opened its massive open-pit at Marmora, the company also added an ore dock a short distance north of Picton Harbour. Ten years later, Canada Cement added its own operation.

Twenty years later, the mine closed. A proposal to ship nepheline syenite (a medium-grained igneous rock used in the manufacture of glass and porcelain) from the mines north of Havelock failed to materialize. When the cement shipments declined, the then owner, CNR, chose to abandon the line. Proposals for tour trains fell on deaf political ears, and in 1995 rail removal began.

The Heritage

Picton

The bustling port of Picton was full of bobbing schooners, steamers, skiffs, and fishing boats — before the railway came to town. The first railway station was a simple two-storey wooden structure typical of many of the first-generation stations in Canada. When the Canadian Northern Railway purchased the entire COR line, stations and tracks were replaced and upgraded.

The Picton station was relocated and converted to a house, and a more elaborate brick structure with decorative gables was constructed to replace it. But, with the end of passenger service in the 1970s, it too was put up for sale. Today, it is part of a lumber store, shorn of its decorative features and overwhelmed by additions to the building. The original station is also still around, now a real estate office at the corner of Lake Street and Main Street West. The branch line to the former ore dock and to what is now Essroc, the current owner of the cement operation, remains evident on the ground.

Picton to Trenton

From Picton to near Trenton, the roadbed, cleared of its tracks in the 1990s, is now a popular rail trail cutting across the countryside. Unfortunately, early efforts to convert the Central Ontario Railway into a tourist rail line were thwarted by political disinterest.

The first station out of Picton was at Bloomfield, where trackside industries included Aylmer Canning and Sun Joy Foods. Now a house, the station still stands on Stanley Street near its original site, south of the main street. Bloomfield, with its spas, pottery, gift shops, and chocolate shop, has become a popular destination for day visitors. Bikes are rented for tours along the trail or on the county's many scenic winding back roads.

The busy fishing port of Wellington was the next major station, although the tracks were located some distance north of the wharfs. The main business for the line, as in the rest of the county, was the shipping of farm products, in particular canned goods from Wellington's three canneries. The station has long since been removed.

From Wellington, the trail veers inland to Hillier, a smaller community with a larger station building, as well as a Canadian Canners cannery. By the 1970s, the station had been removed and a section tool house placed on its foundation.

The next stop, Consecon, was a busy fishing port and mill town even before the tracks reached it. Years later, after track was lifted, a trio of rail-side buildings at Consecon Station presented a valuable piece of the county's rural railway heritage. Although the station eventually deteriorated and collapsed, the two other structures — a freight shed and an elevator — still survive, but there is little local interest in saving them.

From Consecon to the Murray Canal the trail skirts the Lake Ontario shoreline, providing a scenic section for users. At Wellers Bay, the COR had grand dreams of establishing a major port to export the iron then being extracted from the mines at Coe Hill and Marmora.

Regrettably, local disinterest allowed the quaint little wooden Consecon station building to rot and eventually collapse. Although a freight shed and grain elevator remain, the station ground is now vacant and overgrown.

But the harbour proved inadequate and today only a vague outline of the dock is visible.

Need for a dock in Wellers Bay was further negated with the opening, in 1888, of the Murray Canal, which provided a much needed shortcut linking the Bay of Quinte with Wellers Bay. The Central Ontario Railway constructed a swing bridge to carry its trains across the canal. The bridge now rests on the side of the canal, a short distance west of Highway 33. The trail continues only a short distance beyond this, extending along the north shore of the Bay of Quinte before being swallowed up by housing lots.

Trenton

The right-of-way, occasionally visible, follows Highway 33 almost into Trenton, where the Central Ontario Railway roundhouse survives as a retail outlet. Here, it met the tracks of the CNoR's main Toronto to Ottawa line, part of the burgeoning Mackenzie and Mann railway empire. After the CNoR acquired the Prince Edward County Railway, they replaced Trenton's smaller station from that line with an elegant brick station. It was demolished in 1963 to make way for a parking lot.

111

Sadly, Trenton has not been especially kind to its railway heritage, and the wonderful two-and-half-storey station built by the Canadian Northern Railway was removed to make way for a parking lot. Courtesy of the Ron Brown collection.

The routes of the CNoR and COR have utterly vanished from the downtown area of Trenton. Only the bridge piers show where the CNoR span once crossed the Trent River. The Central Ontario roadbed, meanwhile, made its way north following the west bank of the river, but it, too, has largely been built over.

While the right-of-way remains evident beneath the CPR bridge on Front Street, an active spur line, the last remaining bit of COR trackage, runs from Wooler Street northward to pass beneath the Grand Trunk (now

CN) overpass on Telephone Road, a short distance west of Stockdale Road. Established to serve a feed mill to the north, the spur line connects with the tracks of the Canadian National. Again, both the early CPR station and the Grand Trunk station are gone. VIA Rail passengers are left to huddle in a small glass shelter.

CHAPTER 18

The Central Ontario Railway: Trenton to Maynooth

The History

No sooner had the Prince Edward County section of the Central Ontario Railway reached its junction with the Grand Trunk, than plans were underway to extend it to the gold fields of Eldorado in the rugged hills north of Madoc. Although the Belleville and North Hastings Railway had earlier reached the same destination, its line was short-lived. It was the COR route that would survive for another hundred years.

By 1889, the main line had reached the iron-ore country of Coe Hill, with branches reaching into various other mineral locations — the Belmar branch to the gold mines in Cordova, and the Ontario, Belmont, and Northern Railway to the iron deposits of Marmora. The Bessemer and Barry's Bay Railway, which was intended to reach Barry's Bay on the Ottawa, Arnprior, and Parry Sound line, failed to extend beyond the Childs Iron Mine, a short distance from Detlor station on the main COR line.

In 1899, what would later become the main route for the COR was being built northward from Ormsby Junction (thus turning the Coe Hill tracks into a branch line) to Bancroft. The optimistic idea was to reach the Ottawa, Arnprior, and Parry Sound Railway, but at Whitney, on the edge of Algonquin Park, rather than Barry's Bay.

In 1909, the COR, along with the Prince Edward County Railway, was acquired by the Canadian Northern Railway. Under the new owners, the tracks were eventually hammered into Bancroft, a one-time logging town in Hastings County, and then on to Maynooth. But, even under the new ownership, the end of the line fell well short of a link with the OA&PS. It ended ignominiously in the middle of the bush at a location called Wallace. Before long, the mining branches began to fall victim to dwindling deposits. The Cordova branch was gone by 1941, the line north from Maynooth to Wallace ended in 1965, that to the Childs Mine the same year, and the Coe Hill branch the year after. The main route to Bancroft and Maynooth managed to keep going until 1985, when it, along with everything north of Trenton, fell silent.

Most of the old right-of-way is now a rail trail, in most places too rugged for cycling, but suitable for hiking, although most commonly used for snowmobiling. That portion north of Glen Ross, where the tracks once crossed the Trent River and Canal, goes by the name of Hastings Heritage Trail. The portion south of Glen Ross is called the Lower Trent Trail and is for non-motorized use only.

The Heritage

From Trenton Junction to Glen Ross

Although track remains in place beneath the CNR overpass on Telephone Road near Trenton's VIA Rail shelter, some earlier structures add to the heritage of the site, including maintenance structures and a former railway hotel. The starting point for the Lower Trent Trail lies on Stockdale Road, just to the north. The trail then follows the Trent River, although for the most part remains back from the riverbank, and passes the historic milling town of Glen Miller. Here, a side trail leads to the unusual Bleasdell Boulder.

No ordinary rock, this massive Canadian Shield boulder is the size of a small house. Known by geologists as an "erratic," it had been carried great distances by the advancing ice sheets of 50,000 years ago and deposited, in this case, on a limestone plain. The distinctiveness of this feature has earned it its own conservation area, with paths leading from a parking lot to the giant rock and an information plaque explaining the phenomenon. Another path also connects the rail trail to the erratic. At this point, road access is via Highway 33.

The rail trail next passes the eastern boundary of the community of Batawa.[1] Founded by shoemaker Thomas Bata in 1939, Batawa remained a functioning company town until the plant closed in 1998. Today, most of the company houses are gone, leaving little more than vacant lots defined by abandoned driveways, steps, and sidewalks. Both the factory and one-time Bata office still stand beside the trail. Across from them is Pioneer Park, operated by the local municipality, Sydney Township. Here, information plaques relate to early settlers and to Bata himself.

The station site in Frankford, the next station stop, today functions as the trailhead for the Lower Trent Trail, with maps and trail information on a display board. Although the station was relocated to Stockdale, the foundation remains visible in Station Park at the corner of Wellington and Miller Streets, just west of the river. Frankford lines the Trent River, and it is here that Highway 33 crosses the river, leaving the Glen Ross Road to follow the trail northward.

Glen Ross to Marmora

From Frankford, the road winds through scenic rural countryside with the river never too far to the east and the rail trail to the west. At Glen Ross the trail crosses the Trent River on a 120-metre trestle. To cross the Trent Canal, a short distance beyond, the Central Ontario Railway built a swing bridge, one that now sits in a permanently opened position on the south bank of the canal. At this point the right-of-way becomes the Hastings Heritage Trail.

West of Stirling, at Anson Junction, the COR crossed the tracks of the Grand Junction Railway, a route connecting Belleville with Peterborough. No major settlement grew here, and the stop was served only by a shed-sized station with a handful of houses nearby. Today, the site marks the meeting of a pair of rail trails.

On its way to its strategic junction with the Ontario and Quebec Railway at Bonarlaw, the trail passes the sleepy hamlets of Springbrook and Crookston, places that once offered building sites at their station grounds for mills and small industries needing railway-shipping facilities. Despite its significance as a railway junction, the community of Bonarlaw remains little more than a roadside hamlet. Where trains once met, two rail trails now intersect. The O&Q Trail (now part of the Trans Canada Trail) follows the ghost rail line from a point east of Havelock to near Glen Tay in eastern Ontario. While the trails are used primarily for ATVs and snowmobiles, and appear well-groomed, shrubs now obscure the station grounds.

Marmora

Thanks to its long association with the iron mines, Marmora remains a bustling town located on Highway 7. While the COR's Hastings Heritage Trail lies a few kilometres to the east of the town, the station has been moved to a park on the south side of the highway. The branch line to Cordova, although abandoned since 1941, is visible as a laneway beside the Crowe River in downtown Marmora. Here, various industrial ruins lie beside it, including machinery and foundations from a sawmill operation. From this point to Cordova the roadbed of the branch line is overgrown and mostly obscured. The village of Cordova remains a heritage backwater with a number of early mining-era buildings, although no mine has operated here in decades.

The most visible reminder of Marmora's mining days is the "big hole," a monstrous open pit that is filling with water, but, which, from the 1950s to the 1970s, supplied iron ore to be hauled down the railway for transport to the company steel mills in the United States. The Marmoraton Iron Mine, owned by the Bethlehem Steel Mills of New York, began operation in 1955 by stripping away the fifty metres of limestone lying on top of the deposit. Eventually, the open pit would reach a depth of nearly two hundred metres and cover an area or more than two hundred hectares. More than 1.3 million tonnes of ore were processed at the site, filling more than thirty ore cars each day, which were then hauled to the wharves on the Bay of Quinte, near Picton. A lookout point east of Marmora on Highway 7 overlooks the mighty crater.

Eldorado

From Marmora, the trail winds its way through the rugged hills of the Eldorado gold fields. The community of Malone (on the Deloro Road, a winding route travelling northeasterly from Highway 7) once boasted three gold mines, but is now nearly a ghost town. As is Eldorado.

The site of Ontario's first gold mine, Eldorado was born on the back of a land swindle. While gold surely existed, it was in much smaller quantities than the speculators were letting on. Nonetheless, in 1867 the first mine opened and Eldorado boomed into a raucous town of eighty buildings. When the swindle was uncovered, the boom collapsed. With the arrival of the Central Ontario Railway, the village struggled on although its grand buildings had vanished or lay in ruin. Today, the station platform is still visible beside the trail, and one of the community's first hotels stands nearby. Several other structures, which straggle along Highway 62, present a ghostly aura of the town's boom and bust.

Eldorado to Bancroft

North of Eldorado, at Bannockburn on Highway 62, the COR meets the long-vanished roadbed of the Bay of Quinte Railway. Although no trace of the latter road-bed survives, that line's two-stall engine house remains, though it is located down a private lane, out of view of Station Road.

From here, the trail makes its way into some of the rugged bushland that discouraged pioneer settlement to the north. The first attempt to open the area to settlement involved the building of the Hastings Colonization Road. As with the other roads in this development scheme, the land along the road would be free, provided the settler would clear his lot and build a cabin. But the soil proved worthless and most of the farmers headed west, leaving behind abandoned farms and a string of ghost towns.

The mill village of Millbridge lay on the Hastings Road and is now a ghostly remnant of its pioneer days. Located where the tracks of the COR passed a few kilometres to the east, Millbridge Station never developed into a village but offers one of the more striking trail-heritage sights. Here, the former Hogan's Hotel was built to serve travellers planning to travel the Hastings Road. This large brick hotel seems strangely out of place in the woods that surround it. Both it and the trail lie east of Highway 62 on the Stony Settlement Road.

The trail then returns to the woodlands until it reaches Gilmour, once a remote logging community. Today, it has become a modern rural community with newer homes lining the Weslemkoon Lake Road. The station lasted until the1980s. The hotel still stands beside the trail, now a private home.

From the Central Ontario station at Brinklow, the Coe Hill branch, once the main line, headed west to the iron mines. The right-of-way has been developed as a trail here, and the station survives in the local fairgrounds. A small municipal office containing an information centre occupies the former station grounds.

Situated in the middle of what is now a forest, Hogan's railway hotel in the ghost town of Millbridge Station once hosted passengers travelling on the Central Ontario Railway. The site of the hotel and Millbridge Station lies east of Highway 62, north of the town of Madoc.

From the Coe Hill junction (known as Ormsby Junction) the trail winds its way once more through the rugged hill country of north Hastings, through Turiff and Detlor, where the Bessemer branch led to the Childs Mine. Bronson Station, the next stop, which was simply a shed, was moved to a property north of Bancroft. The trail then finally enters the busy tourist and rock collectors' heaven of Bancroft.

Bancroft

It is said that the area around Bancroft offers rockhounds a greater variety of collectible semi-precious crystals and minerals than any other area on Earth. None of the mines were particularly large, however, and were certainly not the reason the Central Ontario Railway was attracted here. Rather, lumber was the enticement, with Bancroft having begun as a lumber-mill town. The farms carved into the surrounding hills provided farm produce for shipping, as well. The station, a storey-and-a-half building with a steeply pitched roof and small dormer, still stands on the right-of-way just west of the main street. After serving as mining museum and tourist office, it lies vacant at this writing.

Today, Bancroft's annual "Gemboree" attracts thousands of rockhounds and dealers, and has turned the town into a tourist destination, busy year-round.

Bancroft to Maynooth

Just beyond the Canadian Tire at the north end of Bancroft, an oddly named road lies to the west. Y Road represents the railway "Y" that formed the junction of the COR with the equally ill-fated Irondale, Bancroft, and Ottawa Railway. The two branches of the Y remain visible, one of the portions now a gravel lane.

Once more the trail heads for the hills, where farm clearings mix with forested hillsides. The partial ghost

In Hastings County, the massive station in tiny Maynooth still stands just east of that village, although its heritage has been horribly neglected. Now derelict, the two-storey structure was the de facto northern terminus of the Central Ontario Railway. It also housed the offices of the line's supervisory staff.

town of Hybla lies a short distance east of Highway 62 on the Hybla Road. A few early structures, some vacant, reflect the days when Hybla was a centre for shipping products such as feldspar from the mines in the nearby hills. A similar station stop stood at Graphite, named for the mineral mined near here. The area has evolved into a small cottage community.

Maynooth offers a varied and conflicting chapter in the history of North Hastings. It was once the junction point of two colonization roads — the north-to-south Hastings Road and the east-to-west Peterson Road. The Central Ontario Railway arrived here and built a massive two-storey station of concrete and laid out rail yards. A couple of kilometres to the east of the village, a small satellite settlement developed around the station.

Today, the yards are overgrown and the station, while still standing thanks to its concrete construction, is criminally neglected. Despite a Facebook page effort to obtain federal funding through the Community Adjustment Fund, it would seem that no one cares to preserve the history in this area. While the trail continues for a short distance north, the heritage does not. Lake St. Peter once contained a small station (now gone) and is now largely a seasonal community; little of the past remains at Wallace either.

CHAPTER 19

The Canadian Northern Railway: Ontario's Forgotten Main Line from Toronto to Hawkesbury

The History

By the 1890s railway fever was peaking. But in 1895 a determined pair of railway builders began an empire of their own. William Mackenzie and Donald Mann (both later knighted) acquired a modest railway charter in Manitoba known as the Lake Manitoba Railway and Canal Company. Their strategy was clear from the start: acquire small lines or unused charters to create yet another transcontinental link.

In 1906 they began construction on a line that would lead south from Parry Sound to Toronto and north to Capreol, to link with a main line they were planning to the west coast. But they also had their sights set on a main line from Toronto to Ottawa and Montreal. As early as the 1850s, the Grand Trunk Railway had already grabbed the prime locations close to the shore of Lake Ontario, with access to the major ports. If they were to build a successful main line to Ottawa, Mackenzie and Mann's line needed to stay well to the north of the lake.

The Canadian Northern Railway (CNoR)'s entry route into Toronto came from the north with the completion of its line from Parry Sound in 1906. From a junction in the Don Valley, near today's Don Mills Road, they began to build their Ottawa line in 1911. It led northeast through northern Scarborough, never coming close to the lake until it swung south into Port Hope and Cobourg. Even there it had no link of its own to these ports. While the line ran by the lake through Belleville and Deseronto, it then turned northeast again to venture across the rocky terrain of the Frontenac Dome (an extensive geological outcropping of the pink granite of the Canadian Shield), and on through Sydenham and Smiths Falls, before gaining flatter terrain for its run into Ottawa in 1913.

From there the line followed the shore of the Ottawa River to Hawkesbury, where it crossed the Ottawa River and sent separate branches to Montreal and Quebec City. By 1918, however, the war had taken its toll on railway revenues, and the Canadian Northern, like so many others, was bankrupt. That year the Canadian

National Railway was created by the government of Canada to acquire such failing lines. By doing so, it came to possess several redundant routes: the CNoR's main line to Ottawa and Montreal was one of these.

With the former Grand Trunk main line along the shore of Lake Ontario being much more profitable, the CNR began abandoning portions of the CNoR as early as 1925, particularly that section between Toronto and Napanee where it ran close to the tracks of the old Grand Trunk. The Port Hope to Trenton portion was gone in 1924–25, the Trenton to Deseronto in 1931, the Don Valley to Port Hope in 1937, and the Ottawa to Hawkesbury between 1938 and 1940. The section between Strathcona and Smiths Falls remained in place until 1984. Between Smiths Falls and Ottawa, the line still serves VIA Rail. Beyond Ottawa to Hawkesbury, little remains of this brave venture.

The Heritage

Toronto

Each day motorists by the thousands inch along Toronto's Don Valley Parkway and pass beneath the massive Bloor Viaduct. If they have the time to notice, they will see that the valley floor is filled with grasses and ponds, an effort to restore a natural valley ecosystem. Few will be aware that this same floodplain once held the marshalling yards for Mackenzie and Mann's ambitious Canadian Northern Railway. In 1906, the CNoR was completing its line down the Don Valley and needed appropriate lands for yards, an engine house, and repair shops. They placed the yards in the Don Valley and the shops and other facilities in the planned community of Leaside.

In Toronto, the CNoR shared Union Station with the Grand Trunk Railway until progress on a new union station proved too slow. In 1916, they moved into the CPR's new North Toronto union station.

Leaside

To access the Leaside location from their route in the Don Valley, Mackenzie and Mann constructed a spur line from the tracks at a point near the crossroads of today's Leslie Street and York Mills Road. Although those rails were recently lifted, the legacy of the CNoR remains firmly planted in Leaside.

As they did in Mount Royal in Montreal, Mackenzie and Mann hired a firm of town planners to design a model community that would develop around their facilities. Despite laying out an elaborate pattern of winding urban roads, the housing boom did not reach Leaside until after the CNoR had folded. Handsome brick homes today line streets that were named after such railway luminaries as Hanna and Bessborough. And despite the absence of the tracks, the original CNoR engine house and station still stand on Esandar Road, east of Laird Avenue. In the valley, they placed a wooden two-storey station with the trademark CNoR pyramid roof. Known as Todmorden, after a nearby mill complex, this station marked the junction where the CNoR would branch out on its eastward route to Ottawa and Montreal.

While the CNoR tracks and station are long gone, the remains of the bridge abutments over the Don River are still evident, as is the roadbed that follows a line of hydro poles along the wall of the Taylor Creek Ravine. Farther along the valley, the outdoor tracks of the TTC subway trace that roadbed. Meanwhile, the route that continues up the Don Valley is now part of CN Rail but is used primarily by GO Transit, VIA Rail, and the ONR's Northlander train.

Toronto to Port Hope

The route of the Ottawa branch through Scarborough surfaces only in rare instances, such as marking property boundaries or in the form of a short footpath in Thomson Memorial Park, located on Brimley Road. The village of Malvern, with its CNoR station, has long been overwhelmed by recent suburban industry.

The alignment eventually leaves the urban sprawl behind, but remains indistinguishable until it crosses modern Highway 12, about five kilometres north of Whitby. A bridge abutment still survives here on the west side of the highway, and a building housing a medical clinic represents either the station agent's house or the station. The CNoR gave this station the name of "Brinlook," a word derived from Brooklin, the nearest village at the time. The Whitby and Port Perry Railway had already used the village name for its own station.

East of Oshawa, the solitary rural Solina station still remains in its original location on the Canadian Northern Railway right-of-way. Most of this has been turned over to adjacent property owners, and it is rarely identifiable.

From here to Taunton Road and Simcoe Street in Oshawa, the right-of-way has largely been obliterated by new development. Forced to remain well north of the lakeshore, the Canadian North Railway called its station here Oshawa North. The building, a long two-and-a-half-storey structure with a series of dormers in the roofline, was constructed after a pattern the CNoR repeated along its lakeshore line. It still survives as a dwelling on nearby Wayne Street.

Similar stations were situated in Orono, Colborne, and Grafton. Just a few kilometres east of Oshawa, on Solina Road, south of Taunton Road, a rare rural CNoR station (now a private dwelling) still survives on the original right-of-way.

Too far north to call its next station after Bowmanville, the CNoR named the location on Liberty Street after Tyrone, a historic mill village to the north. Tyrone, where a water-powered saw- and gristmill still operates as it has since 1846, was near the site of the McLaughlin Carriage Works, the forerunner to General Motors Canada.

The next stop, Orono, retains its heritage main street and a street called Station Street, although neither tracks

The Canadian Northern Railway designed elaborate stations, such as this one in Port Hope, as well as others at Cobourg and Belleville. The latter two were demolished.

nor a station remain. The right-of-way, despite the name, is simply a suburban road.

Port Hope

The rural stations of Osaca and Crooked River once stood between Orono and Port Hope, but no sign remains of either today.

Port Hope, however, offers a potpourri of CNoR heritage, from the bridge abutments over the Ganaraska River to the surviving station on Ontario Street. One of its grander buildings, the châteauesque brick building was designed by architect Ralph Benjamin Pratt, the designer of many of the CNoR's larger urban stations. Although the roadbed has vanished, the building now serves as a provincial government office.

Cobourg to Napanee

From Port Hope to Cobourg, the right-of-way is only vaguely marked by utility poles, and in parts of Cobourg it disappears altogether. The Cobourg station, identical to the one in Port Hope, was located to the north of the present VIA Rail station, amid a small network of rail-workers' homes. Those early houses on Buchanan and Station Streets now mingle with larger, more modern dwellings. The right-of-way here is marked by hydro lines paralleling Buchanan Street.

East of Cobourg, the CNoR closely followed the routes of the GT and CPR, today marked only by vegetation lines and utility poles. The station, south of Grafton, was located beside Cannery Lane, where an early house represents the sole survivor of a cannery operation, which at one time included a boarding house and some workers' cabins. Foundations of the cannery remain by the right-of-way, almost totally hidden by vegetation.

The Colborne station stood near Division and Arthur Streets, while the one in Brighton, a single-storey structure, was located on Richardson, where it served as a lumber-yard office until it, too, was removed. Brighton's GT station, dating from 1857, survives as the Memory Junction Museum, complete with a full-size steam train and much rail memorabilia.

Between Brighton and Trenton, as if to emphasize their redundancy, the three rail lines — CP, GT, and CNoR — ran side by side, within hailing distance of each other. In order to enter Trenton, the CNoR had acquired the charter of the Prince Edward County Railway, and replaced Trenton's simple PEC wooden station with an elegant three-storey brick building. It was later demolished to make way for a parking lot. The piers for the bridge over the Trent River, and the former roundhouse, which now houses retail outlets, survive.

Again, between Belleville and Napanee, most evidence of this short-lived line has been obliterated. In passing through Belleville, the CNoR subsequently shared tracks with the CPR and built a station in the Port Hope style. After falling into the heavy hands of the CPR, this station, not surprisingly, was demolished; it once stood by the still-active CPR tracks near Church Street South.

East of Belleville, the route followed the shore of the Bay of Quinte, where evidence of a causeway is still apparent. South of Shannonville, Beach Road was built on the roadbed for a short stretch along the bayshore, but from there, into the heart of Deseronto, the line is not identifiable.

From Deseronto to Sydenham, the CNoR assumed the tracks of Rathbun's Road, the Bay of Quinte Railway (BQ). The only station to survive on that stretch is the one at Newburgh. The right-of-way here is clearly visible from the outskirts of Deseronto to Napanee, where a short industrial spur still occupies the CNoR/BQ roadbed.

Napanee to Sydenham

From the Strathcona Paper Mills a short distance northeast of Napanee, the route of the CNoR has been converted into the Cataraqui Trail, a multi-purpose rail trail that follows the right-of-way for 104 kilometres to the outskirts of Smiths Falls. Parts of the trail, consisting of fine gravel, are well-maintained and suitable for hikers and cyclists. In other parts, the coarse stones make such usage more difficult.

In Newburgh, a short distance northeast of Napanee, flooding from the Napanee River forced the CNoR to relocate the original Bay of Quinte tracks farther away from the threat. Although the Canadian National removed the CNoR station, that of the BQ still stands on the first right-of-way. In Yarker, the CNoR again needed to reroute its tracks by adding a new trestle to eliminate an awkward "Y," built earlier by the BQ. While the CNoR bridge remains in place and is now part of the Cataraqui Trail, only the stone abutments of the earlier BQ bridge remain.

Once in the village of Harrowsmith, the CNoR/BQ shared both a right-of-way and a station with the Kingston and Pembroke Railway. For a number of years the station remained at the end of Ottawa Street, near its original location, but, although it outlived the demise of both rail lines as a private home, it is now gone. The station platform, however, is still visible beside Colborne Road. Harrowsmith retains a valuable collection of early homes that date back to the days of rail and earlier.

The current iron bridge crossing Harrowsmith Road between Harrowsmith and Sydenham was added by the CNoR and is the third of three. The abutments of the previous two are still visible at the roadside. East of the trestle, the rail trail crosses a valley on a high causeway, beneath which is one of the railway's "cattle passes."

These were basically culverts allowing farmers to herd their cattle from pasture to pasture under the tracks.

While the trail has been built upon through the village of Sydenham, it re-emerges conveniently at the local beer store, where the station formerly stood. During the BQ days this was the end of the line. Here, deposits of mica were loaded from barges on Sydenham Lake onto the waiting rail cars. Sydenham remains a picturesque cottage and commuter community with many early stores and hotels, and it is a popular destination for Kingstonians.

Sydenham to Smiths Falls

Between Sydenham and Smiths Falls, and on into Ottawa, all of the trackage was built by a confident CNoR, convinced that it could compete with the CP and GT for traffic.

From Sydenham, the Cataraqui Trail leads east following a scenic, if sometimes rugged, route through granite rock cuts and along scenic lakeshores. At historic Chaffey's Locks the CNoR's high iron-rail bridge crosses the Rideau Canal.

This historic lock-station community, which dates from 1832, contains many early canal-era homes and buildings, including the Opinicon Lodge[1] and an early mill. The lockmaster's house, fortified to defend against a possible American attack, now houses the Lockmaster's House Museum. Here the canal, along with the fortifications in Kingston, form the UNESCO Rideau Canal and Kingston Fortifications World Heritage Site.

From Chaffey's to Smiths Falls, the landscape changes sharply as the right-of-way emerges from the Canadian Shield to follow the more flat and fertile farmland through communities such as Portland and Lombardy. Finally, the trail reaches its eastern terminus at the western end of Smiths Falls.

Smiths Falls

Although the town traces its roots to the Rideau Canal, Smiths Falls offers much in the way of railway heritage. The community began as a mill town on the Rideau River and boomed in 1832 with the completion of the Rideau Canal. The tracks of the CNoR reached town in 1908, crossing the canal on a bascule bridge that now remains open permanently.

Built in 1914, the turreted CNoR station is now the location of the Railway Museum of Eastern Ontario. Displays inside the museum feature steam engines, coaches, boxcars, cabooses, and a rare dental rail car that carried this popular service to remote railway communities lacking a dentist. Smiths Falls also offers the Rideau Canal Museum and the Heritage House Museum, the latter located in a former mill-owner's house, where it displays a rare two-storey outhouse.

While the CNoR museum is on the west side of town on William Street, much rail activity takes place on the east side of town, where the CPR still operates an extensive sorting yard and divisional point. This historic site came to be with the building of the Ontario and Quebec Railway in 1884, but expanded when the CPR's lakeshore route was completed to this point in 1912. The large station has been saved and houses a community theatre. VIA Rail's Ottawa trains still stop here.

Ottawa to Hawkesbury

From Smiths Falls to Ottawa the route remains very active, carrying several VIA Rail trains daily. For the brief time that the CNoR operated in Ottawa, it used a small station located at Hurdman Avenue. With the takeover of the CNoR by the CNR, passenger service was moved to Union Station in downtown Ottawa.

From Ottawa east to Hawkesbury the route of the CNoR has largely been usurped by various roads. The eastern end of the Queensway in Ottawa, then Highway 174 and the old Highway 17, were all built on the CNoR roadbed. The Cumberland station still survives near the right-of-way and is now a private residence. Farther east, at the Indian River, the CNoR bridge piers stand like sentinels in the water.

From the Indian River into Hawkesbury, the rail bed heads inland, most of it now ploughed under, but re-emerges as an industrial spur at L'Orignal, where Ontario's oldest county courthouse stands as it has since 1825. The spur is operated by the Ontario L'Orignal Railway, which connects to the CNR line at Glen Robertson. The Hawkesbury station stood on Higginson Avenue and displayed the traditional CNoR two-storey pyramid-roof structure used by the company on all its lines throughout Canada. None have survived in Ontario, a fitting end for a rail line with such unrealized dreams.

The Canadian Northern Railway's bascule bridge in Smiths Falls is now one of Ontario's most historic railway bridges. A Scherzer rolling lift bridge, it was built in 1915 and operated manually for more than sixty years. It ceased functioning in 1978, and five years later became a National Historic Site. The bridge remains in a permanently open position over the Rideau Canal.

PART THREE:

The Ghost Rail Lines of the Southwest

GHOST RAIL LINES IN
SOUTHWESTERN ONTARIO

Geogian Bay

Wiarton

Meaford

Owen
Sound

Southampton
Park Head

Collingwood

Ceylon (Flesherton)

Paisley

Chesley

Kincardine

Durham

Dundalk

Hanover

Walkerton

Shelburne

Teeswater

Mt. Forest

Wingham

Orangeville

PALMERSTON

Goderich   Blyth   Listowel

Inglewood

Fergus

Monkton   Elmira

Lake
Huron

Georgetown (VIA)

GUELPH (VIA)

Kitchener (VIA)

Exeter

STRATFORD (VIA)

Galt

St. Marys (VIA)

Lucan

Hamilton

PARIS (VIA)

Forest

Woodstock (VIA)

Brantford (VIA)

Caledonia

Sarnia (VIA)

LONDON VIA

Waterford

Petrolia

Tillsonburg

Simcoe

Glencoe (VIA)

ST. THOMAS

Port Dover

Port Stanley   Port Burwell   Port Rowan

N

RAIL HUB   O

(VIA) Chatham   Ridgetown

Ghost Rail Lines

Active Rail Lines

Windsor (VIA)

Amherstburg Leamington

Lake Erie

Map Not to Scale

CHAPTER 20

The Credit Valley Line: Cataract to Elora

The History

One of Ontario's leading early railway promoters was George Laidlaw. His involvement in the Gooderham and Worts Distillery in Toronto enabled him to recognize the need to import raw material to Toronto by rail. After having promoted the Toronto and Nipissing and the Toronto, Grey, and Bruce Railways to the northeast and northwest respectively, he then turned his considerable energies to adding a line to Ontario's southwest.

In 1871, he obtained a charter to build the Credit Valley Railway (CVR) from Streetsville to Orangeville, following the spectacular gorge in the valley of the Credit River. In 1872, the charter permitted an extension to Elora, and in 1873 to Galt (now Cambridge) and Woodstock. From there the line was to lead into St. Thomas and link with the Canada Southern Railway, thus establishing access to the resources and markets of Ontario's prospering southwest. The branch to Elora would link with the main CVR main line at Cataract Junction, deep within the Credit Valley gorge.

Construction was slow and money scarce. Finally, in 1881, with the company nearly bankrupt, trains began travelling from its main facilities at Parkdale in Toronto to St. Thomas. Worried about the Credit Valley Railway's financial situation, Laidlaw convinced the Canadian Pacific Railway to acquire it in 1883. This, however, meant that the once-competing lines, the Toronto, Grey, and Bruce Railway, which the CPR also owned, and the CVR, were too close to be economically viable, especially between Orangeville and Toronto. As a result, one of Canada's earliest railway closures saw the CPR abandon the TG&B portion south of Melville Junction in 1933, a short distance south of Orangeville. This left the CPR with the former Credit Valley route from Toronto to Melville Junction, and with the Toronto, Grey, and Bruce tracks from Melville Junction into Orangeville. With the severity of the area's snowstorms, the Credit Valley Railway was the first rail line in North America to use the rotary snow plough.[1]

The original CVR Orangeville station, which lay north of Broadway in the flats east of the town's core area, was also removed at this time. The section between Cataract Junction and Elora continued operating until it was abandoned in 1987 and the tracks lifted. Today, that route has become another popular rail trail known as the Cataract to Elora Trail.

Otherwise, much of the Credit Valley Railway remains in active use. From Toronto to St. Thomas, it falls under the control of the CPR's St. Lawrence and Hudson Railway. In 2000, that portion of the CVR from Brampton to Melville Junction and of the former Toronto, Grey, and Bruce line from Melville to Orangeville was sold by the CPR to the Orangeville and Brampton Railway. It is this railway line that operates the popular tour trains in the Forks of the Credit canyon, as well as shipping a variety of products from Orangeville to Brampton.

The Heritage

Cataract Junction

Once a busy Credit Valley Railway junction point, the former site of Cataract Junction is now a ghost town. At its peak, the village contained stores, a hotel, and gristmills, as well as the station with its yards and even a roundhouse. Today, only vague bits of rubble lie amid weeds and shrubs. The ruins of John Deagle's mill lie near a foaming waterfall deep in the gorge, a gristmill that Deagle converted into a power plant that supplied electrical power to the area for more than fifty years.

On the clifftop above the gorge sits the village of Cataract with its small grid of streets. The place started as a boomtown during a phoney gold rush, then fell silent, only to be revived with the arrival of the CVR. After the station closed and the junction village was abandoned,

the village above managed to struggle on. Today, it is the home of rural commuters who travel in to cities such as Brampton and Orangeville.

Starting in the centre of Cataract, an early road that wound into the gorge has become a popular hiking trail, with links to both the Cataract to Elora Trail and the famous Bruce Trail. The Cataract Trail begins at this old roadway and climbs westward out of the gorge. Only metres away, trains from the Brampton and Orangeville line rumble beneath the trail's footbridge.

Despite being an ideal location for a trailhead, the local municipality has prohibited street parking everywhere in Cataract and along many of the roads leading into it — a short-sightedness that diminishes the value of having a rail trail in the first place. Nor has there been any attempt to offer a historic plaque or trail information to visitors.

Hillsburgh

From Cataract, the trail crosses Mississauga Road and leads to the village of Erin. Here, where the rail line crosses the north end of Erin, there is a plaque and parking is available for trail-users. No buildings related to the rail operations remain in Erin; however, Hillsburgh, the next stop on the line, offers a much more interesting access, with a historic plaque displaying early photos of the station that once stood here.

A similar treatment lies at the access in Orton, a relic village with a former railway hotel still standing. Across the street is Joy's Cupboard, a gift shop occupying the former general store. Orton lies on the Erin East Garafraxa Townline Road, about midway between County Roads 24 and 26. The trail access here also offers a photo of the Orton station and historical information.

Belwood Lake is a reservoir on the Grand River, to the east of Fergus, created to help abate the damaging spring floods that once plagued the river valley. It also forced the Credit Valley Railway to reroute its tracks along the south shore of the reservoir where the station once stood, and, until recent years, a feed mill. The village of Belwood sits on the north shore of the lake, now best-known as a small resort community.

Fergus

This picturesque mill town more resembles a Scottish highland village than an Ontario mill town. With its main street of mostly stone buildings, some sporting a distinctively Scottish flair, and its landscaped riverbank, Fergus ranks among Ontario's more scenic towns.

Unfortunately, that care did not extend to its rail heritage, as the station and tracks of the Credit Valley

The ruins of the Deagle Mill, which operated as a flour mill before it was converted in 1899 to a hydro plant, located at Cataract Junction ghost town, south of Orangeville, forms a popular attraction for both Bruce Trail users and passengers on the Credit Valley Flyer tour train. The hydro plant was closed down in 1947, when water levels became too low for effective operation.

Railway are long gone. Even the rail trail is left to make its way through the town streets. The stations of both the Credit Valley and the Wellington, Grey, and Bruce Railways stood near each other at the west end of the town, near Hill and George Streets. Here, with new industries moving in, the former yards are little more than an overgrown clearing, while an early railway hotel, now converted to apartments, is the sole vestige of the town's railway heritage.

Elora

The tracks of the Credit Valley Railway ended in Elora, at the corner of John and Mary Streets, where a sign declaring "Station Lane" marks a new housing development on the old station grounds. The rail trail has its terminus at Gerrie Street, just north of Wellington Road 18, or Mill Street. The famous Elora Quarry swimming hole lies on the south side of Mill Street.

Like Fergus, Elora is full of heritage treasures. A string of historic stores line Mill Street, leading up to the Elora Mill Inn and Spa, a popular hotel and restaurant. Behind the mill, a photogenic waterfall tumbles into the Elora Gorge, a five-kilometre limestone canyon of frothing rapids and unusual rock formations with names such as the "Tooth of Time."

Wellington Road 18 connects the two communities of Fergus and Elora, only six kilometres apart. Midway along, the Wellington County Museum and Archives occupies a massive and historic "House of Industry," one of the county's more cherished historic sites. Also connecting the two towns is a short walking trail along the roadbed of the Wellington, Grey, and Bruce Railway, which includes a vertigo-inducing rail trestle high above the Grand River.

CHAPTER 21

The Toronto, Grey, and Bruce Railway: Toronto to Owen Sound

The History

By the mid-1860s, railway building in Ontario was well underway. Both the Great Western and the Grand Trunk Railways had built their trunk lines west from Lake Ontario toward Lake Huron and the American border. But the region that lay north of these lines remained in its pioneer infancy. Only a few crude trails allowed travellers to reach the far shores of either Georgian Bay or Lake Huron.

The first notion for a rail link into this semi-forested region was formulated in 1864, and foresaw a horse-drawn tramway that would bring cordwood to the Grand Trunk Railway at Brampton, since at that time engines had not yet converted to coal. Its first proposed name was the Orangeville Tram Company. The plan was soon revised to use steam engines, and the name became the Toronto and Owen Sound Central Railway. It, too, failed to materialize.

The proposal, however, didn't remain dormant for long. In 1868, under the urging of Toronto rail-promoter George Laidlaw, the Toronto, Grey, and Bruce Railway (TG&B) became incorporated. The original plan was for a narrow-gauge route that would lead from Toronto to Orangeville, Mount Forest, and Southampton on Lake Huron, with a branch line to Owen Sound. The sod-turning took place in Weston in 1869, and by 1871 the first trains began arriving in Orangeville.

By the next year, track-laying headed north from Orangeville, reaching Dundalk in late 1872. By the following August, regular service to Owen Sound had begun. By the next year, tracks for what had originally been intended as the main line began heading west from Fraxa Junction, near Orangeville, to Wingham. The builders had anticipated that a connection there with the Wellington, Grey, and Bruce Railway (WG&B) would provide them with their link to Lake Huron at Kincardine. But the WG&B declined the proposal and the touted main line ended up as a simple branch line into the village of Teeswater, many kilometres from any water. Another branch line led west from Saugeen Junction, north of Dundalk, and ended up by the Saugeen River in Walkerton, again nowhere near the lake.

For the most part, the branch lines hauled lumber, cattle, and other farm products, while the new main line to Owen Sound was busy loading up on grain from the western grain boats. The stations en route developed into busy shipping hubs. Orangeville became the TG&B's main divisional point, with sorting yards, a freight shed, bunkhouses, a station restaurant, and later a large station building that sported a "witch's hat" roof. However, in 1883, the TG&B was absorbed into the vast CPR network by means of a 999-year lease with the CPR-controlled Ontario and Quebec Railway.

Interestingly, another railway had reached Orangeville just a few years earlier — the Credit Valley Railway, which was built from Toronto to St. Thomas to connect with the American lines there. From Streetsville junction, it extended a branch into Orangeville, arriving there in 1879.

The CPR, which came to control the CVR as well, now had two nearly parallel lines linking Toronto to Orangeville, with a crossover at Melville Junction just to the south of Orangeville. But the original TG&B section south of Orangeville was a very winding route with a particularly steep curve through the Caledon Hills known as the "Horseshoe." It was here in 1907 that a Toronto-bound passenger train went into the curve too fast and jumped the tracks, killing seven and injuring 114. In the inquest that followed, the engineer and conductor were found to have been negligent, and possibly intoxicated.

In 1933, the CPR abandoned the redundant Bolton to Melville portion of the Toronto, Grey, and Bruce Railway, using the tracks of the Credit Valley Railway instead. It did, however, retain the TG&B route from Melville into Orangeville and on to Owen Sound and Teeswater. In 1984, the Walkerton branch was abandoned, and four years later the Teeswater branch. Finally, despite objections from the many railway customers in

Owen Sound, the CPR abandoned that section of the route in 1994, as far south as Orangeville.

Today, the Brampton and Orangeville Railway uses the surviving portion of the Credit Valley Railway line to haul industrial products from Orangeville and Brampton, as well as operating a popular tour train along the Forks of Credit Canyon, arguably southern Ontario's most scenic tour-train route.

At first the stations built by the Toronto, Grey, and Bruce were simple, usually single-storey with low, wide rooflines. Larger communities, however, warranted a two-storey structure in which to include accommodation for the agent and his family. Within a few years, however, the CPR began replacing the older buildings with its newer roster of station designs. Some sported a bell-caste roof with dormers puncturing the upper floor rooflines. The new station at Orangeville contained the interesting conical roof above the waiting room, known as the "witch's hat," a design element the CPR also used in Parry Sound and Goderich.

In 1908, the CPR embarked on a new branch line from Bolton to Sudbury Junction to link with its transcontinental route. When the Toronto, Grey, and Bruce was abandoned west of Bolton, that branch became the CPR's main west coast line.

The Heritage

Toronto

From the beginning, the Toronto, Grey, and Bruce shared the Grand Trunk's Union Station on the Toronto waterfront, although it did establish a wharf and terminus of its own at Queen's Quay, near the foot of Bathurst Street. Construction for a condominium building to be built on the site in 2004 unearthed the buried ruins of that wharf.

From Toronto to Bolton, the route of the TG&B remains part of the CPR main line, while the abandoned portion west of Bolton is now scarcely evident. Between Bolton and Melville Junction the right-of-way has been incorporated into fields, residential yards, and, occasionally, laneways.

On Airport Road, three kilometres south of the village of Caledon East, Mono Road, so named by the railway, once contained a number of stores and hotels, as well as a grain elevator. These are now gone, as is the right-of-way. North of Mono Road, the tracks entered the difficult terrain of the Oak Ridge Moraine, the site of the fatal "horseshoe" train wreck. That infamous curve is no longer discernable, although the name lives on in the nearby Horseshoe Road.

At the south end of Toiless Road, in the village of Caledon (originally called Charleston), a private home was once the TG&B station for that community, and the right-of-way has been incorporated into private yards.

The tracks of the CVR and TG&B were only a couple of kilometres apart as they approached the next stop, Alton. Those of the Toronto, Grey, and Bruce line lay farther from the core of this mill village, where a hotel once stood near the station.

Orangeville

The site of the Credit Valley Railway station in Orangeville, on the north side of Broadway and east of the downtown, is buried beneath commercial development. The attractive Toronto, Grey, and Bruce station has also gone, but not very far. It is now a popular restaurant and bar, fittingly known as the Old Train Station, just a block south of Broadway. The TG&B station grounds remain busy with freight and

passenger cars of the new Orangeville-Brampton Railway (OBR) line, which built a new classic-style station to serve the many tourists riding the scenic tour train.

Today, the tracks of the TG&B end at the east side of County Road 11, west of Orangeville. On the west side sits the site of Fraxa Junction, the dividing point of the branches to Owen Sound and Teeswater respectively.

The Owen Sound Branch

Shelburne

North of Fraxa, the right-of-way is to officially become a rail trail, as it is being used at time of writing, albeit informally. The stations between Fraxa and Shelburne were just simple sheds, and one of these shed-sized stations, the one from the rural flag stop of Crombies, is now housed in the Dufferin County Museum on Airport Road.

While the original station at Shelburne was a two-storey structure, it was replaced with a single-storey station and is now a private home south of the town. Although the station grounds have been cleared, a feed mill still operates beside the right-of-way, the town's only connection to its train days.

A main street of heritage buildings, including a handsome town hall, developed with the arrival of the railway. With the building of the line, Shelburne grew from a population of seventy in 1869 to more than seven hundred in less than a decade. The town, however, is better known today for its annual old-time fiddle competition held annually in early August.

The one-time village of Melancthon, the next station stop on Highway 10 north of Shelburne, is now a ghost village, with no indication that either a train station or even a village ever existed here. Corbetton, another station stop a short distance north, offers a mix of recent and early homes, a few of which owe their origins to the arrival of the railway.

Dundalk

A much larger community, Dundalk, in Grey County, could claim a two-storey station. Its main street of solid commercial buildings testifies to the role that the TG&B played in its growth. Here, too, a feed mill dates from the days of the railway.

From the north end of Dundalk, the Grey Rail Trail begins, offering hiking opportunities along this historic rail corridor. At Proton Station, on Highway 10, an eerily quiet street of rail-era homes and buildings, including a one-time store, still survive. When the TG&B decided to build its station at Proton, it bypassed the earlier village of Inistioge, once three kilometres to the east on Highway 10 and just southeast of County Road 34. Here only a cemetery remains; Inistioge has vanished.

The site of Saugeen Junction never developed into a settlement of any substance. The station remained little

A wall mural in Dundalk celebrates that town's Canadian Pacific Railway heritage.

more than a shed for the train crews and possibly one or two passengers. Its location lies on West Back Line Road, between Grey County Roads 170 and 180. Here a small trestle still crosses over the Saugeen River.

Because it was located a few kilometres west of the main part of the village, the station for Flesherton developed into a satellite village named Ceylon. Here, the roadbed is part of the trail network. A few rail-era buildings, including a former railway hotel, now a private residence, mark the site. The station can now be found on a farm in the Beaver Valley.

Markdale

The station sites for the next string of stops — Markdale, Berkeley, and Holland Centre — are very similar, with little or no evidence of railway structures and only the Grey Rail Trail to reflect the heritage of the line. The Markdale station was removed to nearby Townsend Lake and converted into a fine home. The villages that line Highway 10 began not as railway towns, but rather as stopping places on the pioneer settlement road, the Sydenham Road.

Chatsworth, too, gained its early importance not from the rail line, but rather from its role as the junction of two early settlement roads, the Sydenham and the Garafraxa Roads.

Owen Sound

The arrival of the first Toronto, Grey, and Bruce Railway train to Owen Sound in August 1873 changed the face of this community forever. While it had gained an early lease on life as a protected harbour and shipping point, as well as being the terminus of the Sydenham Road, the rails brought new industries and the vital grain elevators.

Now grain ships could unload and return to the western lakehead faster than ever, and the grain would make its way quickly to the Atlantic ports.

The first station was, as were most of the others, a simple single-storey wide-roofed structure. After the Second World War, the CPR replaced it with a more modern style of building, typical of the internationalist style that the rail line had begun using on its post-war stations. When the rails were lifted, the station was closed and remains so. The asphalt platform is now cracked and weedy, while the former sorting yards next to it have been turned into a dog park. The waterfront has been beautified with benches and landscaping, but other than an historic plaque, the rail heritage of the TG&B goes uncelebrated.

North of the station, the right-of-way now forms the Tom Thomson Trail, allowing cyclists and hikers to follow the shoreline of Georgian Bay until the trail turns inland to link with the Grey Rail Trail near the southeast end of the city.

The Teeswater Branch

It was meant to be the main line of the Toronto, Grey, and Bruce Railway, but when the Wellington, Grey, and Bruce Railway refused permission to use their tracks to access Lake Huron, the Toronto, Grey, and Bruce ended this branch line at the inland mill town of Teeswater.

Grand Valley

From Fraxa Junction, the Teeswater branch headed west, coming first to the mill town of Waldemar in Dufferin County. The tracks crossed the Grand River on a steel trestle just to the north of Station Street, where the abutments remain. East of the river stood the station, now sitting behind a private home opposite its original site. Barely visible from the road, it retains all its original features. A few early buildings in the area date from the pre-rail days when Waldemar was a gristmill town.

From Waldemar, a rail trail now follows the roadbed. Known as the Upper Grand Trailway, it leads to the next station stop, Grand Valley, where a trailhead and information plaque stand on the east side of County Road 25 at the south end of this picturesque village situated along the bank of the Grand River.

The trail runs west from the road to the site of the former station, which has become a private home a short distance away. The groomed part of the trail ends here, although the trail extends to the town of Arthur. While the roadbed here has been obliterated by new development, the station now enjoys new life as a private residence on Conestoga Street, where it also retains many of its original features.

Mount Forest

From Arthur, the roadbed parallels Highway 6 until it reaches Mount Forest. Villages along the way, such as Petherton (now nearly vanished), Kenilworth, and Riverstown, at one time could claim a Toronto, Grey, and Bruce station. Although the hamlet had only seventy-five residents, the TG&B was obliged to locate a station in Kenilworth as a condition of the funding received from the township. All evidence of these features have been removed and the roadbed is barely visible.

At one point, Mount Forest was to be the TG&B terminus for this branch. When those plans changed, the route was redirected to the west, just touching the south end of town; only a spur line entered the town. Here, too, the TG&B linked with the WG&B, but no evidence of either line or of its structures can be found.

Mount Forest to Teeswater

The same holds true for the section of line leading from Mount Forest to Teeswater and Wingham. From Mount Forest the line swung to the southwest toward Harriston, where again it intersected the tracks of the WG&B. As with Mount Forest, all evidence of its existence has been obscured.

West of Harriston, the Toronto, Grey, and Bruce passed through a string of one-time mill villages that had developed along the Maitland River: Fordwich, Gorrie, and Wroxeter. All three have seen their prosperity dwindle with the demise of the railway and the arrival of the auto age. Today, most people drive to Harriston or Wingham for their shopping and other needs.

A few businesses continue to function in Fordwich, while both Gorrie and Wroxeter have declined to the point where their commercial cores could be called "ghost downtowns." Wroxeter, however, has attempted, with some success, to reverse that image by installing streetscaping, new businesses, and a highway sign that now proudly proclaims it as a "Former Ghost Town." Gorrie can claim its historic gristmill as part of a riverside park.

But their railway heritage goes unrecognized and is mostly invisible. In Fordwich, new housing now lines "Station Street," while the roadbed remains vaguely evident at the north end of Gorrie. The Wroxeter and Gorrie station stood halfway between the two villages.

Wingham

From Wroxeter, the Toronto, Grey, and Bruce line swung northwest to a point where the line split with the main branch leading north to Teeswater, its terminus, and a spur line into Wingham. At the junction known as

Glenannan, a station-style name board celebrates the railway, stating "site of post office 1861–1954, The Railway 1874–1988." This is the only physical evidence of the line.

It was not until 1887 that the TG&B extended its short branch line southwest from Glenannan into Wingham. On the way, the route crosses farm fields unnoticed until it reappears in Wingham as a walking path along the Maitland River and passes beneath the former CNR bridge, now part of another walking path.

Teeswater

For a Bruce County town that was once the terminus of a railway line, today's Teeswater is a very quiet place where only a few businesses remain open. An architecturally elegant three-storey hotel also still stands on the main street, although, being some distance north of the station grounds, it was unlikely to have been a railway hotel. As for the station site, only the configuration of the streets and property lines give any indication of the Toronto, Grey, and Bruce's presence. Industrial Road marks the site.

The Walkerton Branch

Priceville

From a point called Saugeen Junction, north of Dundalk on the Owen Sound main line, the TG&B headed west toward Hanover and Walkerton, where the branch terminated. While the location of the junction is visible on the Grey Rail Trail north of the Saugeen River bridge, it is only intermittently visible from there to Hanover.

The handsome station at Priceville, the next stop en route, today stands proudly as a private home on Grey County Road 4, its name board still prominently on the front. Priceville offers a small treasure trove of early heritage buildings along its main street, many dating from its more prosperous days as a mill town.

Durham

From Priceville the roadbed winds its way around the steep morainic hills of Grey County and into the busy highway town of Durham. Although the rail line has largely vanished, the Town of Durham has planked in the large trestle across the Saugeen River, converting it into part of a walking path. West of that, however, the roadbed has been covered by new housing.

The line continues in obscurity to Hanover, where the station grounds are now vacant. A series of walking paths here follow the roadbeds of both the TG&B and WG&B. One path leads across the new pedestrian bridge built on the piers of the Toronto, Grey, and Bruce's Saugeen River bridge, then follows the roadbed a short distance to the east.

Walkerton

Between Hanover and Walkerton the route is now an ATV and snowmobile trail ending at the eastern limits of the town of Walkerton. The water tank and turntable, which stood on the east side of the river, have been built over; however, a lookout point on the west bank of the Saugeen River is called the "CPR Bridge Lookout." It rests on one of that line's bridge abutments. A historic plaque describes how the bridge remained in use until 1954 and consisted of three iron spans. The station grounds themselves form part of a park and are no longer evident. A memorial park in town is dedicated to the recent tainted-water scandal.

As with Hanover and Durham, Walkerton remains a busy village serving the farmers and residents of its hinterland, a prosperity that can, in part, be attributed to the heritage of the Toronto, Grey, and Bruce Railway.

CHAPTER 22

The Buffalo, Brantford, and Goderich Railway: Fort Erie to Stratford

The History

In 1853 the citizens of Brantford were unhappy. For a quarter of a century they had depended on the Grand River Canal — a narrow and seasonal waterway — to export their products and import their needs; but the canal was fast becoming inadequate, and the locks were small, only capable of accommodating schooners and barges, not larger steamers. That year they received word that Ontario's first main-line railway, the Great Western Railway, was going to bypass them. Instead of routing its tracks through Brantford, the line would pass to the north, going straight from Hamilton through Paris.

But even before that, a group of concerned citizens had been lobbying for a line from Buffalo. Lacking government funding, in 1850 they formed a stock company that they called the Buffalo, Brantford, and Goderich Railway (BB&G) to build a line from, as the name suggests, Fort Erie to the port of Goderich on Lake Huron.

The rails of the BB&G reached Caledonia in 1853 and Brantford the following year. To celebrate the arrival of that first train, Brantford hosted a dinner and ball in the train shops, followed by a display of fireworks. Two years later, the line was renamed the Buffalo and Lake Huron Railway (B&LH). It reached Goderich in 1858. Grain ships from the Lakehead now called at the Port of Goderich at frequent intervals, but that was not the only business that the new rail line inspired. Because the tracks passed close to the warm waters and sandy beaches of the Lake Erie shore, more and more American tourists boarded the coaches to vacation at the exclusive summer resort communities now appearing along the shore.

When the Grand Trunk Railway absorbed the B&LH in 1864 and the Great Western's main line in 1882, it finally extended the long-sought-after link from a point east of Harrisburg, located on the now-abandoned former main line east of Paris, into Brantford, and abandoned the GW's original alignment between Harrisburg and Paris. Other abandonments were relatively late in coming. The section of track between Paris Junction and Tavistock was abandoned in 1981, that between Fort Erie and

Caledonia in 1985, and the one between Tavistock and Stratford in 1987.

Other portions of the Buffalo, Brantford, and Goderich route, however, remain in active use to this day. Freights still rumble along the tracks between Brantford and Caledonia, carrying gypsum from the Georgia Pacific plant in that town and coal to the controversial coal-fired power plant in Nanticoke, which required construction of a new branch line from Garnet on the H&NW line to Nanticoke on Lake Erie.

VIA Rail's Toronto to Windsor trains now travel the small Buffalo, Brantford, and Goderich segment from Brantford to Paris Junction, as do CN freight trains. Also still in use is the section between Stratford and Goderich, where trains on the busy short line, the Goderich and Exeter Railway, transport salt and grain from Goderich to Stratford to connect with the CN's main line there.

The Heritage

Fort Erie

Although the Buffalo, Brantford, and Goderich was the first railway to enter Fort Erie, it was not the only one. In fact, with the completion of the International Railway Bridge in 1873, Fort Erie (or Bridgeburg as it was then called) became a funnel for the Grand Trunk, the Canada Southern, and the Toronto, Hamilton, and Buffalo railways as well. Sorting yards covered much of the town and the main street developed parallel to the tracks.

Prior to the completion of the bridge, the BB&G located its original station by the docks of the Buffalo to Fort Erie ferry. Once the bridge opened, however, all railway facilities were moved to that location. Fort Erie soon became home of Canada's third largest rail yard.

Today, most of Fort Erie's rail lines are gone, and no stations remain on-site. The CNR demolished its attractive Bridgeburg station in 1973, one of the few in its station roster that had a "witch's hat" or conical roof above the waiting room.

The town's railway heritage does survive on the grounds of the Fort Erie Railway Museum, where two former stations and railway rolling stock have been placed, among them the massive CNR steam engine #6218 that operated from 1948 into the 1960s. One station, which controlled traffic over the International Railway Bridge, was relocated from a site within the town, and the other from the community of Ridgeway. The downtown business association also promotes their retail district as "Bridgeburg Station." It is unfortunate that the original station no longer remains as the focus of the designation.

Port Colborne

From Fort Erie to Port Colborne, the abandoned right-of-way is now the Friendship Trail, a well-maintained and popular rail trail of finely crushed gravel. It passes through a variety of villages, many of which served as gateways to beach communities. One such destination was the Erie Beach Amusement Park, now reduced to an intriguing set of forgotten ruins in a woodlot. The trail terminates at the east end of Port Colborne, where the rusting rails from a branch of the Welland Railway remain in place on Durham Street.

Port Colborne began with the building of the Welland Canal in 1828. Ultimately, it became a junction on the Buffalo, Brantford, and Goderich and the Welland railways. The original station stood on the east side of the canal. Later, after the Grand Trunk took over the line's operations, it replaced that early station with a larger brick structure, which still stands on the west side of the canal. Here, too, the old limestone walls of the second Welland Canal (there were four canals altogether) survive beside the wider and newer walls. The abutments of the railway swing bridge can also be seen beside the canal.

With the completion of a new Welland Canal bypass around Welland in 1972, the tracks of the Welland Railway were rerouted to follow the west side of the canal. Near the station, these rails converge with those of the original Buffalo, Brantford, and Goderich alignment and follow that ancient route for a few hundred metres, then angle away to serve the grain elevators still in use in Port Colborne's harbour.

Near the western end of Port Colborne an exclusive station served the needs of the American residents of the Solid Comfort resort community. Many of the grand summer homes of these Tennesseans still stand along Tennessee Avenue. Beyond the end of that short stretch of track, the rail trail resumes, known here as the Wainfleet Trail, passing the Wainfleet Wetland Conservation Area. For nearly a century the Wainfleet peat bog, Ontario's most extensive, produced tonnes of peat for the Ontario Peat Company factory located a short distance north of the BB&G line. That operation had a short narrow-gauge rail line of its own, portions of which still lurk in the bog to this day.

Dunnville

Between Port Colborne and Dunnville the tracks ran straight across the level farmland of the Lake Erie backshore. Little stations at Lowlands and Wainfleet served not just the local farmers but the vacationers, as well. The diminutive station from Wainfleet, with its distinctive "witch's hat" roof, survives today as a summer home on Augustine Road, south of Regional Road 3.

Dunnville, near where the Grand River flows into Lake Erie, traces its existence back to the Grand River Navigation Canal, when the port became the head of navigation for Lake Erie vessels. With the arrival of the BB&G, Dunnville boomed into a busy regional centre, a role it still plays. The wooden station there, which the Grand Trunk used to replace the old BB&G building, was an elaborate affair with a tower overlooking the tracks and two towers facing the roadside. After the station burned down, the CNR replaced it with a simple shed, also later destroyed by fire.

Caledonia

From Dunnville to Caledonia the route of the Buffalo, Brantford, and Goderich swung inland to roughly parallel the Grand River. At Canfield Junction, about ten kilometres east of Cayuga, it crossed the tracks of the Canada Air Line and the Canada Southern Line, which ran side by side at this point. It then crossed through the village of Canfield. This route is used as a snowmobile trail today. In Canfield, the only surviving rail-era building is a one-time feed mill. As the old right-of-way makes its way toward Caledonia, it passes near the former villages of Cooks Mills and Indiana, both now ghost towns.

At Caledonia, the route of the BB&G encounters active trackage and the preserved station built in 1906 by the Grand Trunk. Caledonia, too, retains a transportation heritage of other eras. Along Haldimand County Road 54, a number of Grand River Canal buildings remain, including a lockmaster's house. The bridge, which carries Argyle Street across the Grand River, is an eight-span bow-string bridge, the longest of this type in Ontario. At the eastern approach to the bridge stands a red-brick house, once occupied by the keeper of the tollgate in the 1850s, when an earlier wooden bridge crossed the Grand.

Today, the restored Caledonia station houses a museum and serves as the offices of the Caledonia Chamber of Commerce.

The Edinburgh Square Heritage and Cultural Centre on Caithness Street contains the original town hall, a striking brick building built in 1857. Displays include an original jail cell and depictions of the gypsum industry that once prospered along the banks of the Grand River.

Paris Junction

The tracks of the Buffalo, Brantford, and Goderich Railway remain in use from Caledonia to Brantford as a busy short line, hauling products from the Georgia

Pacific gypsum plant and other town-based industries. From Brantford to Paris Junction, the BB&G carries the CN's main line from Toronto to London and Sarnia. VIA Rail trains pass this way eight times a day, calling at the strikingly handsome Brantford station with its slate roof and soaring tower.

Paris Junction formed the meeting point of the original Great Western tracks from Hamilton to Sarnia, and those of the BB&G. The section of original GW track, which ran between Harrisburg and Paris Junction, was removed in 1938 and all evidence of its existence has largely vanished. The only vestiges of this historic link are the bridge piers standing in the waters of the Grand River.

While several sidings remain at the Junction, as well as a one-time railway hotel and other period houses and businesses, today's trains speed through as if the old Buffalo, Brantford, and Goderich never existed.

Paris Junction to Stratford

The tracks from Paris Junction to Tavistock were lifted in 1981, and the roadbed has largely vanished. A line of vegetation here and there across the farm fields is the only indication that there was a rail line here at all. Most of the route has been either ploughed under or built over.

At the village of Drumbo, the Buffalo, Brantford, and Goderich crossed the tracks of the Credit Valley Railway, still an active CPR line, though the right-of-way to that crossing is now a mere laneway. Through Bright, the next stop, the right-of-way is visible on the east side of Oxford County Road 8 but has been buried beneath a new housing development to the west.

In the midst of farm country on Blandford Road, north of County Road 8, the community of Ratho was originally planned for big things; an extensive town site was laid out in anticipation of the BB&G locating a major facility here. But the railway ignored the place, and Ratho remained a small country station. A pair of ninety-degree turns in the road, however, reflect a portion of the intended street network, and a large brick building still stands — once a hoped-for hotel.

Through Tavistock the right-of-way is virtually untraceable, although a one-time freight shed has somehow managed to survive, as has the station, now a residence on Jacob Street. The original station grounds now sport a Tim Hortons.

From there, it's cross country to Stratford, where the BB&G located its original station on Falstaff Street. In fact, the town could once claim four stations. When the Grand Trunk Railway amalgamated the various lines, it added repair shops and a locomotive shop, as well as a railway YMCA. A railway nursery supplied garden plants to the stations along the line. Although these structures are gone, Stratford still remains a hub of railway activity. The yards are full of freight cars for both the CN and the Goderich and Exeter short line, while the large brick GT station remains a destination for Shakespeare lovers who prefer to travel to the town's many theatres in the comfort of a VIA Rail train.

Goderich

Goderich served as the terminus for the Canada Company,[1] a British colonization consortium established in 1826 to settle the territory known as the Huron Tract. Having blazed a trail through the dense forest from Guelph to Lake Huron, it was here, in 1827, that William "Tiger" Dunlop, Warden of the Woods for the Canada Company, recognized the potential for harbour facilities and traced out the town site. Goderich has been around for a while!

The town of Goderich today is a relatively quiet community located well away from the madness of the 400-series highways. Its many heritage features include the unique eight-sided main town square copied from a two-thousand-year-old town plan devised by a Roman architect named Marcus Vetruvius. The eight-sided jail is now one of Ontario's most visited jail museums and is said to have been the site of Ontario's last public hanging. Heritage homes, hotels, and churches, even a castle, are everywhere in this historic community. Scenic vistas extend across the harbour and the valley of the Maitland River from lookout points high atop the Lake Huron bluff.

Goderich continues to be a busy railway town as the western terminus of the Goderich and Exeter Railway. At the end of East Street, the delightful brick station with its two towers, built by the Grand Trunk, still stands by the yards, although it is now a business office. The harbour remains one of the busiest on Lake Huron, with grain ships that ease into port, fishing tugs that bob in the water, and a flotilla of private yachts and sailboats that crowd the marina. All here owe their thanks to the long-forgotten Buffalo, Brantford, and Goderich Railway and the angry citizens of Brantford who made the line a reality.

CHAPTER 23

The Toronto, Hamilton, and Buffalo Railway: Hamilton to Waterford

The History

This unusual rail line may be the only railway in Ontario whose entire abandoned portion has become a superb rail trail.

Initially, the company received its charter in 1884. The intent was to build a line from Toronto to Fort Erie and Buffalo to provide Ontario's burgeoning cities with easy access to American lines. Up until that time such routes as the Grand Trunk and Canada Southern had failed to provide such vital connections.

In 1892, the Toronto, Hamilton, and Buffalo (TH&B) began by taking over a failing line known as the Brantford, Waterford, and Lake Erie Railway, which had already laid twenty-six kilometres of track between Brantford and Waterford. By acquiring the route, the TH&B obtained its vital link to an American line — the Canada Southern at Waterford — which at that time was under the control of Michigan Central. The line was extended east from Hamilton to Welland in 1894, from which point the TH&B ran along the tracks of the Canada Southern Railway to Fort Erie and Buffalo. Finally, in 1896, the line obtained the right to use the Grand Trunk's tracks to run their trains from Hamilton into Toronto.

For several years the Toronto, Hamilton, and Buffalo was owned jointly by the New York Central, the Michigan Central, and the Canada Southern, but the largest shareholder was the Canadian Pacific Railway. Finally, in 1977, the Canadian line acquired total control.

In 1916, the TH&B finished a branch line to Port Maitland on Lake Erie, where they imported their coal supply from Ashtabula. The coal shipments lasted only until 1932, although the line still remains in use to access industries at Port Maitland. The main yards for the TH&B were located at Aberdeen Street in Hamilton's west end. While the lines remain active east of Hamilton, those west of the city to Brantford and Waterford were abandoned in 1989, and are now a popular rail trail.

The Heritage

Hamilton

In 1930, with Hamilton's streets becoming ever more congested with cars, the city council convinced the Toronto, Hamilton, and Buffalo to construct bridges along its line through the city. To do so, the railway needed to remove its fine old Italianate station on Hunter Street. It replaced the ornate station with an equally compelling art moderne–style station, which today serves regional buses and GO Transit. The Aberdeen Street yards remain a busy hub of rail activity, although most structures have been removed.

In 1989, the abandoned Hamilton to Brantford section of the line became one of Ontario's first rail

Built in 1977, the Sulphur Springs replica "station" building resembles a train station both outside and in. Today, it serves as a trail centre located in the Dundas Valley Conservation Area on Governor's Road, west of Dundas.

trails. Although the trail commences in Hamilton on Ewen Road, just west of McMaster University, the most fitting place to access it is in the Dundas Valley Conservation Area. Here, in 1977, the local conservation authority constructed a replica railway station using the plans of the Grimsby station, which had been destroyed by fire. Outside is a stretch of track with historic rail cars, including the "Manitoba," an executive car built for the CPR in 1927, and a 1931 self-propelled baggage car. The original intent had been to operate a tour train along the CPR tracks; however, a washout along the line forced the railway to remove the tracks, quashing the plan.

The rail trail winds its way from the "station," through a scenic hardwood forest, on its way to Summit, where a shelter once awaited passengers. The Mineral Springs station, east of the Summit station, was the main gateway to the Sulphur Springs Hotel and Spa, once operating on Sulphur Springs Road, a few metres south of the rail trail. It used the "healing" waters of a nearby mineral spring to attract customers. The hotel was destroyed by fire in 1910.

The next stop of significance was at Jerseyville, where a standard Toronto, Hamilton, and Buffalo-plan station stood. That building is now in the Westfield Heritage Village near Hamilton. The TH&B steam engine #103 and a shed-sized station from Summit are also part of the village. Little in the way of rail-era structures remains in the village, however.

Brantford

The rail trail continues into Brantford, where it terminates at the intersection of Mohawk and Greenwich Streets. Here, hikers and cyclists can see the remains of another "ghost" transportation system — the Grand River Canal.

This early water-transport route, made navigable through the use of six lock stations, followed the Grand River from Brantford to Lake Erie. As with the rail lines, this canal has left a legacy of busy towns such as Caledonia, Cayuga, and Dunnville, as well as relic villages such as York and Middleport, and ghost towns such as Newport and Indiana. Ruthven, the grand mansion of the Indiana's founder, David Thompson, is now a National Historic Site. The area's Mohawk heritage is on display in the nearby Woodlands Cultural Centre and the Royal Chapel of the Mohawks. Dating from 1785, this simple but elegant chapel is Ontario's oldest wooden church.

Some Toronto, Hamilton, and Buffalo track remains in use within the city of Brantford. Alongside it stands the TH&B's finest station outside of Hamilton. Built of brick on a stone base, it contains two dormers in its roofline.

Bridges can offer as much railway heritage as stations and rolling stock, and Brantford has preserved two. Those built by both the Brantford, Norfolk, and Port Burwell and the Toronto, Hamilton, and Buffalo have been incorporated into riverside walkways along the Grand River, just south of Colborne Street, the city's main street. This is the same street where, in 2010, city council, despite strenuous protest against such a move, voted to demolish no fewer than forty-two historic commercial buildings.

The rail trail resumes at the Shoppers Drug Mart at the corner of Colborne Street and the South Access Road, as does the one that follows the Lake Erie and Northern (LE&N) rail trail. Both trails lead to Mt. Pleasant, at Mt. Pleasant Road and Burtch Road, where that of the LE&N ends, but where the TH&B trail continues. This section of the Hamilton to Brantford Rail Trail was officially opened in October 2010.

As the trail winds through rolling farm country, it passes through the village of Scotland before it approaches Waterford. Here, the trail merges with the

Waterford Heritage Trail, which uses the former route of the Lake Erie and Northern Railway. The roadbed of the Toronto, Hamilton, and Buffalo, no longer a groomed trail at this point, continues across Mechanic Street in Waterford, where it ends at Nanticoke Creek. While the high-level bridge of the Lake Erie and Northern remains prominently in place, the Toronto, Hamilton, and Buffalo's smaller trestles are gone. On the south shore of the pond, the TH&B line merged with that of the Canada Southern, thus marking the western terminus of the line.

The town of Waterford has much heritage to offer. In addition to the magnificent Lake Erie and Northern bridge, it also retains its Michigan Central train station, a typical American-style station with wide overhangs and board-and-batten siding. The main street of Waterford also retains its history feel with a variety of early railway hotels and an eclectic array of shops.

Following its abandonment by the railway, the Toronto, Hamilton, and Buffalo station building in Brantford has served on and off as a restaurant. At time of writing, it was vacant and up for sale.

CHAPTER 24

The Brantford, Norfolk, and Port Burwell Railway: Brantford to Port Burwell

The History

With more than one hundred railway charters granted in Ontario, it is inevitable that at least three would become enmeshed with each other. These three would be the Brantford, Norfolk, and Port Burwell, the Tillsonburg, Lake Erie, and Pacific, and the St. Marys and Western Ontario railways.

Anxious to establish a link on Lake Erie, business interests in Brantford, along with the Great Western Railway, incorporated the Brantford, Norfolk, and Port Burwell (BN&PB), and by 1876 had completed a line to Tillsonburg in Oxford County, where it linked with the Great Western's "loop line" — the Canada Air Line. But when the Grand Trunk took over the GW in 1882, it showed little interest in completing the line to Port Burwell. It did, after all, have links of its own to Lake Erie at both Port Dover and Port Rowan.

But other business interests in Port Burwell and Tillsonburg, just as anxious to have the link completed, incorporated the Tillsonburg, Lake Erie, and Pacific Railway (TLE&P) in 1890. Six years later, the line opened between Port Burwell and Tillsonburg. The tracks, which connected with the Great Western station in downtown Tillsonburg, were extended in 1898 to link with the Canada Southern Railway at the north end of town.

Meanwhile, north of Tillsonburg, business interests in Ingersoll, on the CPR's Credit Valley line to St. Thomas, saw a benefit in extending the TLE&P their way. In 1902, they were jubilant when the line reached their town. By 1911, the tracks had been extended a further sixteen kilometres to the village of Zorra, already on the CPR's main line to Windsor.

Concurrently, the government approved a charter to build the St. Marys and Western Railway (SM&W) from St. Marys south to a point near Woodstock, then west to a point on Lake Huron. It soon became apparent that the easiest route would involve linking the new line with the Tillsonburg, Lake Erie, and Pacific at Zorra. By the next year, the connection was made, and the entire route from Port Burwell to St. Marys became part of the CPR's ever-growing network. The Port Burwell link was particularly important to the CPR since their coal supply from Ashtabula, Ohio, was delivered there. The Brantford to Tillsonburg section, meanwhile, became part of the Grand Trunk network.

The CPR and CNR continued to operate on these lines until 1987, when the corporations abandoned those portions between Brantford and Tillsonburg and between Port Burwell and Tillsonburg. The St. Marys branch followed suit a few years later. The CPR section between Tillsonburg and Ingersoll, however, remains in use.

The Heritage

Brantford

Originally, the Brantford, Norfolk, and Port Burwell (BN&BP) station was located in West Brantford, until a bridge across the Grand River could be completed. Once it opened, the railway operated from a point near today's Market Street, about a block south of the main street. Later, when the Great Western purchased the line in 1877, it moved operations into its Colborne Street station. No sooner had the bridge been opened, however, when a portion collapsed under the weight of a passing train. Fortunately, no one was injured.

The bridge was rebuilt and still stands today, forming part of the city's trail network. However, south of Brantford, while the rights-of-way of both the Lake Erie and Northern and the Toronto, Hamilton, and Buffalo have become busy rail trails, that of the BN&PB has largely vanished.

Through Burford and Harley, communities southwest of Brantford, newer development has intruded on the rights-of-way.

Tillsonburg

While the route of the Brantford, Norfolk, and Port Burwell Railway has been overrun with Tillsonburg's urban growth, the stations built by the Great Western and the Tillsonburg, Lake Erie, and Pacific both stand in the mid-town area. The TLE&P was moved from its original site to abut that of the Great Western at the corner of Bridge and Bidwell Streets, and now houses a daycare, while the former GW station is an art gallery.

West of the conjoined stations, a walkway leads across the high trestle over Big Otter Creek. At the south end of the town stands the modern station of the Trillium Railway, a short line operating between St. Thomas and Delhi on what remains of the Canada Air Line.

From Tillsonburg to Port Burwell the right-of-way continues through Staffordville and Eden, and remains visible, although no rail-era buildings remain on the station grounds. Eden's diminutive station building was moved to a private property, where it is collapsing from neglect.

Port Burwell

The tracks descend the valley of the Big Otter Creek to the Lake Erie harbour at Port Burwell, where the low wooden station, turntable, and sorting yards were laid out. Today, the grounds are vacant. Port Burwell compensates for the loss of its railway heritage by careful preservation of its marine heritage. On the main street, high above the station grounds, Ontario's oldest wooden lighthouse, built in 1840, is the village's proud symbol. Nearby, the local museum offers a treasure trove of marine artifacts.

Ingersoll

CP trains still haul freight through Ingersoll from both St. Thomas and Tillsonburg. The abandoned portion of the St. Marys and Western line begins at a recycling depot near the east end of the town. Although the CPR station in Ingersoll no longer stands, that of the Great Western, built in the 1870s and now on the CN line, is hanging on by a thread. Although designated under the Federal Railway Station Protection Act, the derelict, historic brick station hasn't seen any maintenance or upkeep, and awaits a saviour.

St. Marys

As the vacant right-of-way makes its way northwest toward St. Marys, it crosses the CPR main line at Zorra, where the station grounds are now the site of a communications tower. Here, the extensive Lefarge Cement Company has carved a vast quarry into the landscape. Most of the roadbed north of this point is largely either ploughed under or built over. Although a small iron bridge still stands at the south end of the village of Embro, the station grounds themselves are now a housing development.

While the town of St. Marys can boast of two surviving historic stations, that of the CPR was demolished in the early 1990s to make way for a parking lot.

From Embro the right-of-way continues northwest until it reaches Lakeside (on Plover Mills Road between Oxford County Roads 119 and 6), where it passes the shore of Sunova Lake. The station, built in the CPR "Swiss Cottage" style, now stands in the churchyard of Christ Anglican Church, near its original site.

The roadbed then enters the south end of St. Marys beside the vast St. Marys Cement Company operations, and parallels the Thames River, where it is now a walkway. Sadly, the CPR station, built in a style identical to its other terminus at Port Burwell, could not be saved, although it remained standing into the 1990s. The site is now a parking lot.

St. Marys is a town well worth visiting. Its vast collection of stunning stone buildings reflects the presence of the limestone outcroppings and the town's early prosperity as both a mill town and stone-quarrying centre. Heritage buildings include a three-storey stone "opera house" designed to resemble a medieval castle, and one of Timothy Eaton's first stores. A short distance north of the main street, the Grand Trunk trestle, built in 1856, looms high above the river, now part of a local walking trail.

The trains still stop in St. Marys, but these are at the VIA Rail station at the east end of town, where passengers board from an attractive brick station built by the Grand Trunk in 1904. The GT's original stone station, built at St. Marys Junction in 1857, also remains, and is undergoing restoration at the time of writing.

Despite its intentions, the St. Marys and Western Railway, like so many other lines, fell short of its hoped-for destination, and never made it beyond this point.

CHAPTER 25

The Canada Air Line: Welland to Glencoe

The History

Not to be confused with the modern form of air flight, the term "air line" was used by the railways to mean the shortest route between two points (unlike some air carriers). That is precisely what the Great Western wanted when it created what was yet another American shortcut across Ontario's southern peninsula.

To compete with the proposed Canada Southern Railway, another American shortcut between Buffalo and Michigan, the Great Western obtained a charter for the Canada Air Line (CAL) in 1869. It formally became part of the GW in 1871. Known also as a "loop" line, the CAL helped the Great Western avoid the need to double track its main line. Built from Glencoe, west of London, on the Great Western's Toronto to Windsor line, its route went directly to Fort Erie. The line opened in 1873, as did the Canada Southern Railway (CASO).

With the building of the third Welland Canal in the 1870s, the Canada Air Line constructed a tunnel underneath the waterway, a structure that remains a ghost of itself today, having been abandoned when the tracks were relocated.

The CAL gave many communities in the area duplicate rail service, especially where it and the CASO literally lay within metres of each other; in several instances their stations faced each other across the tracks. In 1882, the Great Western merged with the expanding Grand Trunk Railway, which shortly afterward began upgrading the tracks and replacing many of the older, simpler GW stations.

Much of the line remained in use under the CNR until recent times. In 1996, the section from Delhi to Welland was abandoned, while that between St. Thomas and Glencoe was removed in 2010. Two portions of this line remain in use — the sections operated by the Trillium Railway, from its yards in Tillsonburg, east to Delhi and west to St. Thomas. Here the tracks connect with those of the CN line north to London. Another small section between Fort Erie and Welland also still carries freight.

The Heritage

Moulton

Between Welland and Cayuga, the rail line had little impact on the growth of communities, most of which remained only a cluster of houses and stores. Moulton, on Niagara Road 7, a short distance south of Niagara Road 45, is a good example, and an early general store and several other early structures survive. The right-of-way, however, is a barely visible, overgrown path. The Moulton station is a short distance to the south.

Cayuga

From Moulton to Canfield Junction, a few kilometres east of Cayuga, the Canada Air Line again ran very close to the Canada Southern Railway. It crossed the Buffalo, Brantford, and Goderich line at Canfield Junction. A small village grew around the junction, where the three sets of tracks converged, but the rights-of-way of all three have largely disappeared.

West of Canfield, the CASO veered to the north of Cayuga, the county seat, while the CAL established a small depot at the northern limit of the town. The

A concerned rail lover moved the original Moulton station, a small waiting room with a decorative bell-caste roof, onto a private lot, where it can be seen from the road.

rail bed here remains visible as it passes beneath the Highway 54 bridge. While the railway buildings are long gone, the abandoned shell of a feed mill recalls train time.

A short distance west, the massive Canada Air Line trestle over Grand River, one of the line's largest, is visible from Highway 3. Decewsville and Nelles Corners were the next westerly station stops. While little evidence has survived at the former, a large feed mill still marks the roadbed in the latter.

Jarvis

Jarvis presents a valuable railway-heritage landscape. The attractive station, on the east side of Highway 6, formerly served not just the Canada Air Line but the Hamilton and Northwestern Railway (H&NW), as well. Now restored, it serves as the outlet for Michaud Fine Woodworking. On the west side, a historic feed mill still stands. While the roadbed of the CAL can still be seen on the south side of the station, the route of the H&NW, which passed on its north side, has all but vanished.

The attractive Jarvis station remains part of the Norfolk County community's heritage landscape.

At Renton, on Highway 3, a large one-time railway hotel overlooks the roadbed.

Simcoe

Simcoe was also a focus of a number of converging rail lines, including those of the Stratford and Port Dover (also known as the Port Dover and Huron [PD&H]) and the Lake Erie and Northern. In 1904, the Grand Trunk constructed an elaborate station with two towers, one on the track side and the other over the entrance. The station, which was shared with the PD&H, burned down in 1930 and for a time was replaced by a rail coach.

Today, the station grounds are the site of a transportation depot, although the street pattern and a few early rail-era buildings recall Simcoe's railway heydays. The station grounds lie along 1st Street, north of Highway 3 and west of Highway 24. Although the grounds are vacant, the County of Norfolk is converting many of the rail lines into rail trails: the Lynn Valley Trail to the south, the LE&N trail to the north, and the roadbed of the CAL, west to Delhi.

From Delhi west to St. Thomas, the Trillium Railway and the St. Thomas and Eastern Railway provide freight service to communities such as Aylmer, Courtland, and Tillsonburg, shipping products such as ethanol, fertilizer, and lubricating oil. Its main base of operations is located at the south end of Tillsonburg.

St. Thomas

The tracks of the Canada Air Line crossed those of the Canada Southern Railway at Yarmouth Junction to the east, and entered St. Thomas north of the main street. The tracks also crossed those of the Credit Valley Railway at today's Burwell Road. Here, the active rails of the CAL meet those of the former London and Port Stanley Railway, which connects the line with the CN main line in London.

Of the many railway structures that stood at the CAL's Flora Street yards, few remain. In contrast, the grand station and shops of the CASO still survive, the station now part of a major restoration, while the shops are part of the Elgin County Railway Museum. The town has also preserved a historic switching tower, which governed train movements between the L&PS and the CASO.

West of St. George Street, the tracks of the CAL once crossed Kettle Creek on a trestle that is still visible from a nearby park.

St. Thomas to Glencoe

West of St. Thomas, rails remain in place for a few kilometres to Paynes Mills, but west of there they have been lifted. A switching tower still stands in this once-busy mill town.

At Lawrence Station, on Middlesex County Road 18, a cluster of homes lies west of the freshly abandoned roadbed, a few of which recall the early days of rail traffic. No railway-related structures survive, however. The tracks crossed the Thames River on a trestle just east of Iona Road. To the west, the village of Middlemiss grew up around the railway. Although the name Mill Street still survives beside the right-of-way, there is little to recall its railway heritage.

West of Middlemiss, two more small trestles carried the tracks over a pair of tributaries of the Thames River. From there it was straight across flat farmland into Glencoe, where the tracks merged with those of the Great Western main line. Near Main and McRae Streets in downtown Glencoe, the station, a later Grand

Trunk structure, still stands, although slightly back from its original site.

Built in 1904, this station is the community's sixth railway station, the others having burned or become outdated. The station, surmounted by a corner tower, contained separate men's and ladies' waiting rooms. Vacated in 1993, it was moved and restored by various community organizations. The tracks today remain busy, and a small shelter provides protection for VIA Rail passengers travelling the Toronto to Windsor corridor.

CHAPTER 26

The Port Dover and Huron, and the Stratford and Huron Railways: Port Dover to Owen Sound

The History

Keeping track of Ontario's early rail lines can be like negotiating a maze. Grand proposals came and went, as did even more grandiose names. The Port Dover and Huron Railway (PD&H) was incorporated in 1874 to open a link from Lake Erie to the main east–west lines then crossing Ontario. This would be done by constructing a route from Port Dover, on Lake Erie, to Stratford, where it would link into the Grand Trunk system. On the way, it would also connect with the Great Western at Woodstock, as well as the Canada Air Line and the Canada Southern. By 1876, its trains were running.

Meanwhile, the Stratford and Huron Railway (S&H) came about to link Stratford on the Grand Trunk with Southampton on Lake Huron. The terminus, however, was later changed to Wiarton on Georgian Bay. In both cases, the terrain was comparatively level, although rivers had to be bridged and morainic hills circumvented. Work began in 1877 and finished four years later. That year, 1881, the two lines merged under the management of the Grand Trunk, actively in the process of accumulating as many independent lines as possible.

Another little line appeared on the scene at this time. The Georgian Bay and Wellington Railway (GB&W) had an ambitious plan to build from Guelph north to Owen Sound. But realizing that this was more than it could afford, its proponents scaled back its proposal and opted instead to build a line from Palmerston, then a burgeoning railway hub, to Durham. When the Grand Trunk assumed control of the line, it opted instead to access Owen Sound from Park Head, a junction between the Owen Sound and Wiarton branches on the Stratford and Huron (S&H), just south of Wiarton. This allowed the route a gentler grade down the Niagara Escarpment. It also changed the name of the company to the Grand Trunk, Georgian Bay, and Lake Erie Railway.

In this way, the Grand Trunk assembled a sprawling rail network now competitive with that of its rival, the Great Western: namely a lengthy north–south main line from Port Dover to Wiarton with branches to Durham and Owen Sound.

In the end, the rivalry meant little — by 1882 the Great Western and the Grand Trunk had merged. With that merger some sections of track became redundant and were removed, including the WG&B's Listowel to Harriston section and the LE&H's duplicate track between Stratford and Tavistock.

The Heritage: Stratford to Port Dover

Stratford to Woodstock

As Stratford boomed into southwestern Ontario's major rail hub, nearly every rail line that came to town had its own station. The Port Dover and Huron Railway was no different, with a station near Falstaff and Nile Streets. In 1913, the current grand station was built to replace all the smaller stations. Today, it continues to serve passengers travelling on the six daily VIA Rail trains that use the original route of the Grand Trunk.

As for the PD&H, its tracks angled southeast from the rail yards in Stratford and made their way across country to Tavistock, closely paralleling those built by the Buffalo, Brantford, and Goderich Railway years earlier. Under the Grand Trunk these became redundant and by 1881 were lifted.

Where the right-of-way heads south from Tavistock the land has been sold to adjacent owners, and, except where a tell-tale treeline marks the route, the roadbed has vanished. Hickson, just east of Highway 59, is one of those historic relic villages with little new development. Although the roadbed is not identifiable in town, off one concession road to the south it becomes the Hickson Nature Trail and follows the roadbed to the northern outskirts of Woodstock.

Woodstock, too, has retained its rail heritage, with the classic CPR station still used by that line, and the Great Western's VIA Rail station, a photogenic two-storey structure with hip-gable rooflines. This building remains one of Ontario's most attractive surviving GW stations. Both structures are federally designated heritage stations. Any signs of the PD&H, however, have long vanished, as has its station, which stood at Peel and Huron Streets.

Woodstock to Port Dover

South of Woodstock, the roadbed is discernable only as a line of vegetation and telephone poles. It crosses Highway 59 where the Curries station, south of the former hamlet, still stands, although much altered in appearance.

In Norwich, the Port Dover and Huron crossed the tracks of the Brantford, Norfolk, and Port Burwell line at the south end of the town. The PD&H had its own station on the main street, west of the highway, but new development has removed any trace of both station and track. The local museum houses a small railway display, while the right-of-way for the BN&PB is a short walking trail.

The heritage of the PD&H still survives in Otterville. Here the station survived the demise of the railway and remained on its original site until 1991, when the town moved the building to its museum grounds on Oxford County Road 19 and repainted it in the original grey-and-green colour scheme.

From Otterville, the roadbed marks an easterly course to Hawtry, a small village that could claim stations on both the Port Dover and Huron and Canada Southern Railways. The PD&H station was a small single-storey structure that lingered rotting in a woodlot for several years following the lifting of the rails. Any semblance of the village that once clustered about the little station has virtually disappeared, and only a former general store and schoolhouse remain on the otherwise empty streets. Except for a pair of new homes, Hawtry can almost be called a railway ghost village.

At Lasallette, a short distance east of Hawtry, the Port Dover and Huron line built a station and crossing tower where the line crossed that of the CASO. While the Canada Southern Railway route has become a trail, that of the PD&H has vanished.

Simcoe grew into a key railway hub where the tracks of the Canada Air Line, the Lake Erie and Northern, and the Port Dover and Huron all met. Today, no tracks or stations remain anywhere in the town; however, the County of Norfolk has undertaken to convert three of the rail lines into rail trails. That of the LE&N leads north toward Waterford, while the route of the PD&H has become the Lynn Valley Trail, beginning at the south end of Memorial Park and following a scenic, sylvan trail southeast to Port Dover. A small trestle lies within the park, as does the crossing of the Lake Erie and Northern. A third trail is proposed to extend west to Delhi.

Port Dover

In 1875, the PD&H purchased the Port Dover harbour area and proceeded to build its station, turntable, water tank, and engine house there. Under the Port Dover and Huron's subsequent owner, the Grand Trunk, a trans-lake rail ferry service connected Port Dover with Ashtabula, Ohio. The GT later shared the station with the LE&N until that rail line built a station of its own in 1947. In 1960, the CNR closed the station and moved into the LE&N station until 1972, when the tracks from Simcoe to Port Dover were lifted. This station later took on a new role as a municipal-works yard while the older Grand Trunk station subsequently became a car wash, then a gift shop.

The Lynn Valley Trail, which begins at the south end

of Simcoe, follows the right-of-way to Port Dover and ends near the north end of the town. With the booming popularity of Port Dover as a beach destination, any other evidence of the terminus of the PD&H now lies beneath beach-side gift shops and restaurants.

Port Rowan

In 1887, the town of Port Rowan received a charter to build the Norfolk Southern Railway to Simcoe. The line, built as a straight route from the port to Simcoe, had stations at the small communities of Vittoria, Walsh, and St. Williams. The station buildings at both Vittoria and Port Rowan were large, gangly two-storey wooden structures with four dormers on the top floor, where the agents and their families lived. This branch line was abandoned in 1965 and the tracks and stations removed.

Vittoria served as the district seat of the London District of Upper Canada from 1813 to 1826, when the courthouse burned and the seat was moved to London. The village remains full of heritage buildings, many of which reflect the stature of the judiciary and dignitaries who lived there in the town's heyday.

Port Rowan retains a railway freight shed, located beside a feed mill on the site of the rail line. The town is also the jumping-off point for the UNESCO World Biosphere Reserve on Long Point.[1]

The Heritage: Stratford to Wiarton and Owen Sound

Stratford to Palmerston

Little remains of the rail heritage in the smaller communities on the line north of Stratford, such as Gads Hill and

Brunner, although the latter retains a one-time railway hotel, store, and track-side feed mill.

The town of Milverton became a busy commercial centre following the arrival of both the Stratford and Huron (S&H) and the Guelph and Goderich (G&G) railways. The main street still remains busy, with several blocks of substantial commercial buildings. The S&H right-of-way, at the east end of the town, however, is no longer discernable.

From Milverton to Listowel, nothing remains of the right-of-way except the occasional vague trail and line of vegetation. However, from Britton, on Perth County Road 147, to Listowel the roadbed has been turned into a trail that meets the WG&B trail near the water tower south of the main street. The Wellington, Grey, and Bruce station, at the end of Binning Street, still stands in Listowel, now owned and maintained by the Kinsmen as a meeting hall and event venue. A former railway hotel stands nearby.

Palmerston to Hanover

Following the takeover of the Wellington, Grey, and Bruce and the Stratford and Huron lines by the GT, the latter's original trackage to Harriston Junction was lifted and rerouted through Palmerston, which was fast becoming a major rail hub. Here, many railway heritage features remain to celebrate the town's story, including a steam locomotive, pedestrian bridge, and large station that is now a museum.

Similarly, in Harriston, on Highway 23, the Grand Trunk station is still there, complete with an octagonal operator's bay window topped with a Dutch-style gable. Now a senior's drop-in centre, it stands a short distance west of the town's main intersection.

North of Harriston Junction, where the original S&H tracks formed a diamond with those of the WG&B,

the right-of-way has mostly vanished. Some evidence of it remains at the tiny hamlet of Drew Station on Wellington County Road 2 east of Clifford, where the general store still proudly wears the community's "station" name.

Alsfeldt and Ayton, the next two station stops, still retain vestiges of the right-of-way. The winding road to the distant Ayton station grounds is now a dirt trail, still named Station Road. The villages themselves boast various historic reminders of days gone by, including old general stores, and, in the case of Ayton, an early mill.

Neustadt, with its Germanic heritage, has a bit more to offer, especially for the beer connoisseur. Here the rugged old brewery, constructed of local fieldstone, still brews up award-winning suds. A couple of streets away can be found the home that was the birthplace of Canada's outspoken prime minister John George Diefenbaker. Located on Barbara Street, it is administered by the Canadian Royal Heritage Trust. As for the station grounds located east along Queen Street, nothing of the station survives, although the Top End Tavern now occupies the former railway hotel and celebrates that heritage with a wig-wag — a type of railway crossing signal — in front and a caboose out back. This scenic valley village sits on Grey County Road 10, about twelve kilometres north of Clifford

Hanover

Hanover evolved as a bustling furniture-making centre, thanks in large part to the arrival of both the Stratford and Huron Railway and the Walkerton branch of the TG&B. The town is now the area's main destination for shopping, schools, and services.

The station, erected by the Grand Trunk on the S&H line, stood near the corner of 16th and 8th Streets, while that of the Toronto, Grey, and Bruce, built later by the CPR, lay well to the east. While neither station remains, the routes of the TG&B and the S&H have been combined to form a local walking trail.

The trail follows the Stratford and Huron roadbed from roughly the site of its station grounds and leads over a trestle across the Saugeen River. After a half-kilometre, the trail swings onto the roadbed of the TG&B. A new pedestrian bridge has been erected on the piers of that rail line as it also crosses the Saugeen River.

South of Grey County Road 4 and west of 7th Avenue, the trail continues for a short distance on the S&H roadbed along the Saugeen River. There are various access points in the town.

Hanover to Owen Sound

The roadbed makes its way north from Hanover through farm fields. The right-of-way in the farm village of Elmwood shows no evidence of its rail roots, but its station now lies on Concession 12 east of County Road 10, and serves as a private home with the name board proudly posted on the front.

One of western Ontario's more attractive towns, Chesley's main street displays a heritage of yellow-brick buildings. A historic gristmill still stands near the intersection of 2nd Street SW and Thomas Street, west of the main street. But the most striking feature of the town is the railway bridge across the Saugeen River. Now planked in, it forms part of the well-groomed Chesley Heritage Trail. This rail trail leads from the former station grounds on 7th Street, where Heirloom of Canada, a furniture factory dating from the days of rail, still operates, and makes its way through a wooded residential area before crossing the river and coming to an end at Concession 2.

From Chesley to Allenford Station, the trail takes the form of a snowmobile or ATV trail, although not groomed or maintained. Dobbinton, Tara, and Allenford Station no longer have any indication of a railway connection, although Tara retains a small heritage main street. South of Tara, at Alvanly — an almost vanished mill village — a small trestle remains in place west of Mill Street.

Park Head marks the junction of the main line to Wiarton and the branch line to Owen Sound. The junction is situated about 250 metres north of Park Head Road. Both rights-of-way appear here as trails, though only the one to Owen Sound continues as the Keppel Rail Trail. While no rail-era structures remain at the junction, a historic general store sits on the road beside the right-of-way, and a small trestle can be seen a few metres north along the trail.

The route to Wiarton leads north from Park Head and passes through Hepworth, once an important road junction where a pair of early hotels still stand, including one right by the roadbed. For the most part, though, the right-of-way has been obliterated. Only a line of vegetation, and here and there a vague trail mark the way.

Wiarton

Although the route is no longer discernable in Wiarton, the large, towered station was moved from its original site at Claude and George Streets to Bluewater Park, located on the lakefront. The tracks terminated at a dock near the north end of the main street but have been replaced by more recent development.

Wiarton is best known as the home of "Wiarton Willie," a famous groundhog that annually tells the world on February 2 whether or not the upcoming spring is still six weeks away. (It's worth noting that since Wiarton is situated in a snow belt, the answer is usually "yes, at least six weeks.")

Wiarton is the gateway to the wild, cliff-lined Georgian Bay-side shores of the Bruce Peninsula, home to the Fathom Five Marine Park and Georgian Bay National Park by Tobermory, and to the rare and endangered Massassauga rattlesnakes.

Owen Sound

From Park Head the roadbed to Owen Sound is now known as the Keppel Rail Trail. In the village of Shallow Lake, it passes west of the main street, close to the location of the once-famous Shallow Lake Cement Works. A large two-storey wooden station once stood here but survives only as an image on a main street mural. Near the mural the historic grand hotel, built during the peak period of cement production, still stands but is now an apartment building. Shallow Lake is on Highway 6, halfway between Hepworth and Owen Sound. From there the Keppel Trail winds down the face of the Niagara Escarpment, offering trail-users stunning vistas across the fields to the waters of Owen Sound Bay.

Owen Sound's station museum abuts the harbour, which has been landscaped and converted for pedestrian use. A caboose and a set of tracks have been preserved in front of the station.

In Owen Sound, the trail and the line end at the Marine Museum on 1st Avenue West, housed in the station built by the CNR in 1932. Not so fortunate, however, is the former CPR station, which faces it across the harbour. Of more recent vintage, the CPR station now lies vacant and weed-strewn. The town indeed tells a "tale of two stations."

CHAPTER 27

The Guelph and Goderich Line: Guelph to Goderich

The History

By 1890, Ontario's mid-west was already criss-crossed with a growing network of rail lines. The Canadian Pacific Railway had established its Credit Valley line to St. Thomas and London with a link to Hamilton from a location called Guelph Junction. But they had not extended a branch the few kilometres north into the growing city of Guelph. It already enjoyed service from the Grand Trunk Railway as it had since 1857, but the community wanted the CPR to provide a rail link to give the Grand Trunk some competition and thus lower rates.

As early as 1888, the CPR had indicated a desire to build a link to Lake Huron to capture the lucrative grain trade and transport the commodity it to its Toronto docks. But with its Toronto, Grey, and Bruce line already doing exactly that, it was in no rush to extend another grain route through Guelph. In exasperation, the town built a link of its own, calling the little line the Guelph Junction Railway (GJ). As it often did, the CPR leased the short line for 999 years, and in

1907 finally extended it to the lake as the Guelph and Goderich Railway (G&G).

Construction of the G&G proved to be relatively uncomplicated. The terrain was more or less level and free of major obstacles, but bridges were needed to cross the Grand River, the Conestoga River, and the Maitland River in two places. For its stations, the CPR tended to use its common western-plan stations, usually with a second storey to accommodate the agent and family. Shipments from the village stations consisted primarily of grain, lumber, and other farm products. The large elevators in Goderich took in grain from the lake freighters and transferred it onto the Toronto-bound grain trains.

But with the advent of the automobile both freight and passenger traffic dwindled. Passenger service ended in 1961 and freight service in 1987. The CPR applied to abandon the line, using the shorter fifteen-day notification period rather than the ninety days provided for in the new Canadian Transportation Act passed in 1996. Furthermore, that new legislation no longer called for the railway to justify its abandonment, but instead that the line's customers justify its continuation.

To no one's surprise, the railway moved quickly to lift its tracks, remove bridges, and demolish its remaining stations. By 2000, the only known surviving stations were those at Goderich, Blyth, West Montrose, Dorking (on the Listowel branch), Linwood (west of Elmira), and Monckton. All except those in Goderich and Dorking were relocated.

Several portions of the right-of-way have been converted by local municipalities into a piecemeal system of rail trails.

The Heritage

Guelph

The fine brick station that stood in Guelph was scheduled for preservation. During the 1980s it was disassembled brick by brick and stored in a vacant field. But the station was never reassembled, even though an intended foundation remains in place, and no-one seems to know what happened to the bricks.

Tracks actually remain in use from Guelph Junction to the northern portion of the city, where a number of industries still ship product on what is once more a city-owned rail line. Here, too, the owners have inaugurated a dinner train that follows the forests and fields from Guelph to Guelph Junction, a distance of about twenty-five kilometres.

The easternmost rail trail here is known as the Kissing Bridge Trailway, the name inspired by the nickname applied to West Montrose's covered bridge, and has a trailhead on Silver Creek Parkway, north of the city. The first segment of fine-gravel trail base extends

to the Grand River. Here the trestle has been removed, leaving only a line of piers across the river. The trail then detours though the village of West Montrose and through its ancient covered bridge. The simple West Montrose station was relocated to a farm, where it now serves as a shed.

Elmira to Blyth

The trail resumes west of the river and crosses the well-tended and fertile Mennonite farm fields and the north end of Elmira. Here a pet product outlet marks the right-of-way where the trail passes. The stone-dust trail ends at Wallenstein, west of Elmira, where a parking area and an information plaque mark the trail access. Continuing west of Wallenstein, the rail bed consists of gravel and grass. It detours around the old Conestoga River bridge, which, in the same manner as the one over the Grand, was removed, leaving only the cement piers.

A feed mill, which traces its origins to the days of rail, has been modernized and busily serves the community of mainly Mennonite farmers. At Linwood, the trail improves again, although little evidence remains of any former rail activity in this busy Mennonite centre. The station was relocated a short distance north of the rail bed and remodelled. It does, however, still have its name board.

The branch line from Linwood to Listowel was short-lived, being abandoned in 1939. Although that roadbed is no longer visible, the station at Dorking stands on its original site and is now an attractive home. With its full second storey, it is known as the CPR's "Plan 12" station. Although the brick station in Listowel survived for a time as a hydro office, it too is now gone.

While Millbank is still very much a traditional farm village, thanks again to the preponderance of Mennonite

Many of the stations along the Guelph and Goderich line were built to the CPR's Plan 10, such as this one at Blyth. Similar stations also stood at Elmira and Wallenstein.

farmers, the evidence of its rail days have disappeared. Unlike in Linwood, where the trail is well-maintained, the one here is not kept up, and, in fact, terminates with a TRAIL CLOSED sign.

At the next station stop of Milverton, a bustling country town with a number of historic buildings, the right-of-way runs through a small village parkette. Although it enjoys no status as a maintained trail, it remains open, used predominately by ATV owners.

Lying at the intersection of Highway 23 and Perth County Road 86, the village of Monkton for the moment retains some of its rail heritage. A short distance north of the right-of-way, the crumbling wooden station, now vacant, remains, but is in a struggle for survival. Its condition at this writing does not inspire much optimism. By the right-of-way, the historic feed mill still guards the route of the ghost rail line. A one-time railway hotel rounds out the village's heritage landscape.

169

Blyth

From Monkton to Blyth the rail line, still a vacant road-bed, passes through Walton, which, with the removal of the rail line, resembles a ghost town. Blyth, however, has managed to celebrate its rail heritage in a variety of ways. One was the creation, in 1996, of the Blyth Greenway Trail, a short nature trail along the rail bed that features a butterfly garden and the unlikely survival of the railway water tower.

East of the station grounds the CPR once passed through a subway beneath the route of the London, Huron, and Bruce Railway. With the abandonment of the Guelph and Goderich Railway, the CPR destroyed the historic "arch," much to the chagrin of Blyth's history-conscious community. Those enthusiasts did manage to rescue the station, however, and in 1980 the local Snell family bought the building and moved it south on Huron County Road 4 to the Old Mill complex. The station is built in the same style as those that stood in Elmira and Wallenstein.

Blyth to Goderich

From the next station stop at Auburn, the rail bed once more becomes a rail trail. Known as the Goderich-Auburn Rail Trail, it connects the site of Aubun's former bridge crossing over the Maitland River to the Menesetung Bridge over the Maitland River in Goderich. When the latter was built in 1907, it was Ontario's longest railway bridge at that time. The rail trail then becomes the Tiger Dunlop Heritage Trail and follows the rail bed down to the shore of Lake Huron and the site of the CPR's Goderich station.

Without argument, the most interesting station on the former Guelph and Goderich route is the one that nestles below the shore cliff beside Goderich Harbour. The building, on Harbour Street, has been restored by the Town of Goderich and serves as an occasional gallery and event venue.

The Goderich station was constructed of brick and stone in the Richardson Romanesque style, and sports what is known as a "witch's hat," a conical roof that rises above the semicircular waiting room. The tracks are long gone and the station is now owned by the town and used as an event venue.

CHAPTER 28

The Lake Erie and Northern Railway: Galt to Port Dover

The History

During its short-lived heyday, the Lake Erie and Northern Railway (LE&N) offered its passengers some of the most stunning trackside scenery available in Ontario. And the rail trail that follows its path does the same today.

As rail lines go, the LE&N was a latecomer. It started with pressure from community leaders in Brantford for a rail link to the major rail lines — the CPR and the Grand Trunk in Galt, the American lines in Waterford and Simcoe, as well a connection to Port Dover, where they felt they could access cross-lake freight traffic.

Shortly after work on the line commenced in 1913, the CPR took control. Unlike its other routes, and indeed those of most of the contemporary major rail lines, the CPR decided to electrify the line. The route began at the CPR's yards in Galt (Cambridge today), and from there followed the east bank of the Grand River to Paris, where it passed beneath both the former Great Western's Harrisburg to Paris line and the newer Grand Trunk link to Brantford.

In Brantford, the LE&N shared a bi-level station with the Brantford and Hamilton radial line. Passengers would enter from the upper street level and descend to the platform below. From there the line angled across fertile farmlands and a tobacco belt, entering Waterford on a high-level trestle. The route then continued south to Simcoe, where it enjoyed connections with the Canada Air Line (by then the Grand Trunk) and the Stratford and Lake Erie (also by then the Grand Trunk).

Because the Grand Trunk had taken over the harbourfront in Port Dover for its station and roundhouse, the LE&N had to negotiate to use its rival's tracks to access the harbour. The arrangement only lasted until 1923, when the LE&N realized that the hoped-for cross-lake connections were not about to materialize. It vacated the Grand Trunk site (by then part of the CNR) and added its own station closer to the town centre. Trains had started rolling along the eighty-kilometre route in 1916, and instantly proved to be popular with passengers. Trains were running every two hours even though the entire stock of coaches numbered just four.

Passenger traffic peaked at 600,000 trips in 1921, but a mere decade later it was only a third of that; cars and buses were taking over. In 1950, the CPR applied to close passenger service, but the federal regulator, the Canadian Transport Commission, refused. In response, to discourage passenger travel, the CPR began to run its trains at times that were inconvenient for travellers and with instructions that were misleading. The ploy worked. Five years later, passengers gave up and the service ended.

The section from Simcoe to Port Dover was abandoned in 1962 when the remainder of the line switched from electric to diesel. Finally, service from Brantford to Waterford ended in 1989, and the Lake Erie and Northern fell silent.

The Heritage

Galt

In 1938, the Lake Erie and Northern built a handsome new station on Main Street in Galt, using the flat-roofed art-deco style then coming into vogue. Galt remains a busy CPR town straddling the original route of the Lake Erie and Northern. Although the station serving the LE&N is gone, the historic and active CPR station still stands on Malcolm Street. Galt once contained the main shops for the line, but following its closure, all evidence was removed.

Where the LE&N tracks travelled south from Galt, they crossed the line of the Grand Trunk, where they then followed the banks of the Grand River. The section from Galt to Paris is now the Paris to Cambridge Rail Trail, offering stunning views of the Grand River along the way. Access in Cambridge is via the Canadian General-Tower Trailhead on Highway 24 at the south end of the

city. Between Galt and Glen Morris, the trail also passes a natural spring and the stone walls of an early mill.

Glen Morris, a picturesque historic town on Brant County Road 14, grew around a pioneer river crossing. An information kiosk at the trail access point displays photos of early passenger coaches and the old stone house the Lake Erie and Northern used as its station in Glen Morris.

Paris

From Glen Morris to Paris the trail continues along the riverbank. At kilometre marker 61, it encounters the site of the high-level bridge built over the Grand by the Great Western Railway. A ramp and steps lead to the Murphy Overlook on the eastern abutment of the bridge, providing exceptional views from high above the river.

In Paris, the trail access lies at the Jean Rich Foundation Trailhead[1] on Brant County Road 14 on the outskirts of the town. The LE&N brick station stood here until it was demolished by the CPR in the1980s.

Paris offers one of Ontario's more attractive main streets, with period stores, including the current River Lilly store, once the Robert White's Boot and Shoe Store where Alexander Graham Bell placed the world's first long-distance phone call. The dominant Arlington Hotel, with strong links to railway history, was, until recently, a popular boutique hotel. Built in 1850, it was known originally as the Bradford House.

Paris was founded by Hiram Capron and named for the plaster of Paris produced from the extensive gypsum deposits found along the banks of the Grand River. The town is also noted for its collection of rare cobblestone buildings.

The only railway building remaining in the town is the former Grand River Railway station, now a private home.

The Lake Erie and Northern Railway Trail passes beneath the Grand Trunk's high-level bridge that spans the Grand River in Paris. The bridge is still used by CN and VIA Rail.

Brantford to Waterford

The trail resumes south of Highway 2 as the S.C. Johnson Trail, although it deviates from the rail line through Brantford. In fact, rails remain in place on the Lake Erie and Northern route from the north end of Brantford to the former Toronto, Hamilton, and Buffalo tracks in the centre of the city. From its unique bi-level station in Brantford, the rail line crossed the Grand River and continued southward. Although the LE&N bridge is gone, two other railway bridges survive to its immediate north, both now part of city walking trails.

From Brantford to Waterford and on to Simcoe, much of the LE&N was opened as a rail trail between 2008 and 2010. From the Shoppers Drug Mart on Colborne Street West in Brantford, it becomes the Gordon Graves Memorial Pathway, which, along with the former TH&B roadbed, has become a rail trail to

Mount Pleasant. A newly opened section of trail begins at Burtch Road. At the Oakland Road access, an interpretative plaque greets trail-users.

At the community of Mount Pleasant the two trails, the TH&B and the other on the LE&N, meet. The former Lake Erie and Northern station here has been moved to Mount Pleasant Road, where it still stands, although obscured by a row of cedar bushes. That structure displays a standard CPR plan, with a steep roofline and prominent gables.

The sole rail trail follows the route of the TH&B to Waterford, while the roadbed of the LE&N can be discerned only at intervals. However, at Waterford, where the Toronto, Hamilton, and Buffalo ended at its junction with the Canada Southern (by then the Michigan Central), the rail trail swings back onto the route of the LE&N, ending at a high-level bridge. The trail resumes at a new trailhead on Thompson Street on the south side of the river, west of Norfolk County Road 24. Meanwhile, the high-level trestle, which carried the LE&N over the

One of the province's most stunning heritage railway bridges is the one that carried the Lake Erie and Northern Railway across the tracks of the Canada Southern Railway in Waterford.

TH&B and the CASO, remains in place and is subject to a study regarding its incorporation as part of the trail. The former Michigan Central station still survives in Waterford and now houses The Quilt Shop.

Simcoe to Port Dover

From Waterford to Simcoe, the route of the Lake Erie and Northern is known as the Waterford Heritage Trail. It continues through Bloomsburg to Norfolk County Road 13, where it meets Simcoe's newly opened Rotary Sunrise Trail. This trail continues along the LE&N roadbed through Simcoe to meet the Lynn Valley Trail in Memorial Park. This trail then follows the route of the Stratford and Lake Erie line to Port Dover, and connects with the LE&N right-of-way in a wooded area at the south end of the park.

Port Dover

From Simcoe to Port Dover the Lake Erie and Northern right-of-way has largely vanished from the landscape. It does make an appearance in Port Dover at the east end of Chapman Street, where its 1923 station has now been reduced to an inglorious fate as a municipal storage facility. The former Grand Trunk station, which the LE&N briefly used, has been moved, altered, and is now a gift shop near the Port Dover beach.

Port Dover has much to offer, especially during the warm summer months when visitors flock to its sandy beaches or enjoy fresh yellow perch at local restaurants, much as the many earlier travellers who arrived via the electric coaches of the Lake Erie and Northern once did. The town's maritime history is vividly retold in the Port Dover Maritime Museum located in a former fishing-net shed.

CHAPTER 29

The Wellington, Grey, and Bruce Line: Harrisburg to Southampton

The History

It wasn't just the similarity of their names that they had in common, but the Wellington, Grey, and Bruce (WG&B) and the Toronto, Grey, and Bruce also shared a common objective: to capture the Lake Huron grain trade. The TG&B did that by establishing a line from Toronto to Owen Sound, while the WG&B ran theirs to Southampton.

Originally called the Canada North-West Railway company, the WG&B line received its charter to build a line from Lake Huron to Toronto in 1856. But the 1860s proved a poor period for railway building, with Great Britain, the source of much railway funding, seemingly considering entry into the American Civil War fray.

By 1868, however, money started to flow once more, and construction began the following year. By then the proposed route had changed slightly, as had the name. It would now be called the Wellington, Grey, and Bruce, and, rather than linking Lake Huron with Toronto, the destination was to be Guelph and a junction on the Grand Trunk. When the Great Western, the GT's main rival, stepped in to help with the operation of the line, the junction was moved to the GW's main line at Harrisburg.

The new line opened for business from Harrisburg to Southampton in 1872. But municipalities south of Southampton were also clamouring for a rail link. In 1873, a new branch began its circuitous construction south from Palmerston to Listowel, then northwest to Kincardine.

Rivalry among railways was always keen, sometimes even vicious. In 1874, the Toronto, Grey, and Bruce, a CPR line, conspired with the London, Huron, and Bruce, then building northward from London, to cut off the Wellington, Grey, and Bruce's Kincardine branch at Wingham. But the WG&B won out, and, ironically, both the TG&B and the LH&B proceeded no farther than Wingham. The Wellington, Grey, and Bruce, meanwhile, chugged right on through to Kincardine. That branch line opened in 1876.

Six years later, the Great Western, the WG&B's operator, was in financial trouble and amalgamated with the Grand Trunk. As the new owner, the GT began to replace most of the WG&B's simple first-generation stations with new, more stylish structures, many sporting decorative gables, and, in one case, the unusual "witch's hat" roof style. Regrettably, most are now gone, but the deep valleys of the Saugeen and Maitland Rivers did necessitate extensive trestles, some of which survive today.

The main industries around these stations were usually cattle yards and feed mills. But with the abundance of lumber, many of the towns also developed a busy furniture-making industry.

Throughout the 1950s and '60s, as branch-line operations proved uneconomical (largely due to inflexible labour contracts) and mail contracts were being given to truck companies, the lines were shut down, leaving many industries with no ready means of shipment. The section between Wingham and Kincardine closed in 1983, that from Wingham to Listowel followed in 1991, and finally that from Listowel to Palmerston in 1995.

The Heritage

Harrisburg

In 1854, Harrisburg, about ten kilometres east of Paris, became Canada's first railway junction, the point where the Great Western and the Galt and Guelph Railway (G&G) joined together. When the G&G became part of the WG&B, Harrisburg became a major rail town, boasting a large two-storey station to prove it. Streets were laid in the standard railway grid, but in 1904, when the Grand Trunk rerouted its main line from Lynden to the east to Brantford, bypassing Harrisburg, the route suddenly become little more than a branch line between Lynden and Galt. The tracks west of Harrisburg were abandoned, and the once key rail junction became just another stop.

Nearly all evidence of Harrisburg's heady rail days has gone, although the Galt branch managed to operate into the 1980s. While the street patterns persist, and many early homes still line them, the site of the station is now a playing field where the roadbed is scarcely discernable.

Galt

The roadbed remains a clear right-of-way off and on to Galt, and some sections have become a rail trail. Once in the south end of Galt, however, it lies beneath new development and has vanished. At Highway 24 and Myers Road, a caboose boasts the name "Cambridge Station," while the nearby Tim Hortons was built to resemble a railway station. Behind the restaurant, a station-like foundation was built in the 1980s to support a relocated and rebuilt CPR station from Guelph. Unfortunately, that effort has never come to fruition.

The rail line through Galt now lies beneath its asphalt roads. The rails, however, resume immediately north of the Samuelson Street bridge, adjacent to those of the still active CPR.

Guelph

Between Samuelson Street, in Galt, and Guelph Junction the line remains a freight spur, serving industries in Galt and Preston. (It should be noted that there are two Guelph Junctions. That referred to here lies at the west end of Guelph and is under CN ownership. The other, under CPR ownership, is south of Guelph and was the starting point for the Guelph and Goderich Railway.) The active track continues to the yards at Guelph Junction, where it meets the main line of CN Rail. North of those yards the Wellington, Grey, and Bruce route parallels Edinburgh Road north to Woodlawn Road and still serves local industries. No railway buildings remain at Guelph Junction, although the 1911 Grand Trunk station in downtown Guelph still welcomes six VIA Rail trains daily.

Other than tracing the route of the WG&B, Guelph, with its vast collection of stone buildings, the university arboretum, and the stunning Our Lady Immaculate Catholic Church styled after the Cologne Cathedral and perched high atop Guelph's most prominent hill, is well worth a visit.

Elora

Between Guelph and Elora, little remains of the right-of-way. The Elora station once stood on the east side of Wellington County Road 6 but the site is now occupied by new industry. At the east end of town, a rail trail crosses the Grand River on a historic trestle. Built in 1909, the massive bridge rests on two of the original piers that date back to 1869. The third bridge to be built over the river at this location, it saw its last train in 1989. The short trail ends in Fergus at the Price Chopper store.

The first stations in both Fergus and Elora were of the typical wide single-storey design the WG&B adopted for most of its stations. When the station in Fergus burned down, the Grand Trunk replaced it with a more elaborate building, sporting a decorative tower on one corner. The CN unfortunately demolished it in 1982.

A series of small stations that once lined the route between Fergus and Palmerston also reflected the small simple WG&B designs. These stood at Alma, Goldstone, Drayton, and Mooresfield; none survive today. While the roadbed has virtually vanished, feed mills in Drayton and Mooresfield recall the days of rail.

Palmerston

Palmerston, on Wellington County Road 93, had its start as a railway town, and it has done much to celebrate that heritage. It was here, in 1873, that the Wellington, Grey, and Bruce decided to locate its repair shops. A town was surveyed around the yards, and by 1874 Palmerston had nearly 1,700 residents. The yards offered a roundhouse, engine shed, and water tank, and the nearby Queen's Hotel offered rail travellers their overnight accommodation.

In 1910, to help residents traverse the extensive sorting yards, the Grand Trunk constructed a 250-metre bridge to serve pedestrians crossing the sidings, enabling them to avoid the forty trains that puffed into town each day. The bridge has been restored and was reopened in 2008.

Palmerston's station, a large two-storey wooden structure dominated by a high tower, was added by the Grand Trunk in 1900. From the station, rail lines extended out in four directions, two branches being those of the WG&B while the others were originally those of the Stratford and Huron Railway. The CNR took over the GT in 1923, and placed a drop ceiling in the station waiting room and covered the decorative wooden exterior with drab Insulbrick. In 1959, with the demise of steam, the roundhouse and engine house were demolished. The last passenger train left for Guelph in 1970, and in 1982 the station was closed. When the last tracks between Harriston and Stratford were lifted in 1996, the yards fell silent.

That year the town acquired the station and yards, and, along with the Lions Club and an army of volunteers, began the job of restoring the building and converting it into a museum. They removed the drop ceiling and exterior Insulbrick, and today the station is the focus of a proud railway town and the envy of many Wellington, Grey, and Bruce railway towns that have lost their stations and their railway roots.

An aging steam locomotive, now known as "Old 81," stands near the museum. Built by the Grand Trunk in 1910, the engine puffed away until 1959, having served out its final seven years in Palmerston. With the CNR phasing out its steam operation that year, the railway company donated Old 81 to the town. These reminders of Palmerston's railway heritage lie on County Road 93, east of Highway 23.

Walkerton

Between Palmerston and Walkerton, much of the right-of-way is now a rail trail. From behind the L&M grocery store on Palmerston's main street, a crushed-stone trail

While Palmerston in Wellington County no longer forms the rail hub it once did, the grand station built on the Wellington and Bruce Railway line is now preserved as a rail museum. Photo circa 1980s.

leads to Bruce County Road 3 and the site of White's Junction, where the tracks of the Wellington, Grey, and Bruce and the Stratford and Huron lines once met. The trail features stands of prairie grass and a surviving pair of early trestles.

Resuming at Fultons, a tiny flag station, the trail extends into Clifford, a handsome town of yellow-brick buildings. The station grounds here are vacant and over-grown.

At the next major stop, Harriston, the right-of-way has disappeared under roads and buildings, but the old Grand Trunk station still stands, now functioning as a senior citizens' drop-in centre. Paralleled by Highway 9, the rail trail continues through Mildmay, where the former railway hotel remains. In Walkerton, an early furniture factory claims the otherwise vacant station grounds.

North of Walkerton, the Bruce Rail Trail follows the roadbed to Cargill and Pinkerton. The one-time mill town of Cargill, although ghostly quiet today, still claims a number of fine old business buildings, many of which date to the railway era. Its station also still stands, now a private home a short distance north of the community.

Paisley

With its treasure trove of historic buildings, Paisley also claims a railway heritage. Although its simple WG&B station is long gone, the town is the site of two massive trestles. The substantial brick town hall with its tower and a restored fire station stand along the main street where the Teeswater River merges with the Saugeen. West along Mill Street is the reclaimed four-storey wooden gristmill, now a gift and antique store known as Natures' Millworks.

As the roadbed proceeds north from Paisley, it winds through rolling farm country. Between Paisley and Port Elgin, the tiny hamlet of Turners had only a shed for a station, but today retains a historic store behind which the station once stood.

Port Elgin/Southampton

At the south end of Port Elgin, the popular Saugeen Rail Trail begins. This track of crushed stone follows the roadbed through Port Elgin and terminates at Peel Street in Southampton. Historic information plaques and benches make it a tempting way to celebrate the lost heritage of the old Wellington, Grey, and Bruce line. A popular summer town with a busy beach, Port Elgin offers a main street lined with early stores, and, during the summer, a miniature railway ride.

The Saugeen Rail Trail parallels Highway 21 into Southampton, where it stops short of the old railway station. Although the track side of the station was covered over when the station operated as restaurant, the street side of the brick building displays a decorative entrance topped with an elegant gable.

The Kincardine Branch

From Palmerston, the Kincardine branch angles southwest toward Gowanston, where it becomes an undeveloped trail. From Gowanston to Listowel a groomed trail of fine gravel resumes.

Listowel

This busy town contains one of only two stations to survive on this branch. The tracks are gone, but much of the station exterior remains little altered, though the interior has been remodelled to suit the needs of the Kinsmen, who now own the building. Listowel was once the focus

A massive wooden trestle in the heart of Paisley has been planked in to allow pedestrians to stroll high above the waters of the Saugeen River. A second trestle about a kilometre farther is even longer, measuring nearly three hundred metres.

of three different rail lines, the WG&B, the Stratford and Huron, and a branch of the Guelph and Goderich.

From Listowel the rail trail continues south to Atwood, paralleling Highway 23, then makes an abrupt turn to the northwest. This irregular route was created to satisfy the conditions of the various municipalities along the way; those contributing funds to the railway's construction insisted that the line pass through their community.

The trail comes to a sudden end at the hamlet of Henfryn, named in 1875 by the first postmaster, E.C. Davies — in the Welsh language *henfryn* means "old hill." To the east the route falls under the jurisdiction of the Town of North Perth, which maintains the trail. Across the road lies the Municipality of Huron East, which apparently declined the idea of maintaining a rail trail. Henfryn no longer resembles the mill-and-brick-making village it was during the days of rail, and is now almost entirely residential. The WG&B station here was little more than a small combination dwelling and waiting room.

The next stop along the line was Ethel Siding, about a kilometre south of its namesake village. Initially a train-order office with station agent — who handed out the instruction to the engineer as to when the train could proceed — the diminutive depot's time as a passenger shelter ended in the 1970s. Today, only a few buildings remain at the site and the roadbed is now reduced to a lane on the west side of Ethel Line.

Brussels

First named Dingle, the community of Brussels achieved its more refined name following the arrival of the Wellington, Grey, and Bruce Railway. Within a few years of the line's arrival, the village prospered, boasting several mills, factories, and foundries. Before the WG&B arrived, the town's population numbered a little more than three hundred, but with railway in place it grew six times over. The last of the town's mills to close, the Logan Mill remained in operation into the 1960s.

Located at the north end of town, the WG&B's first station was a large structure sporting gable ends and a gable above the operator's bay. Its later replacement was much simpler and survives today in a public park close to its original location.

Wingham

The WG&B line continues northwest through the hamlet of Bluevale, where Walt Disney lived as a child, his father, Elias, having been born here in 1859. (Walt's American mother went to Chicago for his birth, afterward returning to Bluevale.) After leaving the Bluevale station, the line reaches Wingham Junction and the now-vanished tracks of the London, Huron, and Bruce Railway. The site is marked today by a cluster of early homes on Huron County Road 86, near MacLean Line.

Wingham can claim two features that celebrate the heritage of the Wellington, Grey, and Bruce Railway. First, a large steel trestle that crosses the Maitland River at the north end of the main street, which has been planked in to allow a walking trail. And second, just to the east, the old rail station built by the successor Grand Trunk has survived. Two street-side towers that once graced the structure were cut down to the roofline, but an octagonal gable that surmounts the operator's bay window on what was the track side survives, and an overhang, in which a small gable sits above the street entrance, still wraps around the building. Built in 1906, this was the third station built on the site.

Kincardine

Between Wingham and Kincardine, the Wellington, Grey, and Bruce Railway passed through Lucknow and Ripley. Stations in both locations were of the original WG&B design, being single-storey, low, and wide. Built in 1873, they managed to survive into the 1970s, when the CN demolished them. The station grounds show no evidence of the WG&B.

Sadly, this scenario holds true at Kincardine, as well. Here the tracks lined the Lake Huron shore, ending at a beach-side station near the harbour. Several sidings, a cattle yard, and a freight shed marked the terminus of this branch. The yellow-brick station was attractive in design, with pillars to mark its street entrance, a bell-caste roof with hip gables at each end, and an octagonal gable above the operator's bay. As preservation efforts were being considered by the town, the station unfortunately burned down circa the 1960s.

The only tribute to the rail line's heritage that remains today is the nature trail along the beach, called "Station Beach," and a public washroom and storage facility meant to copy the station's design. Kincardine does have several other historic features, including the restored historic Walker House Hotel and the iconic wooden lighthouse museum, still guarding what is now a yacht-filled harbour.

CHAPTER 30

The Canada Southern Railway: Fort Erie to Blenheim

The History

Despite the name of this early rail line, its builders and promoters had little interest in serving Canada. Indeed, its promoters would admit that the objective in constructing the Niagara and Detroit River Railroad (as it was originally called) was to secure the commerce between Buffalo and Detroit.

The need for such a shortcut was identified as early as the 1830s. Despite the vigorous promotion by William Hamilton Merritt, the promoter of the Welland Canal, construction did not begin on the line until the late 1860s. The delay was partially due to the resistance of the Great Western Railway, which already had created such a link connecting Niagara Falls with Windsor and Sarnia, and was not partial to the idea of a rival serving much the same territory.

Following the American Civil War, a new promoter, William A. Thompson, took over. In 1868 he secured the right to construct a line from Fort Erie to Sandwich (an early name for Windsor). At this time, the name Canada Southern (CASO) was adopted and construction began. With few obstacles other than a number of small rivers, the line was quickly built.

With its objective of moving American goods from the Midwest to the Erie Canal and other connections, and ultimately to the Atlantic, the CASO largely ignored Canada's more important urban centres, such as Hamilton, London, Brantford, and Toronto. Indeed, few Ontario communities benefited much from the new line. Lumber and grain were picked up en route, but the driving factor remained hauling American goods.

In 1883, rebuffed in their efforts to share the new International Bridge at Fort Erie, the Canada Southern constructed a cantilever bridge of their own across the foaming rapids of the Niagara River at Niagara Falls, and a yard facility at Montrose at the south end of the tourist town. An excellent view of the cataract from a station known as Victoria Park was the line's main attraction.

The one community to benefit from the Canada Southern was St. Thomas. Here, at the halfway point between the two borders, the CASO established a divisional point along with repair shops and a locomotive works. The town became a major rail centre, with the London and Port Stanley Railway, the Credit Valley Railway, and the Canada Air Line all converging there.

One of Ontario's natural resources in particular attracted the attention of the CASO builders — the discovery of North America's first commercial oil well at Oil Springs, northwest of St. Thomas. Here, the town of Petrolia burst onto the scene, and drillers, promoters, and businesses poured in, and a downtown lined with magnificent stores was soon thriving. To tap into the liquid gold, the Canada Southern added a branch line to Courtright from a point west of St. Thomas. It was meant to connect to the American side, with a line to be built to Chicago, but the American connection was never built and, with the centre of the oil industry moving to Sarnia, the branch line languished.

The main line, however, remained quite busy. The Canada Southern was at various times part of the New York Central and Michigan Central rail systems. Its final American owner was the omnipresent Conrail, which absorbed many American lines. In 1985, it was acquired by CN-CP, a joint company created by the CNR and the CPR at the time. With their many other lines in southern Ontario, CN-CP began to abandon the CASO line, and by 2010 only short sections between Niagara Falls and Attercliffe, east of Cayuga, and between Windsor and Fargo, south of Chatham, remain in use.

In its day, the Canada Southern could claim more than sixty stations. Today, fewer than a dozen remain, most relocated and altered to become private homes. The right-of-way remains obscure and overgrown, with no groomed trails to mark its route. The heritage of this once busy line has been largely ignored, with the striking exception of St. Thomas.

The Heritage

Hagersville

The easternmost section of the Canada Southern remains in use, with the CP still hauling freight from Port Maitland via Attercliffe to Fort Erie. From that point west to Hagersville, however, the CASO is a fading memory. The tiny wooden stations, little more than shelters, have all gone and the right-of-way is overgrown and barely discernable. At Canfield Junction, where the Canada Southern and the Canada Air Line, to its immediate south, ran within metres of each other and crossed the Buffalo Brantford and Goderich pioneer line, a smattering of early rail-workers' homes line Junction Road.

Although the CASO never had a station in Cayuga, the Haldimand County seat of government, it did cross the mighty Grand River on a high trestle not visible from the road. In Hagersville, the Canada Southern formed a diamond where it crossed with the Hamilton and Northwestern Railway. The former CASO station still stands here, now much altered and in the hands of Rail America, a short-line rail operator. A section of the H&NW runs from Hamilton, past the station, and up to the industrial complex in Nanticoke on Lake Erie.

Waterford

From Hagersville to Tillsonburg the right-of-way is more visible and appears to be used as an ATV and snowmobile trail. At the village of Villa Nova, the former Canada Southern station with its distinctive overhang was moved to Norfolk County Road 9 to become a residence.

Waterford, however, has retained much of its railway heritage. The old wooden station with its gable over the operator's bay still stands on site, although the former yards are now grassed over and the road-bed is now a trail. A pair of one-time station hotels still stand, and the town retains the historic flavour of the days when three rail lines converged here. (The Lake Erie and Northern crossed on a high trestle, while the Toronto, Hamilton, and Buffalo formed a junction with the Canada Southern a short distance west of the station.)

From Waterford to Tillsonburg the right-of-way is mostly visible as a trail. Just east of the village of Lasalette, an 1885 bridge with a railway inscription crosses a small creek. Nothing of the Canada Southern remains in the community.

Tillsonburg

Although its rail days are fading, Tillsonburg is still served by the CP from Ingersoll. The Canada Southern once crossed at the north end of town, and the station remains on its original site. Today it houses an office. The former CP station, built by the Tillsonburg Lake Erie and Pacific Railway, was relocated to Bridge Street, and is now a daycare centre, adjacent to the former Great Western station.

St. Thomas

Between Tillsonburg and St. Thomas some parts of the right-of-way remain visible, while other sections have been ploughed under. The little board-and-batten station from Brownsville has been relocated to the Clovermead Apiaries, north of Aylmer, where it serves as a bee-interpretation centre.

The historic little rail-side hamlet of Kingsmill retains a few former workers homes along a small network of side streets. As the Canada Southern moved south toward St. Thomas, east of the town it crossed the Canada Air Line, which remains in use as part of the Trillium Railway.

St. Thomas has one of Ontario's most vivid collections of heritage railway buildings and lore. What began as a small crossroads town on the Talbot Road, St. Thomas watched with anticipation as the Canada Southern struggled to decide where to locate its main rail facilities — a major divisional point with repair facilities was needed halfway between the two borders.

In 1873, the Canada Southern selected a delighted St. Thomas as the location, and built what remains to this day one of Ontario's largest and architecturally most distinctive rail stations. To the south of the station, a wide overgrown field marks the one-time location of the vast rail yards, and, south of these yards, the former locomotive shop now houses the Elgin County Rail Museum and one of Ontario's most extensive collections of historic railway rolling stock.

At the west end of St. Thomas, once the pre-rail centre of the town, a life-size statue of an elephant faces east. This is, of course, a monument to the ill-fated Jumbo, Barnum and Bailey's star attraction that was killed in 1885 when the four-metre-tall elephant, panicked by the sight of an unscheduled, onrushing freight train, stumbled, and was struck from behind. The impact of the train forced the poor animal's tusk into its skull, which was shattered.

The Canada Southern built another of its major trestles here, high above the modest waters of Kettle Creek. The first trestle was built in 1873, but was replaced by the CNR with a more substantial structure in 1927. It remains a most imposing structure when viewed from below.

Made of brick, with Italianate features, the Canada Southern station in St. Thomas extends an incredible 120 metres along the old roadbed. It was considered one of the finest railway stations in its day.

St. Thomas to Ridgetown

Between St. Thomas and Ridgetown, the Canada Southern ran straight across some of Ontario's best farmland, but barely established a presence. A string of feed-mill villages, with names such as Shedden, Iona, and Paynes Mills, sprouted up along the tracks. At Paynes Mills, where the CASO crossed the Canada Air

Line, the former crossing tower still stands, although boarded in and used as a duck house. Former stations from Shedden and Iona have been moved and converted to houses.

Dutton, West Lorne, and Rodney all grew into prairie-like towns, with wide main streets and iconic feed mills. While the streets remain, the mills do not, and the right-of-way is barely discernable. One of the main attractions in Rodney is its jailhouse, North

America's smallest, measuring just 4.5 metres by 5.4 metres. The structure is located at the town fairgrounds east of the main street, and serves as a part-time tourist information centre.

One-time stops at Muirkirk, Highgate, and Ridgetown still have feed elevators but no tracks. Ridgetown's Canada Southern station is apparently still under the ownership of CSX, a North American company that operates rail-freight transportation.

The abandoned portion of the Canada Southern ends at Fargo, west of Ridgetown; from there to Windsor the line is still in use by the CN. (At this writing CN has indicated its intention to abandon the line.) Initially, the original line led directly to Amherstburg, where the railway was proposing to build a bridge across the Detroit River. Instead, the CASO established a new junction at the village of Essex, with a branch to Windsor, and crossed the river there. Stations in both Essex and Amherstburg remain, the latter now an art gallery and the former, a spectacular Romanesque stone station, now a protected heritage structure.

From Comber, where a disused station still stands trackside, a branch line once led south to Leamington. Originally built as the Comber, Leamington, and St.

Ridgetown, located west of St. Thomas, has one of the few country stations to survive along the Canada Southern's Ontario route.

Clair Railway in 1887, it became part of the Canada Southern in 1895. The branch line shipped large amounts of tobacco and sorghum until 1908, when Heinz pickles opened its large factory in Leamington and began specializing in ketchup.

The tracks on this branch line have been removed, and the little stations from Blythswood and Staples moved to serve a new use as private dwellings. In Leamington, the modest board-and-batten Oak Street station still survives on site but is fenced off and awaiting reuse. Along the still-active sections of track, stations from Charing Cross, Buxton, Fletcher, and Tilbury survive, but have been relocated to private property.

The St. Clair Branch

The St. Clair Branch was once the line to the land of the black gold. The Canada Southern originally intended to extend this line across the St. Clair River at Courtwright, then all the way to Chicago. However, the depression of the 1870s put an end to that plan, and the crossing was reduced to a mere barge. Abandoned since the 1960s, little remains of the right-of-way here.

Of the small communities the line once passed through along this section of track, only Melbourne and Alvinston gained any size and importance. At Alvinston, the line crossed that of the Grand Trunk. While the rights-of-way have, for the most part, been obliterated here, hotels and early buildings in these communities still remind visitors of those days of the Canada Southern.

Oil Springs

Of the stations that stood along this branch line, only those from Moore and Oil Springs survive, both having been relocated to local museum grounds. The one at the Oil Springs Museum has been preserved along with many structures dating from the early oil days when local farmers erected a network of jerker rods across their fields to pump oil from the ground. This hundred-year-old system remains in use to this day. The museum grounds also contain the site of North American's first commercial oil well. The Oil Heritage District Driving Route begins at the Oil Springs station and follows the Gumbed Road, where the little pumps still drag the sticky black goo from shallow deposits. Along the route, wood and plastic figures show how the oil was extracted in the early days.

From Oil City on the St. Clair line, little branch lines led south through Oil Springs to Eddy's Mill, then north into Petrolia. Here, the attraction known as Petrolia Discovery recreates the early oil operations when Petrolia was the oil capital of the western world. Charlie Fairbank, the great-great-grandson of J.H. Fairbank, who brought the jerker-rod system to his oil fields in 1860, continues to use the system to extract oil to this day.

The Canada Southern's Petrolia station has become a summer home at Brights Grove on Lake St. Clair. The former Grand Trunk station, by contrast, is one of the visual highlights of Petrolia's historic main street. The brick structure with its three street-side towers has served as a library since the trains stopped calling in the 1930s. Meanwhile, at the end of the line, at Courtright on the St. Clair River, nothing remains to remind visitors that a grand dream also ended here.

PART FOUR:

The Northland's Ghost Rail Lines

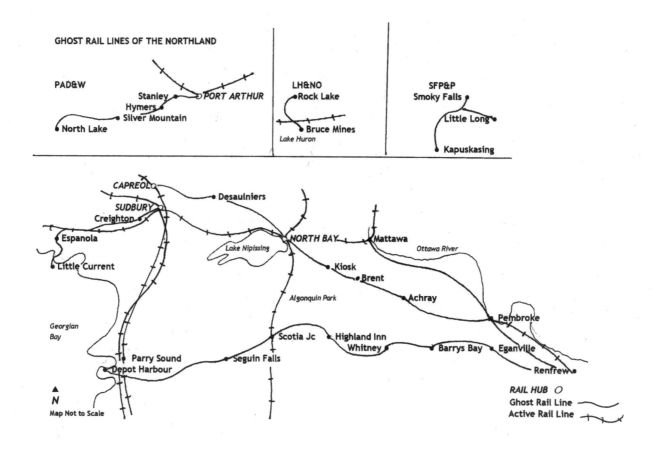

GHOST RAIL LINES OF THE NORTHLAND

PAD&W

Stanley
Hymers
Silver Mountain
North Lake
PORT ARTHUR

LH&NO
Rock Lake
Bruce Mines
Lake Huron

SFP&P
Smoky Falls
Little Long
Kapuskasing

CAPREOL
SUDBURY
Creighton
Desaulniers
Espanola
Little Current
Lake Nipissing
NORTH BAY
Mattawa
Ottawa River
Kiosk
Brent
Achray
Algonquin Park
Pembroke
Georgian Bay
Scotia Jc
Highland Inn
Whitney
Barrys Bay
Eganville
Parry Sound
Depot Harbour
Seguin Falls
Renfrew

N
Map Not to Scale

RAIL HUB O
Ghost Rail Line
Active Rail Line

CHAPTER 31

The Canadian Northern Railway's Algonquin Route: Pembroke to Capreol

The History

Should it ever become a rail trail, the route of the Canadian Northern Railway through the northern section of Algonquin Park would be Ontario's most scenic. For most of its route through the park, the rail bed follows the shores of lakes and rivers created following the last ice age when a huge ice dam burst, allowing a thousand-year torrent of water equivalent to a thousand Niagaras to gouge out a massive canyon. Its remains consist of a chain of lakes connected by the foaming Petawawa River.

In 1914, anxious to complete their long-cherished dream of a transcontinental rail line, the ambitious rail builders, William Mackenzie and Donald Mann, constructed their western link of the Canadian Northern Railway from Ottawa, northwest through Pembroke and the wilds of Algonquin Park. They built major stations at North Bay and Capreol, about twenty kilometres north of Sudbury, adding divisional points at Brent and Capreol. The line then continued northwest toward Geraldton before changing direction and heading southwest to Nipigon and Port Arthur. The route then swung west to Rainy River, where the line crossed into Minnesota before re-emerging on Canadian soil in southern Manitoba.

Traffic between Pembroke and North Bay consisted primarily of serving the scattered sawmill towns such as Kiosk, Brent, and Fossmill. Tourist traffic, however, remained light because, unlike the more ambitious Grand Trunk that crossed the southern portion of the park, the CNoR did not build tourist facilities.

Between North Bay and Capreol, business again consisted primarily of lumber from sawmills at places such as Field and Skead, and ore from mines at Crerar, the site of the Basin Mines. Once the timber was depleted, the sawmills were closed. In 1975 the mill at Kiosk burned and was relocated. Two decades later the massive mill at Field also fell to flames, reducing traffic even more. Through trains had little reason to stop, with passenger service having ended in the mid-1960s.

Finally, in 1996, the section of track between Pembroke and Capreol was abandoned and the track removed.

The Heritage

Pembroke

The Ottawa River town of Pembroke began life as a mill town well before the railways came. The first trains through town in 1885 were those of the CPR, then in the process of building its transcontinental route up the Ottawa Valley.

In 1915, the CNoR extended its line a short distance west of the town, adding a branch line to the town's core. They erected a substantial concrete station with a castle-like tower at the corner of Pembroke and McKay Streets, where a mini-mall now stands. The other station was at Pembroke Junction, where the town spur formed a junction with the main tracks. While rails remain here to a point just west of the town, beyond that only an empty cindered roadbed survives where the line makes its way into Algonquin Park.

Achray

Throughout Algonquin Park, stations consisted of boxcar-sized wooden buildings that had been hauled in on flat cars. Achray was the CNoR's most easterly station within the park and did attract some visitors, including Tom Thomson, who spent time in a nearby cabin, where he painted some of his famous park images. The ranger cabin that he occupied as both painter and fire ranger, which he named the "Outside in Cabin," still stands. Close by, a stone structure was erected in 1933 to serve as the park's eastern office. Achray, accessible by following the Barren Canyon Road, is a popular access point for canoeists.

Lake Traverse

Located a short distance south of kilometre marker 70 on the Barron Canyon Road, a number of railway buildings once stood, including a small station. This was also the site of several mill operations, including that of the Shaw Lumber Camp, set about three kilometres east of what was known as Stuart's Spur. Half a kilometre east of the station, the Pembroke Lumber Company operated a mill between the 1930s and 1977. A water tower and scattered debris are the sole survivors of this busy mill operation.

A few paces north of the Barron Canyon Road, stone chimneys are the lonely remnants of a log mansion built in 1933 as a private lodge for the family of J.R. Booth, the man who built the OA&PS Railway that ran through the southern section of the park. Built in the shape of a turtle, it was known as the "Turtle Club." Sadly, yet typically, the government bought the building in 1973 and demolished it five years later.

Brent

Of all the sites along the CNoR's Algonquin route, Brent offers the greatest number of examples of the route's railway heritage. Before rails arrived on the flat, sandy backshore of Cedar Lake, a Hawkesbury lumber operation had opened a tote road from the Ottawa River and constructed a sawmill. The railway builders found the terrain ideal for a divisional point, located at its halfway mark between Pembroke and North Bay. Here, they built a roundhouse and houses for its train crews and staff.

Meanwhile, the Brent Lumber Company had taken over the Hawkesbury firm and erected a mill to the west of the railway village. Including the mill and rail workers, the village could claim 160 residents who enjoyed the addition of a general store and a school. After the CN took over the CNoR, it upgraded the crew facilities, replaced the station, and added a new bunkhouse that still survives. In the 1960s, the CNR ended passenger service along the line, and the residents were forced to relocate outside the park, turning Brent into a ghost town.

Today, a surprising number of rail-workers' homes survive, now used as summer cottages. The historic general store has become part of Algonquin Outfitters, who equip canoeists for adventures in this more lightly used portion of Algonquin Park. Inside the store are displayed photos and clippings recounting the community's unusual story.

A winding fifty-kilometre dirt road still provides access from Highway 17 to this remote location. The Brent Crater, a circular lake created by a meteorite about 450 million years ago, lies along the route.

Daventry

Now a ghost town, Daventry, west of Brent, was another of Algonquin Park's early mill towns. It once contained two lumber mills and a school where up to sixteen pupils attended daily. Although a few structures survive, the site is not accessible by road.

Kiosk

Prior to the coming of the CNoR, Kiosk, on the north shore of Kioshkokwi Lake, was the site of one of J.R. Booth's many lumber camps. In 1934, when the busy Fassett sawmill complex at Fossmill, farther west, burned to the ground, the lumber company decided to move the operation to the Booth camp. By 1936, the Booth operation had gone, and the Fassett Company negotiated to take over Booth's Algonquin Park limits and built a new mill.

By 1939, forty-four residents had moved into the new town site, and by 1950 the population had grown to 186. Soon, six hundred residents occupied the eighty houses and one bunkhouse, worshiped in a new

Catholic church, and sent pupils to the local school. Three of the earlier Booth buildings still stood at this time. But then fire struck once again, burning the mill to ground in 1973. By this time, the Algonquin Park master plan prohibited mills and towns, and the Ministry of Natural Resources (MNR) gave the residents until 1996 to relocate. Although they fought to remain, the MNR won out and bulldozed all evidence of the town site. Today, all that remains of the once bustling town are the old streets winding through the regenerating forest and the railway trestle across the Amable du Fond River. As with Brent, the location, accessible at the end of Highway 630, is a jump-off point for canoeists and offers a campground and new outfitters store.

Fossmill

Kiosk's predecessor was the mill town of Fossmill. The Fossmill story began in the community of Fassett on the Quebec side of the Ottawa River, several kilometres downstream from today's Hull. After the CNoR built its line through the park, the Fassett Lumber Company acquired the timber limits of William Foster, lumberman owner of the property near the northwestern corner of Algonquin Park. In 1924, Fassett opened a mill and town site along the new rail line. Similar to the stations at Brent and Kiosk, the one in Fossmill was a simple boxcar-sized structure. The community contained thirty-five houses, a church, and a school.

In 1934, a fire consumed the massive mill and lumber yard, and Fossmill's milling days were done. After the lumber company built its new mill at Kiosk, the population quickly dwindled. By 1940, only sixteen homes remained, and by 1955 there were only six. Today, nothing remains save a clearing and the mill pond. The site is not accessible by vehicle.

Kiosk was a sizable town located on the Canadian Northern Railway line, east of North Bay and within the boundaries of Algonquin Provincial Park. In the 1980s, the government ordered everyone out to ensure Algonquin Park's status as a "wilderness" area.

Alderdale

Between the park boundary and North Bay, the only rail-side communities were Wasi, which today has no residents, and Alderdale, a railway village where the surviving structures line the road opposite the former station grounds. The station, another of the boxcar-size buildings typical of the route, was relocated to a farm property a short distance east.

North Bay

By the time the CNoR arrived in North Bay in 1915, the lakeside town could already count two rail lines. In 1884, the CPR had chosen the site as one of its divisional points and had built sorting yards, housing, and a large stone station along the prime lakefront location. In 1911, the Grand Trunk had extended its line from Toronto into Callendar just south of North Bay and entered North

Bay by obtaining running rights along the tracks of the government-owned Temiskaming and Northern Ontario Railway. The CNoR was left to locate its station several blocks inland, and its rail yards to the south of the town.

Because the location represented a key convergence between rail lines running north to south and east to west, the CNoR decided that a grander station was necessary. The company engaged its eastern architect, George Briggs, to design a Richardsonian-style station with rounded arches above its windows. Because the track was elevated, the entrance from the street was one floor below track level.

While North Bay remains a busy and growing city, the CN is no longer part of it. Brian Mulroney's government ended VIA Rail's passenger service to the town in 1990. When CN Rail abandoned the route in 1996, it lifted the tracks and vacated the station.

For a decade the attractive brick building stood empty, visited only by vandals, while the town sought a way to preserve this heritage structure. Happily, they found one. Today the station on Fraser Street is home to the Crisis Centre North Bay, which has converted the interior into office space, and the waiting room, with its marble pillars, into a boardroom. Outside, however, the "ghostly railway" landscape dominates the silent, weedy platform and the empty, overgrown right-of-way.

Down by the lake, the CPR station on Ferguson Street has also become a community facility, although the yards and the roundhouse are gone. Currently the station houses a museum and the Discovery North Bay tourist centre, and rents out event space.

North Bay can also claim a new bus/rail station built by the Ontario Northland Railway (the former T&NO) in 1996. While CN and CP have left town, the ONR remains one of the town's more important employers and is home to the popular Northlander train that travels daily between Toronto and Cochrane. Operating since 1903, Northlander train crews helped rescue victims of the deadly forest fires that ravaged the Matheson and Cochrane areas in the early years of the twentieth century. A provincially run train service operated by the Ontario Northland Transportation Commission, the Northlander still calls at historic stations in places such as Washago, Gravenhurst, Huntsville, South River, Temagami, and Cobalt.

Field

From North Bay, the Canadian Northern rail line made its way northwest, passing through a land of loggers and bush farmers. At Field, a computerized state-of-the-art sawmill and the two-storey stucco CNR station both stood until the late 1990s, when the mill burned and the station was demolished.

Desaulniers, another former mill town west of Field, has become a ghost town. The once busy main street that led to the station now contains only a handful of buildings, including a vacant former hotel. The next stop, River Valley, retains a number of homes and rail-era buildings beside the roadbed, but no evidence of its rail days remain. Field, Desaulniers, and River Valley are all accessible along Highway 539. The roadbed then becomes a dirt trail, passing the site of the Chudleigh station and leading west to Pine Falls Lodge. Beyond that the trail becomes unusable.

Closer to Capreol, the roadbed reaches Skead, a former mill town northeast of Sudbury. While the roadbed is evident, rail buildings are not, although the community still has a "Station Road."

Capreol

In 1915, the two routes of the CNoR, that from Toronto and that from Ottawa, joined at Capreol, located on

Highway 84 about thirty-five kilometres north of Sudbury. Prior to this, the town was only a minor stop on the CNoR's earlier Toronto route that was completed in 1908. The station was then called Orefield. With the completion of the 1915 route from Ottawa, the tracks were moved from the west side of the Vermilion River to the east, to join with the new route. Capreol became a busy junction and divisional point.

The town remains a busy rail centre, this time under the ownership of CN Rail. The original CNoR divisional-style station has been replaced by a newer structure and VIA Rail has added a new passenger station built in a traditional architectural style that incorporates the brackets from the first station. VIA Rail's train, "Canadian," calls here three times a week in each direction, carrying rail lovers between Toronto and Vancouver.

The Northern Ontario Railway Museum and Heritage Centre celebrates the town's rail heritage. Established in the home of the CNR's first superintendent, it is located on Capreol's Bloor Street. A short distance away, Prescott Park contains a steam engine — a Mountain-type 6077, a "rules instruction car" from the days of the railway-school cars — and a caboose.

CHAPTER 32

The Ottawa, Arnprior, and Parry Sound Railway — the "Booth" Line: Renfrew to Depot Harbour

The History

John Rudolphus Booth was a man who liked to take chances.[1] In 1872, this son of a Quebec farmer turned mill owner took a chance and bought out a couple of failing rail lines between Ottawa and the Atlantic seaboard. His goal was to provide a shipping route for the lumber he was sawing in his Ottawa mills. The new line was named the Canada Atlantic Railway (CAR).

This wasn't the first time Booth had taken a risk. Earlier, he had underbid the Ottawa lumber establishment to win the contract to construct Canada's new parliament buildings. He shocked them once more by outbidding them for the prized timber limits in what would later become Algonquin Park. While he was ridiculed for his bid of $40,000, which seemed high at the time, he would later turn down an offer of a million dollars for those same limits.

Now that he had his rail route to the Atlantic, Booth needed one to move the timber from his new limits to his mills. But why, he wondered, should he terminate a new line in the middle of nowhere when he could extend it right to Georgian Bay, which meant he could offer western grain-shippers the shortest, and, therefore cheapest, rail link to the Atlantic ports.

Booth didn't need to look far. The business community in Parry Sound had already chartered the Parry Sound Colonization Railway to connect their port town with the newly opened Northern and Pacific Junction Railway at Burk's Falls. But it was difficult to raise funds, and Booth bought them out.

Although the route from Ottawa that ran up the Ottawa Valley to Wilno was relatively flat and obstacle-free, the troubles began at the entrance to the Black Donald Mountains. The only buildable route into this ancient mountain range was up a narrow pass near Wilno. To gain that access, Booth had to do battle with the mighty CPR, which wanted that route for their Atlantic and Northwestern Railway. Booth won the court challenge, and the CPR was forced to terminate its tracks in Eganville.

As it turned out, the rocky wilds west of that pass were an even more troublesome hurdle. The rocks, rivers, and swamps there meant much blasting, bridging, and filling. Eventually, the route managed to snake its way along the Madawaska River and the shores of Algonquin's many lakes and rivers, until it finally crossed the height of land at Rain Lake. From there, it was a relatively easy route to the shores of Georgian Bay.

But another challenge lay ahead for Booth. The charter of the Parry Sound Colonization Railway (PSC) called for a terminal in Parry Sound, a location that Booth found too pricey and too physically limiting. He opted instead to route the line south of the town and across a narrow channel onto Parry Island, located on First Nations territory. Here, he acquired enough land to build a sizable town, which he named Depot Harbour. When finished, the town contained more than 110 dwellings, a hotel, three churches, and a school. By 1900, its population was 650 and its massive grain elevators could handle fourteen million tonnes of grain a year.

By 1896, the Ottawa, Arnprior, and Parry Sound Railway (OA&PS) was shipping grain and carrying

A 1950s view shows the activity around the Grand Trunk Railway's Highland Inn in Algonquin Park at train time. Train time ended in 1958 when the Canadian National Railway, the Grand Trunk's subsequent owner, ended rail service to the park. Courtesy of the Ron Brown collection.

passengers at a rate of twenty trains a day. Eventually, the good burghers of Parry Sound, who were desperate for a rail link, added a branch from the OA&PS line to their town, calling it the James Bay Junction Railway. In 1908, the CPR ended the community's isolation by building their Toronto to Sudbury line through the town, as did the Canadian Northern Railway.

Booth sold his line to Grand Trunk Railway for $14 million in 1904. Impressed with the CPR's promotion of the tourism of the Rocky Mountains, the GT attempted to do the same with Algonquin Park, and built a string of lodges and campgrounds. Tourists would come in from Ottawa in the east and from Toronto in the west via a connection with the former Northern and Pacific Junction Railway at Scotia Junction.

When the then bankrupt GT became part of the Canadian National Railway in 1923, the downturn began. Since the CNR had similar amenities and many other routes for grain-shippers to use, they closed many of Depot Harbour's facilities. In 1933 ice damaged a bridge in Algonquin Park, and when the CNR went to the federal government for funds to rebuild, they were refused. The government, which at the time was battling the Depression by building roads, including Highway 60 through the park, had no money for railways. Service continued to arrive in the park separately from the east and west, but the through trains were finished. Beginning in 1940, sections of the line were abandoned throughout the park. The last to go was the eastern portion, in the 1970s.

In 1945, the elevators and freight shed in Depot Harbour were destroyed by fire, and seven years later the entire Parry Sound Colonization Railway portion of the Booth Line, from Scotia Junction to James Bay Junction, was abandoned. Trains from the west continued to call at the park until 1959, and from the east,

at Whitney, until 1974. Also, CN continued to use the tracks from James Bay Junction into Depot Harbour as a storage track until the 1980s.

The Heritage

Renfrew

Between Renfrew and Whitney, at the eastern boundary of Algonquin Park, the abandoned route of the Ottawa, Arnprior, and Parry Sound Railway has assumed a number of different forms. Within Renfrew, a well-used walking and cycling trail known as the Millennium Trail follows the line up to the Renfrew Junction site, where the K&P Trail begins. The main access for the Millennium Trail can be found at the site of the old Renfrew station at Carswell Street and Renfrew Avenue. But both east and west of Renfrew, while the right-of-way remains visible, in most locations it is not open as a trail.

Eganville

Eganville retains one of only two Booth Line stations still on their original sites. (That from Goshen still survives but it has been moved to a nearby farmyard). The simple single-storey structure has variously served as a tavern and as a private home, and lies well to the west of the village on Highway 512.

With a few breaks, the trail parallels Highway 60 from Eganville through the village of Golden Lake, where it is used as a road. It was from Golden Lake that a short branch called the Pembroke and Southern Railway connected the Booth Line with the CNoR at Pembroke. From Golden Lake to Barry's Bay, the route has evolved into a snowmobile trail for a portion of its length, and, closer to Whitney, a rough roadway along the Madawaska River.

Killaloe

Killaloe celebrates its lost railway heritage with a mural on the post office, a few buildings built in the style of the old Booth station, and preservation of the trestle over Brennan Creek, now part of a local walking path. Killaloe Station Park was opened in 1994 on the former station site, the station itself having been demolished in 1968.

Interestingly, there were once two Killaloes. The original began in the 1840s as a mill site a short distance to the south of the current town. In 1893, when the Booth Line reached what was then called Fort McDonell, the settlement that grew around it became known as Killaloe Station. As the milling operation faded, Killaloe Station became the larger of the two settlements. In 1988, the town dropped the *station* from its name: by then, neither station nor tracks remained.

Wilno, the next station west, marks the site of Canada's first Polish settlement. Its twin-spired St. Mary's Church, built in 1937 and dedicated to Our Lady Queen of Poland, is one of Ontario's most magnificent. A Polish heritage museum stands on the site of the old station, and the annual Polish-Kashub Day is celebrated here on the last Saturday of May.[2]

Opposite the museum, the Wilno general store still retains a Polish sign on the front and stamps mail with the Polish eagle postmark. Unfortunately, amid the celebration of the area's Polish heritage, that of the rail line is nowhere to be seen, although to the west of the heritage centre, the right-of-way is now a rail trail.

Barry's Bay

It is not necessary to travel far from Wilno to enjoy some rail heritage, however. One of the better preservation efforts on this line is found in Barry's Bay, where not only the station been preserved — it is a well-stocked museum — but so too has the old wood water tower, the only such railway relic still standing in Ontario. Even the previously rundown Balmoral Hotel, a one-time railway hotel, has been renovated and is now a popular dining room.

Before the arrival of Booth's railway, Barry's Bay had served as a steamboat landing on the north shore of Kamaniskeg Lake, and was a jumping-off point for travellers on the rough and winding Opeongo Colonization Road.

Madawaska

It is difficult to understand while viewing it today but, except for Depot Harbour, Madawaska was the rail line's most important town. Despite its wilderness location and the objections of the residents of Barry's Bay, Booth chose this location to establish the railway's mid-line divisional point. (Perhaps it was because the place was inside Booth's timber limits, while Barry's Bay was not.) Here he built a five-stall wooden engine house, a large station, and accommodations for his train crews.

When the Grand Trunk acquired the line, it replaced the old roundhouse with a fourteen-stall roundhouse, constructed of the more durable concrete. Sadly, even that could not save this bit of railway heritage, and the crumbling structure was torn down in recent years for safety reasons and for the expansion of a recreation area.

The only bit of rail legacy that Madawaska can claim is the long trestle that crosses the mighty Madawaska River.

Barry's Bay station is the only surviving example of the distinctive station style the lumber baron J.R. Booth used on his Ottawa, Arnprior, and Parry Sound Railway line, which he built in the 1890s to ship not just his lumber but also grain from Depot Harbour.

Algonquin Park

From Madawaska to Whitney, at the eastern boundary of Algonquin Park, the route follows the shore of the river and is now a rough trail. But all ends at the park boundary. Within the park, there is no continuous way to view Booth's old line.

West of Whitney, portions of the roadbed are visible to canoeists paddling the waters of Galeairy Lake. The

Rock Lake Campground offers the next glimpse of the old line. It was here that Booth established a small village and a shed-sized station to serve the nearby sawmills.

Here, too, along the Booth's Rock Trail, are the grounds and remains of the Barclay estate. Built around 1900 by Judge George Barclay, a relative of Booth's, the grand home continued to be used by the family until 1953. Although offered to the Department of Lands and Forest by the family, that government agency treated the mansion as it has treated many of its heritage structures, and demolished it. Today's hiker will find only foundations and the remains of the tennis court and docks as testimony to this part of the park's vanished history.

From Rock Lake to Mew Lake, the route is now part of the six-kilometre Old Railway Bike Trail. Farther along, the Track and Tower Trail reveals the ruins of the two trestles that once crossed the waters of Cache Lake, and follows the right-of-way to the site of the Madawaska River trestle. At fifteen metres above the river and 110 metres long, this was the rail line's grandest. As with all trestles in the park, this structure had its own crossing guard — an employee who would check following each train to ensure that no sparks were left to cause a fire. As with the others, this structure was removed in the 1940s when that section of the rail line was abandoned.

On the northern shores of Cache Lake is the now overgrown site of one of the park's most important rail stops. Here, in 1908, the Grand Trunk built its main Algonquin Park lodge, the legendary Highland Inn. By 1913, it would offer one hundred guest rooms and a dining room. The GT added a pair of more remote and rustic camps, Nominigan Lodge and Camp Minnesing, both of which continue to operate. With the park headquarters located here, as well, the GT constructed one of its large standard-plan stations in front of the Highland Inn.

Trains continued to puff up to the Highland Inn station until 1959, when rail traffic finally succumbed to the automobile, which by now could easily travel the paved Highway 60. The following year, the station, the tracks, and the inn were all removed. A pine plantation covers the foundations of the hotel today. Only the platform remains visible.

A short distance west, on an access road used by cottagers and logging trucks, a short trestle once crossed the narrows of Joe Lake, where a log station catered to tourists at the Algonquin Hotel. A short distance farther along, where the line crossed Potter Creek, stood the Canoe Lake Station. From here, a spur line led to the busy mills and Mowat town site of the Gilmour Lumber Company. Tourists could stay at the Mowat Lodge, a former boarding house for the loggers (it burned down and was replaced). Painter Tom Thomson had been living here before a fateful canoe trip cost him his life in 1917.

Mowat has become a ghost town, with a handful of the old homes still occupied by lessees waiting out their leases. This last vestige of a park mill village may soon be razed into the pages of history.

Scotia Junction Ghost Town

From Algonquin Park's western boundary, into Kearney, located east of Emsdale on Highway 518, the right-of-way has largely vanished. Even this small tourist town shows little evidence that Booth's line ever passed this way.

A short distance west from Kearney the route encounters the ghost town of Scotia Junction, the first of several between here and Georgian Bay.[3] Here, on the current Highway 529, the Booth Line met the tracks of the Northern and Pacific Junction Railway, later assumed by the Grand Trunk. There were once sidings for switching tracks and a small village of homes and boarding houses for the rail workers here. An attractive turreted station also stood within the diamond where two sets of tracks crossed each other. After being destroyed by fire, it was replaced with a simpler structure.

Nearly all of these have vanished. While the right-of-way and the sidings leading from it to the Grand Trunk remain visible, the only track remaining is that of the CN, which carries CN freights and the

Northlander passenger trains of the Ontario Northland between Toronto and Cochrane. While a few newer homes have appeared in the area, only an abandoned store and former hotel remain from the railway days.

Sprucedale

From Fern Glen, a few kilometres west of Scotia Junction, west to Highway 400, the Booth Line has, for several years, been a popular snowmobile trail known as the Seguin Trail. The route is followed closely by Highway 518, which accesses the same communities created by the railway. Just as Sprucedale was the busy hub of the area during rail days, it remains a hub for snowmobilers today.

The historic Sprucedale Hotel offers rest and relaxation but now caters to snowmobilers and other trail-users instead of to travellers on Booth's trains. In addition to its restaurant and beverage room, the hotel offers a small number of modernized guest rooms. Remote by southern Ontario standards, Sprucedale contains a store, school, churches, and several homes that date from Booth's time.

Little, however, remains at the next flag-stop station, Whitehall, which contains little more than an abandoned store. The rail trail then bypasses the village of Bear Lake some distance to the north. Originally called Jarlsberg, this cottage community contains the historic wooden St. Olaf's Church, erected in 1876 by Norwegian setters who came to the area in the 1860s.

Seguin Falls Ghost Town

A short distance south of Highway 518, the ghost town of Seguin Falls tells the tale of two failed transportation routes.

Before the Booth Line arrived, travellers into this area used a rough trail known as the Nipissing Road. It was one of twenty-five colonization roads opened by the government in an effort to entice settlers into the then sparsely inhabited northern woodlands. When the Booth Line arrived, a new Seguin Falls sprang up around the shack-sized station. Hotels, schools, churches, and houses were built, along with a sawmill. Today, all that remains of the hotel is a charred foundation, while only a handful of the village's original buildings still stand. Just west of the village site, concrete piers mark the location of the line's bridge that once spanned the Seguin River.

Swords Ghost Town

West of Seguin Falls, the rail line passed through Orrville, or as the railway station was called, Edgington. Located on Highway 518, Orrville remains a solid little community with active churches and homes, and a one-time blacksmith shop. Unlike the land between here and Scotia Junction, the soils here were more fertile, giving rise to a small farming community.

The community of Swords, also called Maple Lake Station, was the destination for tourists hoping to find a room at the Maple Lake Hotel. Most of the village's buildings are gone now, although the former hotel and store remain as ghostly ruins beside the rail trail. The silent little hamlet lies a few kilometres south of Highway 518.

The Seguin Trail finishes on Highway 400, conveniently at a Tim Hortons. From this location to Rose Point, where a railway swing bridge crosses to Parry Island, the rail trail becomes known as the Rose Point Trail.

Depot Harbour

On the west side of this new and busy four-lane Highway 400, the old Booth Line follows the Rose Point Trail to James Bay Junction, the site of the link built from the Booth Line into the town of Parry Sound. However, once the CPR and the CNoR built their own direct lines into town, the junction was no longer needed.

The Rose Point Trail passes beneath the high overhead bridges of today's CP and CN railways and makes its way to Rose Point. Here stood one of the more attractive of the line's combined hotel-stations. With its picturesque towers, it contained guest rooms and was the jump-off point for travellers, who at that time were required to use a ferry connection to reach the town of Parry Sound.

While the hotel has long since been removed, Booth's original swing bridge, now paved and with the rails removed, carries cars across the narrow channel to the cottages on Parry Island and the homes of the Wasauksing First Nation. Here, the right-of-way becomes a local dirt road leading to the abandoned town site of Depot Harbour, one of Ontario's most extensive ghost-town ruins.

When Booth laid out the town of Depot Harbour it was not without considerable dispute with his First Nations neighbours. Although he ultimately successfully negotiated the original parcel of land for the town site, when he needed additional land, he used the Railway Act to simply expropriate it. This acquisition rankles the residents of Parry Island to this day.

Between 1896 and 1933 the town boomed. The cinder streets were lined with sidewalks, and among the structures were included a hotel, a boarding house, three churches, a school, a small station, and a railway roundhouse, along with 110 dwellings. Piped water and electricity were available to the more than 650 people calling Depot Harbour home.

Two massive grain elevators and a coal dock stood over the long wharf. The harbour was one of the best deep-water natural harbours on the Great Lakes, where as many as twenty grain ships stood at anchor waiting to land their cargo. As the town was alcohol-free, imbibers had to board a small ferry to travel into Parry Harbour, the only "wet" section of Parry Sound, to quench their considerable thirst. This neighbourhood became so rowdy that disgusted Parry Sounders took to calling it "Parry Hoot."

In 1933, with the abandonment of the trestle in Algonquin Park, Depot Harbour lost its main reason for existing. No longer could it offer grain-shippers the shortest rail link to the Atlantic. By this time, the CNR and CPR were hauling grain trains directly from the Lakehead, while large grain ships could travel directly through the newly enlarged Welland Canal to elevators at Toronto, Kingston, and Prescott.

During the Second World War, the elevators stood empty. Across the harbour was the town of Nobel, where the volatile explosive known as cordite was being manufactured for the war. The empty dock seemed like the perfect place to store it. That is until, to celebrate the end of the war, celebrants lit a bonfire. Gusting winds whipped the flames toward the cordite, which erupted into a midnight fireball that lit the streets of Parry Sound ten kilometres away and destroyed the grain elevators.

Over the next decade, the houses of Depot Harbour stood empty, sold off one by one for their wood content. For a period of time, iron-ore pellets were shipped to the docks from mines north of Sudbury for transhipment to the United States, but that trade also ended. The CNR continued to use the spur to the town site as a storage track for a few years, but those rails were eventually ripped up in the late 1980s.

Today, the town site lies empty and overgrown. The only vestiges of the once bustling community and of Booth's grand dream are cracked sidewalks, overgrown foundations, and the crumbling concrete shell of the old railway roundhouse, a fitting but bittersweet tribute to the ghosts of one of Canada's most promising railways.

The crumbling Roman-like ruins of the Depot Harbour roundhouse are a haunting reminder of what was once North America's largest one-man rail operation.

CHAPTER 33

The Lake Huron and Northern Ontario Railway: Bruce Mines to Rock Lake

The History

Bruce Mines, on the north shore of Lake Huron, was one of the north's earliest mining towns. Extraction of copper began here in 1842. Its prosperity, however, has been hit-and-miss, as mines opened then closed, usually after only a brief period of operation.

One of those mines was the Bruce Copper Mine. Opened in the village of Bruce Mines in 1898, the mine built a rail connection from its headframe to its dock on Lake Huron, over a kilometre away. The following year another copper mine opened, this one on the shores of Rock Lake, about twenty-two kilometres to the north. The Bruce Mines and Algoma Railway (BM&A) was incorporated to haul the copper south.

At first, it was connected only to the CPR, which ran its line about three kilometres north of the village, but permission was soon granted to extend the line into the village to connect with the dock along the line built by the Bruce Copper Mine. At the same time it extended a 120-metre, three-track coal dock into Lake

Huron to provide a coal supply, not just for its own equipment but for the CPR as well.

As long as it operated, the ore from the Rock Lake mine was carried to the docks and then by ship to the smelters at Dollar Bay, Michigan. But the mines were short-lived, and by 1904 were silent. But not the railway; that year it amended its charter to build all the way to James Bay, connecting en route with the transcontinental main lines of the CPR and the National Transcontinental Railway.

Following some preliminary surveying for the extended route, the BM&A's only two engines collided and the rail line was shut down. But it was not officially abandoned, and in 1912, after seven years of inactivity, the line re-emerged with new hope, new equipment, and a new name — the Lake Huron and Northern Ontario Railway (LH&NO).

Its saviour had been the Mond Nickel Company of Sudbury. The company was not interested in copper but in a large deposit of quartz, also found on Rock Lake. The company would use the mineral as flux in the furnaces of its smelter at Victoria Mines. But because the line had been inactive for such a long period, the roadbed and bridges were in poor condition. In fact, it became common practice for the brakeman and engineer, when approaching the bridges, to put the throttle on slow and walk across the bridge ahead of the engine, then climb back aboard the slow-moving train. But profits were never enough to cover the line's mortgage payments, and when the Mond mine closed in 1921, so did the rail operations.

The Heritage

Bruce Mines

The town of Bruce Mines, strung along Highway 17, contains a surprising amount of history. A walking tour from the local Bruce Mines Museum, housed in a historic church, guides visitors to the old mine sites. One of these mines, the Simpson Shaft, has been restored to re-create the crude nature of early mine operations. Tours also show visitors the early back streets and hotels,

To attract tourists, the town of Bruce Mines has reconstructed a small copper mine of the type that attracted the railway line to the then bustling mining town.

a one-time lockup, and the remains of a coal dock on Jacks Island.

The station that originally served the village stood a block north of Highway 17, close to Highway 638, but nothing remains at the site. The main station for the line was the one it shared with the Canadian Pacific at Bruce Station, where the two lines crossed. Its original station was replaced in 1923 with a western-standard plan station, but it was torn down in the 1970s. The CPR track here remains busy, linking with the CPR's main lines in northern Michigan. Located three kilometres north of Bruce Mines, Bruce Station developed as a separate satellite hamlet and still contains a few rail-era structures.

Rydal Bank

The mill town of Rydal Bank was once a stop on the Lake Huron and Northern Ontario (LH&NO) line, where passengers would await their train in the comfort of the Maple Leaf Hotel. The right-of-way here is no longer discernable except for a laneway paralleling it.

West of Rydal Bank, Plummer Road lies on the right-of-way as it follows the south shore of Ottertail Lake. On the west side of the lake, the right-of-way swings north near the site of the line's small trestle bridge across the Thessalon River, where the McCarthy station was located along Centre Line Road, north of Plummer Road. The right-of-way, abandoned for eighty years, has now faded into the landscape.

Rock Lake

The cliff-lined shore of Rock Lake is a very scenic one. At the base of those cliffs, the roadbed remains visible where it once skirted the lakeshore. East of Centre Line Road, along Highway 638, a side road leads south to the former miners' community of Rock Lake, now a summer cottage community. From here, the tracks continued for two more kilometres to the site of the mine.

The back roads in the area north of Bruce Mines are among Ontario's most scenic hidden treasures. From Rock Lake, Highway 638 winds west around lofty ridges and dips into wide valleys where fields and forests abound. In one of those valleys, the hamlet of Leeburn contains what may well be Ontario's smallest general store.

The highway continues west to meet Highway 17 — the Trans Canada Highway — at Echo Bay. Not only is this route a quiet and attractive alternative to the busier Highway 17, it also offers a peek into the heritage of one of Ontario's long-lost railway lines.

CHAPTER 34

The Manitoulin and North Shore Railway: Sudbury to Little Current

The History

The Manitoulin and North Shore Railway (M&NS) received its original charter in 1888 with a mandate to build a line from Sudbury across Manitoulin Island. From there, it would operate a ferry to Tobermory, and then run a line down the length of the Bruce Peninsula to Wiarton and Owen Sound. Not surprisingly, these ambitions succumbed to reality, and nothing was built.

Finally, in 1900, Francis Clergue, CEO of the Superior Corporation (which owned the Algoma Central Railway in Sault Ste. Marie and large ore mines to the north around Wawa), bought a pair of mines near Sudbury — the Gertrude and the Crean. But he needed a means of shipping the ore to market, so when the CPR passed on the prospect, Clergue himself purchased the charter of the M&NS line.

Initially, the Superior Corporation built the line only as far as its Gertrude Mine. In 1903, when Clergue's empire collapsed, construction on the M&NS stopped. By 1907, however, Clergue had been replaced and construction resumed. By 1909 the line had been extended to the Crean Mine, crossing the Vermilion River on a thirty-metre-long trestle, then crossing the Spanish River on an even longer sixty-metre trestle. Two years later, the tracks reached Espanola and what would be the line's major customer, the E.B. Eddy pulp mill. At this time the name was changed, becoming the Algoma Eastern Railway (AER), likely a tribute to the Algoma Central Railway, another line founded by Clergue.

In 1913 the line finally reached Little Current by way of its two-hundred-metre swing bridge over the North Channel of Lake Huron. For nearly two decades the line prospered, but then the Great Depression struck. Mines closed and the Superior Corporation began to look for a financial saviour. The rescuer appeared in 1930 in the form of the CPR's leasing of the line for its usual 999 years. But because the CPR had its own line that paralleled that of the AER, it began to abandon redundant trackage. By 1935, the tracks to the hazardous O'Donnell roast yard were gone, and by the 1950s everything west of Creighton had been abandoned.

The Lafarge Cement Works at McGregor Bay switched to trucks in the 1990s, and the Lawson Quarry closed, causing the AER to vanish from the railway landscape. Only two former portions of the line continue to see rail traffic: that from the CPR junction at McKerrow to Espanola, and the short link to the Clarabelle Mine at Sudbury. Consistent with CPR's "heritage" policy, all stations were demolished.

The Heritage

Sudbury

The M&NS line originally started at the Canadian Northern Railway station, once located in the Flour Mill District of Sudbury. The fine old stone-and-brick station, however, fell victim to a frenzy of urban renewal, a scheme that unfortunately failed to consider the city's railway heritage.

The Manitoulin and Northern Shore switched to using the CPR's downtown station, a châteauesque station now minus its dormer. From there, VIA Rail passengers board the Lake Superior, the local train that travels between Sudbury and White River, along the "Ghost Town Trail." Many busy sawmill towns that once lined this rail route have been reduced to ghost towns over the years, although the train continues to access many summer camps and lodges along the line.

The M&NS's Sudbury yard, formerly located on Frood Road, has now vanished, although the current CPR line still follows the original Manitoulin and North Shore route.

Creighton

The active portion of the M&NS line abruptly ends at the ghost town of Creighton. It was here that the International Nickel Company of Canada (INCO) extracted nickel ore from a deep shaft and created an extensive town site. The town included some 1,100 residents, four hundred houses, along with churches and schools, a bustling main street, and a two-storey train station.

In 1988, citing costly upgrades to the water and sewer systems, INCO closed the town and removed the buildings. Only the remains of foundations and cement sidewalks mark the site. Former residents, however, have created a parkette with an information plaque outlining the appearance of the town when they could still call it home. This historic site lies on Regional Road 24, east of Highway 144.

West of Creighton, INCO still owns the trackless right-of-way that leads to the sites of two former mines, the Gertrude Mine, about three kilometres west of Creighton, and the O'Donnell roast yard. The environmental disaster that was the O'Donnell roast yard was where, until 1928, the mining company roasted the mined ore in open pits. By the time the government forced it to close, the damage had been done. The area around the roasting yards remains barren to this day.

West of the Vermilion River, a rough trail follows the rail line up to the Crean Hill Mine, which still operates despite the fact that the town that once housed the workers is gone. A short distance west of Crean Hill Mine lies the Victoria Mine. In this case, the miners' town was five kilometres south on the still-active CPR Sault Ste. Marie line. But it, too, is now a ghost town, its once well-populated network of streets reduced to cinder trails in a field.

Espanola

As the right-of-way continues west, now a summer trail, it crosses the Spanish River near the community of

Turbine, so named because of a hydro dam to the north. A few remnants of the log cribbing still remain visible in the river.

Between Turbine and Nairn, located north of Highway 17, about halfway between Sudbury and Espanola, the right-of-way that follows the river becomes an access road leading to the hydro dam at Nairn Falls. The active CPR line also passes through Nairn, which owes its grid street pattern to the planners who laid out every railway town the same. The former CPR station has been moved and is now a residence in the town.

From Nairn to McKerrow the right-of-way lies in a forest regeneration area. At McKerrow, the Manitoulin and North Shore formed a junction with the CPR. The M&NS tracks remain in use for a few kilometres, servicing the pulp mill in Espanola.

Originally a company town, it was laid out around the massive E.B. Eddy paper mill, which is now owned by Domtar. The station, a simple two-storey structure resembling the one at Creighton, lasted until nearly 1990, when, not surprisingly, it was demolished.

Willisville

The right-of-way continues south from Espanola until is forced to find a way through the La Cloche Mountains, a wall of pure-white quartzite and one of the most spectacular mountain ranges in eastern Canada. Along this stretch, the line has only recently been abandoned, and the right-of-way remains clearly visible.

Willisville, on the Willisville Road a short distance east of Highway 6, is a company town built by INCO in 1943 to house workers for the Lawson Quarry. The small, uniform homes line a network of streets. Behind one of these homes, the diminutive Willisville station survives as a shed. Near the Willisville Road, Highway

6 climbs to the summit of the La Cloche Mountains to offer one of the most expansive vistas of white hills, forests, and lakes that the region has to offer.

The right-of-way next winds though the community of Whitefish Falls, and crosses onto Birch Island. Throughout this section, the right-of-way is some distance from Highway 6.

La Cloche Island, a large island lying in the North Channel between Manitoulin Island and the mainland, was the former site of the major McGregor Bay port, where the railway picked up cement for INCO's Sudbury super stack. The port remained active into the 1990s.

Little Current

The roadbed criss-crosses Highway 6 from Birch Island to what was once the site of Turner, on the south shore of Great La Cloche Island. Originally a coal dock, Turner became a busy pellet shipment centre. The remains at the site stood until 1998.

From here, the highway crosses the North Channel on a former railway bridge and onto Manitoulin Island. In 1943, this bridge was planked in to allow vehicular traffic. It is a tribute to the railway heritage of the Manitoulin and North Shore Railway that the only land access to the world's largest freshwater island is its railway bridge. The line, however, failed to fulfill its original objective of extending south beyond Little Current. Despite the preservation of the bridge, now an island icon, the site of the station and cattle yards are uncelebrated, now ignominiously marked by a beer store and oil tanks.

Little Current's railway swing bridge represents the only land access to Manitoulin Island, the world's largest freshwater island.

CHAPTER 35

The Port Arthur and Duluth Railway — the "Pee-Dee" Line: Thunder Bay to Rock Lake

The History

Dubbed the "ghost rail line to nowhere," the Port Arthur and Duluth Railway (PA&D) started off in Port Arthur — but failed to make it anywhere near Duluth.

Interest in a railway to the west of Fort William dates back to 1872 and the incorporation of the Thunder Bay Silver Mines Railway. However, its charter lapsed and tracks were never laid. In 1875, the CPR chose rival Fort William over Port Arthur as the initial terminus for its grand trans-national railway project. Concerned over the lack of access to those vital CPR rails, the citizens of Prince Arthur's Landing (as Port Arthur was then called) requested a link, but were rebuffed.

In 1887, the prospect of a railway for Port Arthur resurfaced with the Thunder Bay Colonization Railway. This scheme, proposed in conjunction with rail builders in Duluth, would build a rail line from either end and link them up at the site of a promising iron-ore deposit on Gunflint Lake, near the Ontario-Minnesota border.

The line from Duluth would be called the Duluth and Iron Range Railroad.

By then re-named the Port Arthur, Duluth, and Western Railway (PAD&W), in 1893 the Canadian section made it to the border, one hundred kilometres away, and then eight kilometres to the Gunflint Iron Mine in Minnesota. But the American section never arrived. For a few years the mine produced meagre quantities of iron ore, as did a handful of silver mines along the route.

But the silver market collapsed and the mines closed, and by 1898 the railway was bankrupt, earning it a nickname — the "Poverty, Agony, Distress, and Welfare" line. In 1909, a fire destroyed the vital three-hundred-metre trestle over North Lake, and the line lost its Minnesota link, ending at the North Lake station on the Canadian border. This misfortune caught the attention of William Mackenzie and Donald Mann, the builders of the Canadian Northern Railway. They were looking for an entry into Port Arthur for their line to Rainy River, and the PAD&W's twenty-five-kilometre section of track from Stanley (about fifteen kilometres west of today's Thunder Bay) into Port Arthur provided an ideal opportunity.

Since the CNoR only needed the kilometres from Stanley Junction to Port Arthur, the remaining eighty kilometres west of that point gradually fell into disuse. In 1938, the section that lay west of Mackies, on Highway 588 about thirty kilometres southwest of Stanley, was abandoned by the CNR, by then the owner of the Canadian Northern. Even Stanley had become a backwater once the CNoR had straightened the route to bypass the community.

In 1958, the Ontario government converted much of the rail bed into a highway, and today only a few metres of track remain in place near the Twin City area of Thunder Bay.

The Heritage

Port Arthur

When Mackenzie and Mann acquired their cherished link to Port Arthur, they constructed one of that rail line's grandest station structures on the waterfront. Built of brick and stone, it featured two of their iconic pyramid roofs, along with wheat-sheaf carvings in the

One of the finest stations on the Port Arthur, Duluth, and Western Railway line was built by the Canadian Northern Railway at its Port Arthur (now part of Thunder Bay) terminus. The building survives as part of that city's waterfront redevelopment, although trains no longer stop there.

gables. The CPR's station, with its elegant tower, stood across the road. While highway widening cost the city this valuable heritage building, that of the Canadian Northern remained and is now a designated heritage building dominating the renovated waterfront.

From Port Arthur, the route of the railway angled across Fort William, crossing the CPR near Westfort, the site of the CPR's original groundbreaking. Beyond the end of the track at Twin City, the roadbed remains in evidence. At Rosslyn, the Slate River station, for many years used for storage, survived until 1989. The Rosslyn Road follows the old railway roadbed to the early junction of Stanley.

During its few years as a key junction for the Canadian Northern Railway, Stanley could boast a two-storey station, a water tower, and a hotel. Today, only a few early buildings linger, as does the roadbed, which continues to be a vehicular roadway leading west. After two kilometres, the road crosses the Kaministiquia River on the line's only surviving trestle, a steel bridge built by the CNR in 1922.

With the arrival of the Port Arthur, Duluth, and Western Railway, Hymers, west of Stanley, became a busy shipping point. Today this one-time railway town, with its grid street network, has evolved into a dormitory community for the city of Thunder Bay. Although no sign of the old rail line remains here, its heritage is celebrated in a historical plaque located on the former grounds of the PAD&W station. The museum, housed in a former schoolhouse, contains much of the railway's history.

Silver Mountain

South of Hymers, Highway 588 is known as the Silver Mountain Highway, since it led to a high plateau where the legendary Silver Mountain Mine sprang to life with much promise. But the mine folded after producing for only a few years, and the remains of that operation now lie atop the mountain that borders this scenic road. Here, the rail line followed the banks of Whitefish Creek, where a set of bridge abutments remains.

In Nolalu (an acronym for North Land Lumber Company) the tracks ran up the centre of the main street. But both tracks and early buildings have vanished. West of Nolalu, the rail line crossed the Beaver Dam Creek on a number of small wooden trestles whose sparse remains are still visible. Although some distance from the actual mines, the Silver Mountain station is the only other Canadian Northern station to survive on the old PAD&W. It displays the standard CNoR plan, with a high pyramid roof atop a square two-storey station house. It now serves as the Silver Mountain Station restaurant.

West of the Silver Mountain station, Highway 588 follows the roadbed along the scenic shores of Whitefish Lake, and then enters the historic Finnish community of Suomi. Thirteen kilometres west of Suomi, the highway crosses Sandstone Creek, where a dirt road leads along its shores. Here, it follows the route of the rail bed to the shores of Addie Lake, where the old rail line remains drivable for only a short distance, beyond which lie the Minnesota border and the site of the North Lake station.

North Lake

Following the fire that destroyed the three-hundred-metre trestle crossing the lake, North Lake became the western terminus for the failing line. The station was built in 1911 according to the CNoR's standard plan. It closed in 1923. The building was still standing in 1977, when it was moved and rebuilt on the shores of Addie Lake as part of the plan for a proposed park. That plan never materialized and the station was eventually destroyed by fire.

CHAPTER 36

The Smoky Falls Railway: Kapuskasing to Smoky Falls

The History

With a name like the "Smoky Falls Railway" (SFR), it's easy to conjure up a romantic image of steam engines puffing through mountain passes and rivers foaming through a deep gorge. This "Smoky" line, however, delivered no such reality. Rather, it began simply as a logging railway meant to haul raw materials to one of Ontario's most northerly pulp mills, the Spruce Falls Power and Paper Company, in Kapuskasing, Ontario.

Before rail lines or pulp mills intruded into this northern landscape, the Mattagami River was a busy fur-trading route along which the largely indigenous Cree population paddled their pelts to the many outposts. Then, in 1905, the federal government created another transcontinental railway line called the National Transcontinental Railway. Its route led from Quebec City, through the remote forests of northern Quebec and Ontario, across the Prairies (where it was called the Grand Trunk Pacific), and finally to Prince Rupert in British Columbia.

Kapuskasing, or "Kap" as it is locally known, began as a station stop on this line. Initially, it was called MacPherson Station. During the First World War it served as a prisoner of war camp. Located as it was in such remote and bug-infested surroundings, escapes were non-existent. Post-war, the Ontario government, planning to build on the existing infrastructure, approached the Kimberly-Clark Company to establish a paper mill by the waterfalls on the river. In 1921, the Spruce Falls Power and Paper Company created a new town site, with 150 homes, a one-hundred-room hotel, and a twenty-two-bed hospital. This modern town site was called Kapuskasing, Cree for "bend in the river."

By 1922, the sulphite mill was turning out 115 tonnes of pulp a day. To access the more remote forest stands, the company began construction of the Spruce Falls Power and Paper Company Railway; the mill by then was producing newsprint as well. The railway led to Smoky Falls, about sixty kilometres north of Kapuskasing, where the company could obtain more power for their plant. A town site was created there.

In 1960, the Ontario government opened a town site of its own to house workers who were building a massive hydro dam in the area. Known as the Little Long Colony, it included a recreation hall, a four-room school, a supermarket, an office building, as well as dorms for single employees and houses for families. It was not an ideal place to call home, however, as the blackflies were so ferocious that frequent aerial spraying was required. In fact, the hordes were so unnerving that they inspired one former resident, Wade Hemsworth, to write what some call Ontario's unofficial anthem — "The Blackfly Song."

To service the hydro town site, the Smoky Falls Railway extended a spur line into the Little Long hydro community and provided daily passenger trains from Kapuskasing. Known as the "Little Long Express," it left Kap each day at noon, except on Sundays, when it left in the evening. The journey through the endless tamarack and spruce forests could take anywhere from two to three hours.

Ontario Hydro acquired its own equipment for this line, including an engine, two baggage cars, and four coaches — two of which were wooden and two steel.

Station stops were at Smoky Falls, Neshin Junction, and Lake Bennet, in addition to the later expansion to Little Long. In 1946, the Census of Canada recorded nearly one hundred residents at Smoky Falls, and at its peak (between 1960 and 1966) six hundred at the Little Long hydro camp.

The first road appeared in 1974, built from Fraserdale, on the Ontario Northland Railway, to Smoky Falls, about forty-five kilometres to the west. With it, the need for a railway to Smoky Falls ended; the line was removed, the bridges were burned, and the engines were put into service at the mill. Some equipment was put to use on the Ontario Northland Railway spur line created for the construction of the Otter Rapids Dam on the Abitibi River. Two of the coaches, both sleepers, were left behind to serve as rudimentary accommodation for hunters and fishers, while a third coach now rests with the York and Durham Heritage Railway in Uxbridge.

Before the tracks were lifted, a former employee, Ron Morel, had hopes of creating a tourist railway along the southernmost portion of the line, but his dream sadly died along with him.

The Heritage

The only station to survive with any relevance to this rail line is the one at Kapuskasing. It was from the CNR station that passengers were transferred to the Smoky Falls Railway platform on the west side of the Kapuskasing River. This station still stands in good shape and functions today as a bus station and traveller information centre. A preserved train beside the station is now the Ron Morel Museum, which is housed in two railway coaches headed by CNR engine #5107.

The lower section of the line is no longer usable, since there are no longer any bridges. However, the determined explorer can take the Pearce Hall Road, a public-private logging road leading north from Highway 11, a short distance east of the town. After forty kilometres, the route joins the railway's old roadbed. The old coaches lie a short distance west of here. Farther along, the road parallels the rail bed for a short distance. The bridges are out here, too. Then, at a *Y* in the road, the main route heads east to the vacant Little Long campsite.

If you continue for another twenty-two kilometres, you'll find yourself back at the rail line and the ghost town of Smoky Falls, where a number of ruins have survived the closure of the line and the abandonment of the town. Here, the Pearce Hall Road meets with the road to Fraserdale, located forty-five kilometres to the east. From Fraserdale, Highway 807 leads south to Highway 11 and the town of Smooth Rock Falls, another modern-era paper mill town.

East of Smooth Rock Falls, the town of Cochrane remains a railway hub, where most workers are employees of the Ontario Northland Railway. From Cochrane, trains depart daily: the Polar Bear Express destined for Moosonee to the north; the Northlander bound for Toronto to the south.

Kapuskasing, the town site laid out for the paper company in 1923, remains an impressive sight. Despite the commercial strip along Highway 11, the downtown core that lies north of the highway displays its planned traffic circle, now landscaped. The homes here line winding suburban-style roads. Among the town's more impressive buildings are the historic Kapuskasing Inn, the hospital, and the town hall, all constructed in an elegant Tudor style. A scenic avenue follows the curve of the river, providing this railway and mill town with an unexpected visual appeal.

The former passenger station in Kapuskasing provided the link for train passengers arriving from Cochrane to connect with the trains of the Smoky Falls Railway. This image, taken circa *1988, pre-dates the end of passenger service in 1990.*

EPILOGUE

The End of the Line?

Unfortunately, Ontario continues to lose its historic rail lines, even though the pace of abandonments has slowed. In 1986, the CPR's South Shore line tracks were lifted, leaving but a solitary station on site — that in the community of Bourget, east of Ottawa. Launched as the Montreal and Ottawa Railway in 1899 to link those two cities, it passed through a land of fertile farms and level terrain. Bypassing a string of existing Franco-Ontarian farm villages, it had little impact on the landscape and has left few vestiges aside from the Bourget station and bridge piers in the South Nation River. That section which was built in Quebec does survive today, however, and now carries Montreal's commuters between Rigaud Station and downtown Montreal.

The Bytown and Prescott Railway was one of Ontario's first steam railways. Chartered in 1851, it began service in 1854, linking Prescott with Bytown (shortly to be re-named Ottawa). Its main function was to carry logs around the tumultuous Chaudiere Rapids on the Ottawa River and deliver them to the Prescott wharfs on the St. Lawrence River. But within three years

the line was bankrupt and was soon after absorbed by the CPR. The line's original station on Sussex Drive in Ottawa burned down in 1860, and in 1871 began using the CPR's new Broad Street station. Canadian Pacific began abandoning it section by section as early as the 1960s, finally lifting the last rails, those to Manotick, in 1999. While the early stone piers of the bridge over the Rideau River still survive near Sussex Drive, the only remaining portion of the historic line today is the route of Ottawa's "O Train."

Over the past fifteen years, many sections of Northern Ontario's historic lines have likewise vanished. Those portions of the National Transcontinental line, which had been built to link Quebec City with Prince Rupert, British Columbia, were lifted between Cochrane and Senneterre, Quebec, and between Hearst and Nakina, in the 1990s. In 2005, Mackenzie and Mann's Canadian Northern tracks between Longlac and Thunder Bay were also lost, but not without controversy in the communities that it had served, such as Geraldton, Nipigon, and Thunder Bay itself. Today, only the magnificent Port Arthur station and a scenic tunnel at Macdiarmid, now a picnic site, celebrate their legacy.

But controversies continue. The CPR in 2009 announced the abandonment of its Ottawa Valley Railway between Smiths Falls and Mattawa. Fearing a negative economic impact, municipalities such as Smiths Falls and Renfrew County lobbied furiously, without success, for the provincial and the federal government to help in acquiring the line. It was on this line that, in the 1970s and '80s, the CPR demolished nearly its entire stock of wonderful stone railway stations. The sole survivor can be found at Carleton Place, and now serves as a daycare centre.

A parallel line, however, enjoyed a happier fate. Although the CNoR tracks between Pembroke and Capreol were lifted in 1996, those which connect Pembroke with Ottawa remain in place. In late 2010, a rail company — Transport Pontiac-Renfrew — agreed to resume rail operations along it with an eye to possible future passenger service, as well.

Despite the long downward slide of Ontario's rail operations and the abundance of the ghost lines it has produced, perhaps the end of the line is not certain and some of these "ghosts" may indeed survive to find new life in the future.

NOTES

Introduction

1. Although Britain remained officially neutral, concerns arose because Britain was supporting the blockade runners carrying supplies past Union blockades and into Southern ports. As well, Britain was heavily dependent on Southern cotton, and a British shipyard had built two ships for the Confederacy. The British, however, never did enter the war on behalf on the South. See Ephraim Douglass Adams, "Great Britain and the American Civil War," at *www.questia.com*. Originally published in book form in 1958 by Russell and Russell of New York.

2. The Canadian National Railways began with the amalgamation of five financially troubled railways between 1917 and 1923. These included the Intercolonial Railway, the National Transcontinental Railway, the Grand Trunk Pacific, the Canadian Northern, and the Grand Trunk itself. The CNR was formally incorporated in 1919 and at the time was North America's most extensive rail network. See "Canadian National Railway Company," at *www.trainweb.org/ontariorailways/railcn.htm*.

Part One: The Ghost Lines of Central Ontario

Chapter 1

1. St. Lawrence Seaway. Following the rebuilding of the Welland Canal in 1932, the Canadian government was anxious to upgrade the canal along the St. Lawrence River, as well, but the United States balked. Only when the

Canadians threatened to construct an all-Canadian route did the Americans agree to a joint project. Opened in 1959, the new seaway consisted of seven new locks, a major power dam, and the deepening of the waterway to 8.2 metres. During construction, which began in 1954, many towns and villages had to be relocated as did the tracks of the CNR between Cornwall and Cardinal.

2. The long-lasting and fateful Donnelly saga began in the 1850s when a large family of Irish origin named Donnelly and various neighbours began to feud. Barn-burnings and animal molestations were all laid at the feet of the family until, in 1880, a frenzied mob of vigilantes burned their cabin and killed five family members. Although the trial received international attention, no one was ever convicted. Up until recent years, few area residents would discuss this chapter in their local history. Now, the Donnelly home (built by a son following the fire) is available for group tours, while a new Donnelly museum has opened in Lucan. The family gravesite stands in the yard of the church where, ironically, the vigilante committee first formed.

3. Howard Watson was a Sarnia Township councillor who was instrumental in encouraging the development of the trail.

Chapter 2

1. Van Horne stations. To expedite the construction of the Canadian Pacific Railway's transcontinental railway, William Cornelius Van Horne, the line's feisty president, ordered his engineers to design a simple station pattern that could be constructed quickly and one that he could ship to local contractors across the country. Simple and functional, the design was a two-storey house-like structure with a full second floor for the agent's accommodation. The freight room and waiting rooms were located on the ground level, along with the agent's offices. Known as a "Van Horne" station, these buildings appeared at most of the CPR's first station locations until most were later replaced by more decorative buildings in the ensuing twenty years. Eventually the CPR would produce a pattern book with twenty station patterns.

Chapter 4

1. At the urging of St. Catharines businessman William Hamilton Merritt, the Welland Canal was opened in 1829. Its purpose was to provide Canadian shippers with an all-water alternative to the American Erie Canal. Upgrades took place in 1845 and 1887, with the current route opening in 1932. A new bypass around Welland opened in 1973. From its original forty-two wooden locks necessary to mount the cliffs of the Niagara Escarpment, the canal now employs just seven locks.

2. Hutchison House was built in 1836–37 for Peterborough's first doctor, John Hutchison. A cousin, Sandford Fleming, later knighted, lived in the home in the 1840s. Today it is a museum with rooms depicting a period doctor's study and nineteenth-century surveying equipment. Visit *www.hutchisonhouse.ca*. For more on Sir Sanford Fleming, see Jean Murray Cole, ed., *Sir Sanford Fleming: His Early Diaries, 1845–1853* (Toronto: Dundurn Press, 2009).

Chapter 5

1. The Scottish-born George Laidlaw immigrated to Canada in 1855 and began work at the Gooderham and Worts Distillery in Toronto. While employed there he recognized the need to extend rail lines into Ontario's hinterlands. A fan of the less expensive narrow-gauge lines (three foot six versus the five foot six then in vogue), he promoted the Toronto and Nipissing and Toronto, Grey, and Bruce railways. He was also involved in promoting the Credit Valley Railway as well as the Victoria Railway. He died at his Balsam Lake cottage, which was situated near the T&N railway. For more information, see "Narrow Gauge Through the Bush," at *www.narrowgaugethroughthebush.com*.

Chapter 6

1. John Shedden helped build the Toronto, Grey, and Bruce Railway, but was killed on the Toronto Nipissing Railway in 1873.

Chapter 8

1. In 1850, the government of Upper Canada passed the Public Roads Act. Under this law, the government would build twenty-five colonization roads into what were then the unsettled lands of the Canadian Shield. While the stated aim was to offer settlers free land to farm, the unstated goal was to help the influential lumber companies obtain labourers, and horses to work in their lumber camps. Once the lumber was gone, the soil, which the government assured settlers was fertile, proved stony and worthless. As the disheartened moved away — many to the Canadian Prairies — farms and villages were abandoned along this and other such roads.

Chapter 11

1. A wealthy London, Ontario, manufacturer, as well as that city's mayor, Adam Beck was elected as a Conservative MPP to the Ontario Legislature where Premier James Whitney appointed him Power Minister and chairman of

the Ontario Hydro Electric Power Commission. In 1910 he oversaw the building of a 110,000-volt transmission line to Toronto and southwestern Ontario. Always on the lookout for new customers for the electric utility, he actively promoted the development of electric rail lines. Knighted by King George V in 1914, he died in 1925. See Niagara Parks Commission, *www.niagaraparks.com/attractions/sir-adam-beck-history.html*.

2. Librarian and activist Kay Gardner began lobbying in 1970 to save the abandoned CN's old Belt Line tracks from succumbing to development and convert them to an urban trail. She served on Toronto City Council from 1985 until 1997. Two years after it opened, the trail was named the Kay Gardner Beltline Park to honour her efforts.

3. Initiated by Kitchener artist Nicholas Rees in 1996, the Artifacts Project involves the placing of industrial artifacts from early Kitchener industries at strategic points in the city. The Iron Horse Trail displays four such items, including a compression transfer press, a bull gear, a Clemmer punch press, and a trueing fixture. For more information, visit the City of Kitchener website at *http://app.kitchener.ca*.

Part Two: The Ghost Rail Lines of Eastern Ontario

Chapter 12

1. St. Andrews West is an early village, north of Cornwall, which grew along the stage road known as the Montreal Road.

Chapter 13

1. Arthur Child, who grew up in Gananoque, wanted to ensure the preservation of the rich history of the Thousand Islands region. His ideas and generous donations, together with the town's land, municipal, federal, and provincial government funding, as well as additional private and corporate donations, brought about the construction of the Arthur Child Heritage Museum, the centrepiece of the Historic Thousand Islands Village complex.

Chapter 15

1. Colonel George Flower was contracted to build the line, while John and Robert Flower were on the railway's board of directors.

Chapter 18

1. Batawa had its beginnings in 1939 with the arrival of Czech-born Thomas Bata, who was escaping the invasion of his home country by the Nazis. Along with members of one hundred other families who had escaped with him, he opened a shoe factory in Frankford. Later, he built a new factory and a company town around it. Batawa would grow to contain two schools, two churches, a post office, and a bank. With the factory's closing, the population dwindled, houses were moved, and many of its streets are now silent. The Bata Shoe Museum in Toronto was founded by Thomas Bata's widow, Sonia. For more information, see Bruce Ricketts, "Batawa, Built on a Shoe String," at *www.mysteriesofcanada.com*.

Chapter 19

1. Opinicon Lodge dates from the early days of the canal, when it was built as the home of the Chaffey family. In the 1890s, it became a boarding house and later a resort hotel, the role it still serves today.

Part Three: The Ghost Rail Lines of the Southwest

Chapter 20

1. The rotary snow plough was first designed by a Toronto dentist, Dr. J.W. Elliot, a design improved upon by Credit Valley Railway engineer Orange Jull. The device resembled a giant propeller and was placed in front of a railway locomotive, where its rotation hurled the snow to the side of the tracks. But some winters in the Orangeville area were so severe that even the Elliot-Jull ploughs proved ineffective, and trains were occasionally stranded in deep drifts for up to two weeks. This Canadian invention is still widely used by railways throughout North America's snowbelts. See The Canadian Encyclopedia website at *www.encyclopediecanadienne.ca*. See also Wayne Townsend, *Orangeville: The Heart of Dufferin County* (Toronto: Natural Heritage Books, 2006), 235–37.

Chapter 22

1. For more on the Canada Company and Tiger Dunlop, see Robert C. Lee, *The Canada Company and The Huron Tract, 1826–1853: Personalities, Profits, and Politics* (Toronto: Natural Heritage Books, 2004).

Chapter 23

1. In late 2010, the City of Hamilton debated building a new football stadium on this site, but rejected the idea as being too costly.

Chapter 26

1. The Long Point World Biosphere Reserve is one of just three such sites in Ontario, and was designated by UNESCO to help protect the biodiversity of this eighteen-kilometre sand spit that juts out into Lake Erie, its dunes and marshes an important habitat for many species of birds, fish, turtles, and frogs.

Chapter 28

1. In 1996, Jean and Colwyn Rich established the Jean Rich Foundation to financially assist students at the University of Guelph, especially those enrolled in veterinary sciences.

Part Four: The Northland's Ghost Rail Lines

Chapter 32

1. Born in 1827 on a farm near Waterloo, Quebec, John Rudolphus Booth moved to Ottawa in 1855 and began his own milling business. After obtaining the lucrative contract to supply lumber for Canada's new parliament buildings, he acquired the rich timber limits in Algonquin Park. To help move his lumber to the Atlantic, he created the Canada Atlantic Railway. After completing the Ottawa, Arnprior, and Parry Sound Railway to Georgian Bay, he became the largest private railway owner in North America, as well as the owner of a fleet of grain boats. In 1904, he sold the railway to the Grand Trunk for $14 million. He remained active in his business into his nineties, highly respected for his work ethic and his fair treatment of employees. In 1920, at age ninety-two, he was invited to drop the puck at a Stanley Cup hockey game. Booth died in 1925. His home at 252 Metcalfe Street in Ottawa is now a National Historic Site. Information is from the Trinity Western University website, at *http://twu.ca/sites/laurentian/heritage/jrbooth*.

2. The Wilno area was settled in 1859 by Polish immigrants from the Kashubian region of Poland. The area's Polish heritage is still celebrated with the Kashubian language still practised in the rural areas, and in the *kaplichi*, or roadside shrines, found along the area's farm roads. For more information, visit *www.wilno.com*.

3. For more on these vanished villages of the Almaguin District, see Astrid Taim, *Almaguin Chronicles: Memories of the Past* (Toronto: Dundurn Press, 2008).

SUGGESTED READING

Books

Barr, Elinor. *Thunder Bay to Gunflint: The Port Arthur, Duluth, and Western Railway*. Thunder Bay, ON: The Thunder Bay Historical Museum Society, 1999.

Bell, Allan. *A Way to the West: A Canadian Railway Legend*. Barrie, ON: privately published, 1991.

Bennett, Carol, and D.W. McCuaig, *In Search of the K and P: The Story of the Kingston and Pembroke Railway*. Renfrew, ON: Renfrew Advance Ltd., 1981.

Brown, Ron. *Ghost Railways of Ontario*. Peterborough, ON: Broadview Press, 1979.

_____. *Ghost Railways of Ontario, Volume 2*. Toronto: Polar Bear Press, 2000.

_____. *The Train Doesn't Stop Here Anymore: An Illustrated History of Railway Stations in Canada*. Toronto: Dundurn Press, 2008.

Coons, C.F. *The John R. Booth Story*. Ontario Ministry of Natural Resources, 1978.

Cooper, Charles. *Hamilton's Other Railway*. Ottawa: Bytown Railway Society, 2001.

_____. *Narrow Gauge for Us: The Story of the Toronto and Nipissing Railway*. Erin, ON: Boston Mills Press, 1982.

Hansen, Keith. *Last Trains from Lindsay*. Roseneath, ON: Sandy Flats Publications, 2000.

Jackson, John N., and John Burtniak. *Railways in the Niagara Peninsula*. Belleville, ON: Mika Publishing, 1981.

MacKay, Niall. *Over the Hills to Georgian Bay: A Pictorial History of the Ottawa, Arnprior, and Parry Sound Railway*. Erin, ON: Boston Mills Press, 1981.

Mackey, Doug and Paul. *The Fossmill Story: Life in a Railway Lumbering Village on the Edge of Algonquin Park*. Powassan, ON: Past Forward Heritage, 1999.

Mills, John. *Traction on the Grand: The Story of Electric Railways Along Ontario's Grand River Valley*. Ottawa: Railfare Enterprises, 1977.

Newell, Diane, and Ralph Greenhill. *Survivals: Aspects of Industrial Archaeology in Ontario*. Erin, ON: Boston Mills Press, 1989.

A Pictorial History of Algonquin Park. Ontario Ministry of Natural Resources, 1977.

Plomer, James, with Alan R. Capon. *Desperate Venture: Central Ontario Railway*. Belleville, ON: Mika Publishing, 1979.

Robinson, Dean. *Railway Stratford*. Erin, ON: Boston Mills Press, 1989.

Smith, Douglas N.W. *By Rail Road and Water to Gananoque*. Ottawa: Trackside Canada, 1995.

Stamp, Robert M. *Riding the Radials: Toronto's Suburban Electric Streetcar Lines*. Erin, ON: Boston Mills Press, 1989.

Tennant, Robert D. Jr. *Canada Southern Country*. Erin, ON: Boston Mills Press, 1991.

Watson, Peter. *The Great Gorge Route*. Niagara Falls, ON: P. Wilson and Assoc., 1997.

Wilkins, Taylor. *Haliburton by Rail and the IB&O*. Haliburton, ON: self-published, 1992.

Willmot, Elizabeth A. *Meet Me at the Station*. Toronto: Gage Publishing, 1976.

Wilson, Dale. *The Algoma Eastern Railway*. Sudbury, ON: Nickel Belt Rails, 1979.

Wilson, Donald M. *Lost Horizons: The Story of the Rathbun Company and the Bay of Quinte Railway*. Belleville, ON: Mika Publishing, 1983.

_____. *The Ontario and Quebec Railway*. Belleville, ON: Mika Publishing, 1984.

Reports and Booklets

"Booth's Rock Trail: Man and the Algonquin Environment." Whitney, ON: The Friends of Algonquin Park, 2004.

Tay Shore Trail Committee, *Tay Shore Trail*, Report to Council, Tay Township, December 2007.

"Track and Tower Trail: A Look into Algonquin's Past." Whitney, ON: The Friends of Algonquin Park, 2004.

Websites

Caledon Trailway, Ontario Rail Trails. *http://webhome.idirect.com/~brown/*

Cataraqui Trail, "Eastern Ontario's Path to Nature and History." *www.rideau-info.com/cattrail/*

Cataraqui Trail, Ontario Rail Trails. *http://webhome.idirect.com/~brown/cataraqui.htm*

Charles Cooper's Railway Pages. *www.railwaypages.com*

MacDonald, Mady. "Hiking the Dundas Valley." *www.out-there.com/dundas.htm*

"Chrysler Canada Greenway." Essex Region Conservation Authority. *www.erca.org/conservation/area.chrysler_canada_greenway.cfm*

"Craigleith Station Is Now an Historic Heritage Museum." *www.model-railroad-infoguy.com/Craigleith-station.html*

"Elora Cataract Trail." The Elora Cataract Trail Association. *www.trailway.org*

Grand River Railway. *www.trainweb.org/elso/grr.htm*

"Hamilton Brantford Cambridge Trails." Ontario Rail Trails. *http://webhome.idirect.com/~brown/hamilton_cambridge. html*

Harwood Station Museum. *www.harwoodmuseum.ca*

"Historical Background of the Grand Trunk Railway." Mary Smith, curator, St. Marys Museum. *http://stonetown.com/ gttsm/history.htm*

History of the Line (York Durham Heritage Railway). *www.ydhr.on.ca/HistoryOfTheLine.html*

"The Hogg's Bay Trestle." Township of Tay, *www.tay.ca/Community/History/TheHoggsBayTrestle/index.htm*

"The IB&O Trail," Haliburton Highlands Trails and Tours Network. *www.trailsandtours.com/trail/90*

"Iron Horse Trail." *www.trainweb.org/elso/ironhrse.htm*

"The Iron Horse Trail." *www.cycleontario/waterloo-region/City-of-Kitchener/page-2.html*

"The K and P Trail: A New Use for an Abandoned Railway." *http://post.queensu.ca/~ab25/kandptrail/dillon.htm*

"Lake Erie and Northern Railway." *www.trainweb.org/elso/len.htm*

"Lynn Valley Trail." *www.lynnvalleytrail.ca*

"Niagara, St. Catharines, and Toronto Railway." *www.trainweb.org/elso/nst.htm*

"North Simcoe Rail Trail." *www.simcoecountytrails.net/nsrt.htm*

"Palmerston Heritage Railway Museum." *www.palmerstonrailwaymuseum.com*

Petrov, Tom. "Travelling the Abandoned Railways of Ontario." *www.tompetrovphotography.com/abandonedrailway.html*

Railway Depot Museums. *www.rrshs.org/depotmuseums*

Robinson, Jamie. "Bike Back in Time on the Tay Shore Trail." *The Star*, Monday, July 6, 2009. *www.thestar.com/travel/ article/660001*

Saugeen Rail Trail. *www.saugeenrailtrail.com*

"Tay Shore Trail." Simcoe County Trails. *www.simcoecountytrails.net*

"Tiny Trail." Simcoe County Trails. *www.simcoecountytrails.net*

"The Victoria County Recreation Corridor." *www.kawartha.net/~fencom/railtr.htm*

"Thornton–Cookstown Trans Canada Trail." *www.simcoecountytrails.net/tctrail.htm*

"To the Mettawas." The *Times Magazine* archive site. *www.walkervilletimes.com/26/to-the-mettawas.html*

Wyatt, David A. "All-Time List of Canadian Transit Systems, Toronto Region, Ontario." *http://home.cc.umanitoba. ca/~wyatt/alltime/operators.html*

Zandbergen, Lewis. "An Historical Summary of the Stirling Grand Trunk/CN Railway Station." Rotary Club of Stirling. *www.stirlingrotary.ca/history_trainstation.html*

INDEX

ABOUT THE AUTHOR

Author, geographer, and travel writer Ron Brown has long had a love affair with the landscapes of Ontario. His publications include *Top 100 Unusual Things to See in Ontario* and *Ontario's Ghost Town Heritage*. His latest titles are *The Lake Erie Shore: Ontario's Forgotten South Coast*, and *From Queenston to Kingston: The Hidden Heritage of Lake Ontario's Shoreline*. The revised *The Train Doesn't Stop Here Any More* explores the history of railway stations in Ontario.

His travel pieces have been published in the *Toronto Star*, the *Globe and Mail*, the *Canadian Geographic*, and *VIA Rail Magazine*. Ron has provided consulting services to advertisers and filmmakers, and participated on TVO panels involving Ontario's history. CBC radio has claimed that "nobody knows Ontario like Ron Brown." He now lectures on Ontario's heritage, and leads tours to explore heritage landscapes across Ontario. A member of the Travel Media Association of Canada and past chair of The Writers' Union of Canada, Ron lives in Toronto.

Also by Ron Brown

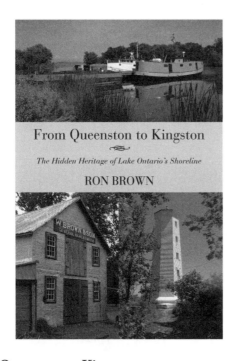

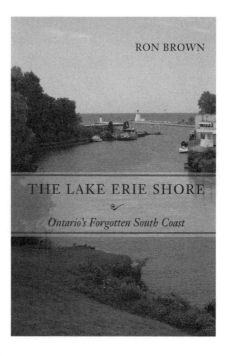

From Queenston to Kingston
The Hidden Heritage of Lake Ontario's Shoreline
978-1554887163 $26.99

Travel with Ron Brown as he probes the shoreline of the Canadian side of Lake Ontario to discover its hidden heritage. Explore "ghost ports," forgotten coves, historical lighthouses, rum-running lore, as well as some unusual natural features, including a mysterious mountain-top lake and the rare alvars of Prince Edward County.

The Lake Erie Shore
Ontario's Forgotten South Coast
978-1554883882 $24.99

The Lake Erie shoreline has witnessed some of Ontario's earliest history, yet remains largely unspoiled. Much of the area's natural features — the wetlands, the Carolinian forests — and its built heritage — fishing ports and military ramparts — provide much of interest for visitors to the region. Discover the stories of the world's largest freshwater fishing fleet, the area's links with the Underground Railroad, the introduction of wineries, and the legacy of the many towns and villages that hug Erie's shore.

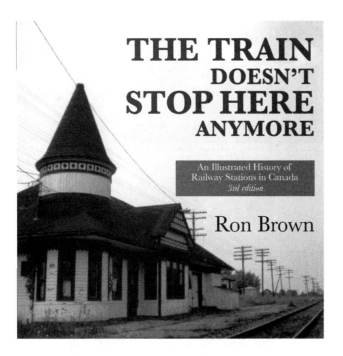